GÁBOR ILON

The Golden Treasure from Szent Vid in Velem

The Costume of a High-Ranking Lady of the Late Bronze Age in the Light of New Studies

BUDAPEST 2015

The publication of this volume was generously funded by
the National Cultural Fund of Hungary,
the Savaria Museum and the Pannon Kulturális Örökség Egyesület

Front Cover
The diadem and the domed roundels of the golden treasure
(photo by Tamás Tárczy)

Back Cover
St. Vid Hill of Velem (photo by the author)

ISBN 978-963-9911-71-0

HU-ISSN 1216-6847

2015

ARCHAEOLINGUA ALAPÍTVÁNY
H-1250 Budapest, Úri u. 49

Desktop editing and layout by Rita Kovács

Printed in Hungary by Prime Rate Kft

ARCHAEOLINGUA

Edited by

ERZSÉBET JEREM and WOLFGANG MEID

Series Minor

36

Commemorating

The 155th anniversary of the birth of Kálmán Miske (b. 1860)
who discovered the golden treasure

The 105th anniversary of the birth of Amália Mozsolics (b. 1910)
who published the first monograph on the golden treasure

The 76th anniversary of the birth of Gábor Bándi (b. 1939)
who directed the archaeological investigations
exploring the largest area of the archaeological site

Table of Contents

Prologue

The golden treasure was discovered in the last days of August in 1929, in the course of an archaeological excavation conducted by Baron Kálmán Miske. The first monograph on this remarkable assemblage, written by Amália Mozsolics, was published twenty-one years later; Gábor Bándi's study, focusing specifically on the diadem of treasure, appeared after a period of thirty-seven years. Yet another thirty-two years elapsed before the present author completed his manuscript. My attention was directed to this golden treasure by Dr. Ottó Trogmayer, who in 1999 organised an exhibition in the Helikon (Festetics) Palace Museum of the most fascinating artefacts kept in various museums of Budapest and of the county seats. This exhibition was accompanied by a bilingual catalogue.* Dr. Trogmayer requested the gold diadem for the exhibition. Before loaning it, I held it in my hands for the very first time and I was horrified to see its terrible condition, as was Dr. Trogmayer. Therefore, after the exhibition and as soon as I was able to, I announced a tender (2003), and as a result, the conservation of the diadem was carried out between 2004 and 2006. At the same time, I believed that I would be able to answer at least some of the questions that had bedevilled archaeological scholarship for so long about this dazzling assemblage. This work lasted for many years: the present volume is a reflection of what I have accomplished as well as a reminder that our work on this spectacular treasure remains unfinished as it was for my predecessors; it shows the options I had at my disposal, and what I have been actually able to achieve.

Kőszeg, August 20, 2014

Gábor Ilon

* László Czoma (ed.): *Ritkaságok, becses óságok. Magyarország megyéinek és fővárosának muzeális kincsei a keszthelyi Festetics-kastélyban 1999–2000. – Raritäten, kostbare Altertümer. Museale Schätze der ungarischen Komitate und der Hauptstadt im Festetics-Schloß in Keszthely 1999–2000.* Keszthely, Helikon (Festesics) Palace Museum, 1999.

1 Introduction: the findspot, the find circumstances and the history of research of the golden treasure

1.1 Kálmán Miske and the archaeological site

Located on the eastern spur of the Alps, the area of St. Vid Hill in Velem was investigated in detail during a topographical survey performed during the past fifteen years (*Figs 1–2*).[1] Many treasures and hoards were found on the hill located not far from the so-called Amber Road, an ancient route that follows the valley of the Gyöngyös Stream (*Fig. 10. 1*). Many researchers had set themselves the task of cataloguing and assessing these assemblages;[2] however, a final, conclusive catalogue still awaits publication. Shortly after their discovery, some parts of these hoards were "recycled": they were melted down and used for producing other artefacts (for example in the bell foundry of Pfistermeister in Kőszeg).[3] Another part has been lost forever, while yet another part was purchased for private collections (Rezső Széchenyi, Kálmán Miske[4]) or for public collections abroad (Graz, Vienna[5]) because their finders sold them. A small part of these treasures and hoards was given to the former Museum of Vas County in Szombathely (present-day Savaria Museum). Some of the treasures were sent to the Hungarian National Museum.[6] This short monograph focuses on one particular assemblage, namely the golden treasure that was discovered in 1929 in the course of an archaeological excavation conducted by Baron Kálmán Miske. Before discussing the findspot and the find circumstances, a brief detour on the relationship between Kálmán Miske (*Fig 6. 1*) and the archaeological site on the St. Vid Hill of Velem seems in order.

This archaeological site was placed on the map of Hungarian archaeology by Flóris Rómer, the "founding father" of Hungarian archaeology. In 1869, he collected fragments of Roman clay water pipes on the hill, which he perhaps gave to the collection of the Benedictine gymnasium of Kőszeg.[7] However, Kálmán

---

1 ILON 2007a; ILON 2013a.

2 CZAJLIK 1993, esp. 317–327; ILON – KÖLTŐ 2000, note 5; FEKETE 2008, 525–540.

3 MISKE 1925, 46; CZAJLIK 1993, 326; FEKETE 2008, 527.

4 MISKE 1925, 47.

5 Miske too donated some artefacts to Vienna. Cf. FOLTINY 1958, 1.

6 MISKE 1897, 13; MISKE 1925, 47.

7 CHERNEL 1877, 15.

Miske can undoubtedly be regarded as the scholar who devoted much of his efforts to unearthing the archaeological relics on the hill and to presenting the findings to the international scholarly community. He was born on November 25, 1860, the sixth child of a landowner in Bodajk, Fejér County. His father was the Lord Lieutenant of Moson County. Maybe this was the reason that he was obliged to attend the Academy of Agriculture in Mosonmagyaróvár,[8] in preparation for the future management of his family's property. At the same time, in my opinion, this academic background explains why he was so open toward geology, pedology and, in this context, chemistry in the course of his archaeological career. We can understand his positive attitude towards chemical analysis,[9] and geological[10] and pedological[11] research in this light.

That he moved to Kőszeg is evidenced only by a letter dated to 1890, which he addressed to Kálmán Chernel, the city's eminent historian. Both of them were highly educated and spoke several languages, they were devoted to history, and were passionate collectors of ancient relics, hoards and antiquities. In this letter, he also inquired about Sarolta, his future wife.[12] After his father's death, Kálmán Miske sold his property in Bodajk in 1900 and created a life for himself in Kőszeg. He had one son from his marriage.[13] Through the mediation of the Chernel family, he became acquainted with the Prince Esterházy[14] and Count Zichy families, which added to his already wide-ranging social connections, initially created through his

---

[8] Vágusz 2010, 58–59.

[9] See Kálmán Miske's unpublished report on the analysis performed by chemist Dr. Ernst Söwy (Silesia): "Analysisek a Velem Szt. Vid 1901. évi szakszerű ásatása alkalmával situsban lelt tárgyakról" [Analyses of artefacts found in situ during the professional archaeological excavation conducted on St. Vid Hill in 1901]. The final section of the report notes that Dr. Otto Helm (Gdańsk) will be performing the analysis of resins. KVM Local History Archives, inv. no. 1484/XXXIX/101; Miske 1908, 20, 26–34.

[10] On March 18, 1908, he applied to the District Mining Inspectorate for the renewal of his license and for the extension of the activity area to Sopron and Veszprém Counties. KVM Local History Archives, inv. no. 1388/XXXIX/4.

[11] In 1931, he commissioned the Hungarian Royal Chemical Institute to perform the analysis of soil samples and to prepare a pedological map for the Musuem of Local History and Homeland Education to be established in Kőszeg. This is reported in a letter dated May 1933 addressed to the Mayor of Kőszeg. KVM Local History Archives, inv. no. 790/XX/22.

[12] Their wedding was held on April 10, 1894.

[13] Vágusz 2010, 58.

[14] This explains why he dedicated his monograph on Velem (Miske 1907, 1908) to the "Honourable Prince Dr. Miklós Esterházy, as a token of friendship and respect".

father's role as Lord Lieutenant. Also, his baronial rank provided solid grounds for his career in the foundation and general management of museums and in the discipline of archaeology. His donations to the Museum of Vas County, which started its activity in 1908, made him its founder and thus he became the keeper of the collection of antiquities from October 12 the same year;[15] he was the very first secular director of the museum from March 12, 1912, to March 15, 1943, the day he passed away in Kőszeg. He was the founder of the Museum of Local History and Homeland Education in Kőszeg that was opened to the public in May 1932, and he also served as Chairman of its Board of Development beforehand.[16]

In the first half of the 1890s, Baron Miske had a personal knowledge of the archaeological relics found on the St. Vid Hill, because he noted the following in 1896: "After various acquisitions, my collection slowly expanded and, due to limited space, I was forced to place the pieces into a glass case in the hallway of my home. After seeing my collection, a peasant woman from Velem informed me that similar antiquities turned up oft-times in their village, and that some of the peasants made a very good living from selling the antiquities, which fetched a good price. During a visit to the place, I was able to see this with my own eyes. The prehistoric settlement, which seems to be an inexhaustible source of artefacts that has been exploited for years, is located in the northwestern part of Velem, on a lone peak, where the castle of the infamous and dreaded Németujváry kindred stood formerly, but where today you find a place of pilgrimage, a chapel dedicated to St. Vid, where artefacts bearing witness to past centuries and millennia can be found at a depth of 1 to 2 meters. *I successfully collected many fascinating minor finds for my collection during the years* [my italics]."[17]

The name of the peasant woman mentioned by Baron Miske was Mrs. György Kápiller. Later, Miske wrote the following about their meeting, the artefacts, and their collectors: "Mrs. György Kápiller of Velem, who frequently delivered butter to my home, admired [the bronze artefacts of Miske's collection in the glass case] and told me that her neighbour, Mihály Szigeti Molnár usually collected things like these in the settlement and said that they were from St. Vid [Hill]. This was on April 12, 1896. While ploughing his land, János Bóna of Velem found a sizeable assemblage of bronze objects in a large vessel at the end of the same year."[18] The majority of these artefacts were acquired by Kelemen Kárpáti, Chairman of the

[15] ILON 2009, 39, 65.
[16] KÁROLYI 1990, 402–403; ILON 2002a, 617.
[17] Miske 1896, 250.
[18] MISKE 1925, 46–47; CZAJLIK 1993, 318; FEKETE 2008, 528.

Cultural Society of Vas County and later director of the Museum of Vas County, for the planned museum in Szombathely, while another part was purchased by Kálmán Miske for the Hungarian National Museum.

After this information had been divulged by the peasant woman, Bonya[19]/Bónya (and not Bóna as recorded by Miske in the above passage) obviously considered selling the bronze finds to Baron Miske for a hefty sum. The villagers regarded the baron as something of an eccentric. In May 1896, Miske wrote the following: "On the 18th day of this month, J. B. of Velem paid me a visit and brought clay vessels with him as well as many fragments of sickles, knives and coils for sale. After I purchased them, he informed me, to my joy, that he had even larger intact pieces in his house."[20] As a cultured gentleman, or simply as a careful amateur collector who jealously guarded his sources from other potential buyers (we must not forget that the museum of Szombathely did not exist at the time,[21] and Miske became the keeper of the collection of antiquities only after 1908), Baron Miske only disclosed the initials (J. B.) of the peasant from Velem in the quoted passage in *Archaeologiai Értesítő*.

In 1896, in cooperation with Count Rezső Széchenyi and Kelemen Kárpáti, Miske conducted what we would today call a control excavation, funded from his own pocket, on the findspot of Hoard I (a and b), as it was then called. This excavation unfortunately ended with no results. The first state-subsidised archaeological excavation, which was supervised by Kárpáti and Miske, took place in July 1898. These excavations, funded by the central budget, were conducted until 1915.[22] From 1901 onwards, archaeological excavations took place under Miske's supervision (*Fig. 5*), lasting for several days or weeks each year. In 1902/03, anthropologist Aurél Török, lecturer at the University of Budapest, assisted Miske; they published the burials dating to the Hunnic Age unearthed on the hill.[23] Lajos Bella of Sopron, who participated as the assigned representative of the Hungarian National Museum, was Miske's colleague in many excavation campaigns. Miske's assistant in the 1910s was Gilbert Neogrády, the co-keeper of the collection of antiquities in the Museum of Szombathely.[24] The

---

19 The cadastral map (*Parzellen Protocoll Gemeinde Velem 1857*) specifies the name of the proprietor spelt as "Bonya".

20 MISKE 1896, 252.

21 The museum was opened on October 11, 1908. TÓTH 2009, 28–29.

22 MISKE 1925, 47.

23 MISKE 1903, 1904.

24 MISKE 1925, 48.

archaeological excavations that lasted until 1929 under his supervision were not continued due to World War 1, the turmoil of the ensuing years (1919–1920), the drastic diminution of his private wealth, his advanced age, the gradual loss of his social relations with high society, and the incomprehensible antipathy of the younger generation of archaeologists.[25] Nonetheless, he successfully managed to carry on his archaeological research as a result of the funding granted by financial institutions of Szombathely (1921), the support of the county bishop (1922),[26] and by renewed state subsidies from 1923 onwards.

Miske conducted and documented his archaeological fieldwork with a meticulous attention to detail. Nothing proves this better than his article in the 1909 issue of the specialist methodological periodical *Múzeumi és Könyvtári Értesítő* [Museological and Library Journal] published by the Ministry of Culture.[27] Regrettably, his archaeological fieldwork in Velem is documented by a few photographs only (*Fig. 5*),[28] a report that includes a chemical analysis, certain passages in the field diary of the archaeological excavations of 1901,[29] a portion of the survey of the burials dating to the Hunnic Age, a few financial reports on the allocation of the state subsidy granted by the Museum of Vas County, the incomplete annual reports and acquisitions registers of the same museum,[30] and his incomplete notes with regard to the golden treasure. These documents

---

25 In his letter dated May 22, 1929, the President of the Hungarian Academy of Sciences informed Miske that the Archaeological Commmittee of the Academy would not recommend the support of his archaeological research in Velem. If, for any reason, support should nonetheless be granted, the Committee would reserve its right to supervise the archaeological research and the Museum of Vas County would not be given a free hand to publish the results. SM Department of History, letterheaded paper of the Hungarian Academy of Sciences, originally filed under no. 1314/1929, among the univentoried records. Ferenc Tompa played no small role in the unfavourable evaluation of Miske's work, which he admitted, very diplomatically, in his obituary of Miske. Cf. TOMPA 1943; for the hostile attitudes of the period's Hungarian scholarship at the time, cf. KÁROLYI 1990, 402.

26 MISKE 1925, 49.

27 MISKE 1909.

28 For instance, the photograph recording the excavation of prehistoric furnaces, published by KÁROLYI 1990, 405.

29 The single field diary known to me. written during the archaeological excavation of 1901, is in the KVM Local History Archives, inv. no. 1477/XXXIX. 94, 1478/XXXIX. 95.

30 E.g. from 1913; cf. ILON 2009, Fig. 7

have been preserved in many different institutions.[31] It seems to me that large portions of Baron Kálmán Miske's archaeological documentation, finished and incomplete manuscripts,[32] drawings and descriptions of artefacts connected with Velem either still lurk undiscovered in various archives or have been lost forever to archaeology.[33]

Realising the significance of this archaeological site, and in an effort to protect it from the hunger for metals and metal ore in Hungary after the Treaty of Trianon, Baron Miske, far ahead of his time, solicited the Deputy and Lord Lieutenant of Vas County in October 1923 to declare the hill and the 1 to 3 km wide zone of land around it a scheduled monument or a protected/conservation area as it would be defined today. Only agriculture would be permitted in that particular zone and any research would exclusively be carried out by the Museum of Vas County and/or any other third party permitted to do so by the museum.[34] However, the ministerial decree for the protection and conservation of the archaeological site only was only issued in the late 1960s and was restricted to the hill.

---

[31] Documents housed in the City Museum of Kőszeg, the Savaria Museum, the Archives of Vas County, the Archives of Kőszeg of the Hungarian National Archives (Szombathely) and in the Hungarian National Museum as well as the documents from the Department of Archaeology of the Eötvös Loránd University, now in the possession of Mária Fekete.

[32] Among these, Vols II and III of his monograph on Velem are undoubtedly the most important. In its three-page leaflet promoting Vol. I, the Carl Konegen publishing house of Vienna wrote the following: "Im zweiten Band wird über die systematischen Grabungen berichtet und die Altersfolge der Funde erörtert werden. Der dritte Band wird über den Fundort und die dort vorkommenden Funde anderer Art, über die botanischen, zoologischen und antropologischen Verhältnisse, über die Untersuchungen der Schlacken und über sonstige spezielle Fragen Aufschluß geben." KVM Local History Archives, uninventoried leaflet.

[33] During the years of the Great War, a part of the building of the Museum of Vas County was used as a school (Miske 1925, 50), but extremely bad conditions existed during the years of World War 2 as well. László Szakonyi, the former laboratory assistant of the museum and later its first official conservator, who lived in the building, hid the gold artefacts of Velem in a chest in his apartment, to prevent them being found by soldiers and looters. Kiss 2009, 329.

[34] Károlyi 1990, 401; Ilon 2009, 51. The undated draught version of a letter addressed to the Deputy Lord Lieutenant specified a range of 1 km. See KVM Local History Archives, inv. no. 393/XXXIX/9. It is possible that he had sent a letter to the Lord Lieutenant as well, in order to get a larger area protected.

1.2 Kálmán Miske and the discovery of the golden treasure

Part of Miske's manuscript, preserved as a result of fortunate circumstances, but earlier unknown to scholarship, describes the date and findspot of the golden treasure relatively accurately.[35] This part of Kálmán Miske's letter of eight pages, written in late 1929 and addressed to Count Albert Apponyi, former Minister of Religion and Public Education, reports the following (*Figs 7–9*):[36] "the archaeological excavation on the St. Vid Hill in the summer of this year brought to light the prehistoric iron mine. [Because research of this type is a special branch of archaeology and not all archaeologists are predisposed to this branch] ... we excavated a cultural stratum that would satisfy the curiosity of the majority of our visitors as well." The trial trenches opened under Miske's supervision to reveal the layers were funded by the Ministry of Religion and Public Education (see *Appendix 2*) during a planned four-day campaign[37] as a result of efficient "lobbying" by Ferenc Tompa (1893–1945, *Fig. 6. 2*), Miske's former assistant in Szombathely, who was by then working in the Hungarian National Museum.

---

[35] I had earlier, inaccurately as it turned out, located the findspot near the chapel. Ilon 2007a, 282; Czajlik 1993, 327. I discovered the letters written by Kálmán Miske that specified the findspot of the treasure under nos 1426/XXXIX. 43 and 1942/XXXIX.109 in the KVM Local History Archives on October 1 and 21, 2013.

[36] The following section of the letter (KVM Local History Archives, inv. no. 1426/ XXXIX. 43) allows the identification of the minister, as there is a reference to a state subsidy granted twenty years earlier. We know the minister held this post between April 8, 1906 and January 17, 1910: "[...] I shall again pay a visit to Your Honour and request the generous patronage of your lordship for St. Vid Hill of Velem *as two decades ago*" [my italics]. One part of the letter, four pages (inv. no. 1942/XXXIX.109) was found in a bundle of documents tied up with a string, labelled "Incomplete manuscripts from Kálmán Miske's bequest". The addressing of "Your Honour" can be found here too. Miske asked for another state subsidy for the purpose of further research on the iron mine he had discovered; this part of the letter is unrelated to the six pages of another letter about the golden treasure. See the list of Hungarian ministers of public education: http://hu.wikipedia.org/wiki/Magyarorsz%C3%A1g_oktat%C3%A1s%C3%BCgyi_miniszetereinek_list%C3%A1ja#Vall.C3.A1s-_.C3.A9s_k.C3.B6zoktat.C3.A1s.C3.BCgyi_miniszterek_.281867-1918.29 (accessed October 2, 2013).

[37] Kálmán Miske's letter of July 10, 1929, addressed to Ferenc Tompa is in the uninventoried material of the HNM Archaeological Archives; Tompa's bequest, box 1. I am grateful to Dr. László Szende, director of the department, for calling my attention to this letter.

Who were the visitors mentioned in Miske's letter? They were German and Austrian archaeologists and scholars who were attending an international conference, for whom Tompa organised an excursion; they visited St. Vid Hill on September 5, 1929 (see *Appendices 1–3*).[38] And where was the trial trench opened to illustrate the chronology of the site? In his letter, Miske described the site as follows:[39] "It was something of a headache to select the appropriate location. I wanted to dig in an area familiar to me, which was now covered by a young forest; this was a place known to me, where I had conducted an archaeological excavation in 1904 and which would reveal 2.1–2.5 meters thick cultural layers overlying each other.[40] But I had to give up this idea." This is because he would have had to remove an immense volume of earth from the area (30–35 m^2) and, also, the owner of the forest would have to be compensated. These factors would have led to excessively high expenses, which he would not have been able to finance. Therefore, Miske opted for a location where, despite the thin cultural layer, the orientation of the three different terraces ("the terracing of the site was oriented variously") could be presented. His letter continues as follows: "Also for this reason, nearly 16 years ago, I decided to continue the excavation of the area that I had explored a year before the outbreak of Great War [1913]: an upper terrace that contained a late La Tène layer with a layer of the First Iron Age underneath, and where I had the opportunity to find and identify a period preceding the Iron Age, so typical of our archaeological site, and a lower terrace where the pre-Iron Age layer so typical for our site would be found under the middle La Tène layer. Choosing this location seemed to be appropriate for another reason, namely because *it lies in the immediate vicinity of Szt. Kut* [a well], where we have already selected a convenient place for the afternoon tea of our distinguished guests, who by that time would be exhausted by the mountain climb and would be hungry, thirsty, and thus in need of some recovery. It seems that my choice was inspired by my personal patron of the St. Vid Hill because I was very fortunate to find *the rectangular foundation of a late La Tène dwelling on the upper terrace* and the burnt remnants of a round, sunken hut from the Late

[38] Relevant letters are kept among the records of the museum's history, SM Department of History, file no. 70, 74–75/1929. Correspondence of Tompa and Miske, list of participants.

[39] KVM Local History Archives, Inv. no. 1942/XXXIX.109; incomplete document.

[40] As far as I know, a similarly thick layer sequence comparable to the one uncovered by Miske has since only been discovered on the plateau of the hill, on the terrace under the chapel. Cf. FEKETE 1986, 59–63, Taf. 10.

Bronze Age on the lower terrace, and what is more, I found a remarkable and valuable *golden treasure* during our work [my italics]." (*Fig. 9*).

The gold treasure, therefore, was discovered a few days before the arrival of the guests, in the last days of August or the first days of September.

His letter continues as follows: "There is a significant chronological difference between the period of manufacture and the deposition of the gold band. It was created by the twisted gold wire technique, and its ornamentation, representing the most advanced bronzeworking technique, determines its period of production. Thus, this artefact can be dated to the Late Bronze Age at the earliest or to the late period of the Early Iron Age at the latest. It was therefore made sometime in 1800–1400 BC. However, its findspot definitely lay in a layer of the late La Tène, more specifically, it was hidden in a spot marked by an upright stone slab in the corner of an unearthed dwelling. This jewellery was not used for the purpose of adornment, but was rather a buried treasure, a hoard of valuables amassed by its former owner. ... If, in this report, I be allowed a flight of fancy, we may imagine that this jewellery was one of the mortuary gifts placed in the burial of a prehistoric inhabitant of the St. Vid Hill of Velem and that it had come to light during the chance discovery of the burial by a late descendant of the late La Tène period. Bronze mortuary gifts were not considered to have had any value and were left undisturbed; only golden treasures that had real value were appropriated. However, it was not used for the purpose of everyday wear, but was instead hoarded because of its obvious value. This should explain why the band was folded, why the masterfully crafted adornment of twisted gold wire spirals was in such a sorry state in its secret hiding place." (*Fig. 9*).

The information related to the treasure in the letter reveals that (a) the trial trench was dug in an area which Miske knew well in terms of its topography and stratigraphy since 1913 because he was still intrigued by Hoard I, but at the same time, he sought to find a spot near the spring that would be convenient for his guests; (b) the trial trench cut across three terraces; (c) the third, lowermost terrace lay roughly at same level as the spring; (d) the golden treasure was buried underneath an upright stone slab in the corner of a late La Tène dwelling on the highest terrace cut by the trial trench.

In his letter, Miske calls Ferenc Tompa his beloved student, who would publish a report on the golden treasure alongside other artefacts (bronze pins, a bronze arrowhead, iron finds, a Celtic brooch and potsherds) found on the archaeological site. He also reported that vessel fragments were placed against the section wall and that the visiting scholars were very much pleased and appreciated the opportunity to take them.

In his letters dated October 3 and 18, 1929, addressed to Ferenc Tompa (see *Appendix 4*), Miske reported on the gold assemblage.[41] More precisely, he proposed that some compensation be paid to the owner (regretfully not named) of the land that had yielded the gold objects and also recommended that its amount be moderate in order to avoid looting by locals. Simultaneously, he asked Tompa to publish a report on the treasure, verified by his letter dated January 8, 1930,[42] in which he asked Tompa where and when he wished to publish this report. However, Tompa's response came in the form of his study in *Bericht der Römisch-Germanischen Kommission*, which contained an extremely brief description of the assemblage, which hardly did any justice to the splendid artefacts.[43]

In an entry on page 84 of the inventory book of the Museum of Vas County (*Fig. 11. 1*) written on March 27, 1941, Amália Mozsolics noted the following regarding the find circumstances: "It was allegedly discovered by a tree in 1929." This is natural in a forested area, but reveals little about the find circumstances. In response to a question asked by Mozsolics in her letter dated April 23, 1941 (see *Appendix 5*) concerning the findspot of the treasure, Ferenc Tompa did not provide additional information.[44] In her book published in 1950, Amália Mozsolics noted the following as regards the findspot of the treasure: "Baron Kálmán von Miske fand im Jahre 1929 bei einer Probegrabung in Velem auf der obersten Terasse am südlichen Abhang unter der Szent Vid (Sankt Veit) Kapelle unter zwei kleineren

---

[41] The gold artefacts are first mentioned in Miske's letter (no. 3), to be published in Mária Fekete's *Leletek és levelek* [Artefacts and Letters]. In another letter (no. 5), he explains that in view of the sensational assemblage, the excessive expenses of the reception of the foreign archaeologists can perhaps be excused. These letters were found in the de-accessioned material of the Department of Archaeology of the Eötvös Loránd University and were given to Mária Fekete by András Mócsy, the then director of the department. I would here like to thank her kind for her permission to quote these still unpublished letters.

[42] The letter can be found in the uninventoried material of the HNM Archaeological Archives, Tompa's bequest, Box 1.

[43] Tompa 1934–35, 105.

[44] See the letter filed under no. 114/1929 in the Archives of the Savaria Museum. Quoted by Fekete 2007, notes 58 and 243. A copy of Mozsolics's letter dated April 23, 1941, addressed to Ferenc Tompa, university professor, filed under no. 1941/43, can be found among the records of the museum's history of the SM Department of History.

Felsen den hier zu besprechenden Goldfund."[45] She essentially repeated the same incorrect description in her monograph published in 1985.[46] Although there are a few terraces on the southern slope of the hill, no archaeological relics have been found on any of them, and no investigation took place in that specific area. Part of Baron Miske's previously quoted letter makes it clear that the treasure was found somewhere near the Szentkút Spring (*Fig. 10. 3*).[47]

Therefore, Amália Mozsolics did not receive additional information on the precise findspot of the treasure. In fact, she believed that it had been found on the terrace under the chapel on the opposite slope of the hill. The term "upper terrace" can only be interpreted in the light of Miske's letter – it was the uppermost terrace cut by the trial trench that extended across three terraces. The lowermost terrace can be assumed to have been located at the altitude of the spring. The description of the slab of stone as a marker is confirmed by Miske's above-quoted letter. It is to be noted that Miske reported a single stone slab under which the gold finds were hidden, not two.

I could verify that the treasure had indeed been found in the proximity of the Szentkút Spring (*Fig. 10. 3*), as described in Miske's letter, during the inspection of the site on April 19, 2013, made together with Szilveszter Katona from Kőszeg (*Fig. 10. 6*).[48] Szilveszter Katona knew about the findspot of the treasure from his grandfather, János Katona,[49] a villager of Velem. In the 1960s and 1970s, János Katona was the caretaker of the St. Vid Chapel (*Fig. 10. 2*). Szilveszter accompanied him from the village up to the hill in his childhood. His grandfather showed him the findspot of the treasure many times. While walking up the hill, they drew water from the Szentkút well,[50] fed by the Szent Vid Spring (*Fig. 10. 3*), and continued walking east-southeast. After leaving the spring, the path, which is in fairly bad condition today, but is still used as a tourist trail (*Fig. 10. 4*), passes the ruins of a building (*Fig. 10. 3*) once used as a scout camp and then a pioneer

[45] MOZSOLICS 1950, 7.

[46] MOZSOLICS 1985, 213; as a result, I too believed, erroneously, that the findspot lay near the chapel. ILON 2007a, 282.

[47] KVM Local History Archives, inv. no. 1942/XXXIX.109.

[48] I was told about him by Ferenc Derdák, surveyor of the Savaria Museum (the co-worker of the museum from 1973 onwards), member of the French-Hungarian archaeological team led by Gábor Bándi and Mária Fekete. I am most grateful to him for sharing this information with me. Szilveszter Katona was born on April 9, 1952 and he currently lives at 108 Várkör in Kőszeg.

[49] He was born on February 25, 1895, and is buried in the cemetery of Velem.

[50] BALOGH – VÉGH 1982, 73: geographical toponym no. 42.

camp in the Socialist era.[51] The path leads along the edge of the terrace to the valley dirt track passing under the plateau of the hill in front of the steps leading to the chapel. According to the cadastral map of 1963, János Katona's land was Plot 2930 and extended to the southeast, to Plot 2981, lying on the other side of the dirt track. The golden treasure was found on a strip of land, Plot 2930, between the path, the spring, and the dirt track. This would be on the left side if viewed from the path and moving toward the chapel, that is 30–60 meters toward north-northeast according to Szilveszter Katona (*Fig. 10. 6*). His grandfather always told him that the findspot lay "next to a common hornbeam bush … practically underneath its leaves, almost no earth had to be dug out." He never talked about slabs of stone or rocks, at least his grandchild could not recall any mention of these. His grandfather told him many times that "the promised compensation was never paid."

In the 1960s, the Bónya family owned a strip of land, Plot 2931, which lay on two or three terraces of slightly varying altitude at the altitude of the spring (!), north of and slightly lower than the land of János Katona, who was their neighbour. When reading out the names of owners recorded in the Land Registry to Szilveszter Katona on the site, he told me that this family, specifically Lajos Bónya, was his grandfather's neighbour. Therefore, in 1896, the peasant woman from Velem was speaking about this piece of land, owned by the Bónya family, and its neighbourhood where the bronze hoards were discovered, some of which Baron Miske had purchased. From his meticulous review of the data, Zoltán Czajlik[52] identified the site where Hoard Ia and Ib, that is, the impressive Hoard I had been found in April and May 1896 (*Figs 3–4*). In my view, Hoard Ia, comprising nearly four hundred objects, was found in a large vessel on April 12, while Hoard Ib, made up of jewellery items, was found in May, with the two lying some 4.5 meters apart. This would conform to what Tudor Soroceanu described as the duality of hoard deposition.[53] With excellent archaeological sense, as well as in the hope of finding another hoard, Kálmán Miske conducted another excavation in 1913 and had a trial trench dug there as a presentation trench. He also hired János Katona, the owner of one of the (neighbouring?) plots, to work as an excavation labourer.

---

51 The digital cadastral map of the settlement dated 2006 still marks the two brick buildings, but they no longer appear on the maps dated 2008 and 2010.

52 Czajlik 1993, 318, Fig. 1, Fig. 2a.

53 Soroceanu 2011, 278, 281, Taf. 3.

To sum up the subject of the "hoards and treasures" plots and their owners: according to the list of properties and lands drawn up in 1857, Simon Bonya was the owner of Plots 2991 and 2993 on the St. Vid Hill, which were most certainly owned by János Bónya in 1911 under registration numbers 2448 and 2450. Therefore, Miske purchased the first bronze finds discovered in Velem from the former owner in 1896. These strips of land (Plot 2931 in 1963) concealed Hoards Ia and Ib, and the neighbouring land owned by János Katona (Plot 2451 or 2452 according to the cadastral map and land registry of 1911, and Plot 2930 in 1963) was probably where the golden treasure was found, most likely at the end of August 1929, but quite certainly before September 5.

Thus, the location of the findspot of the golden treasure[54] is corroborated by two new pieces of information previously unknown to archaeological scholarship: (a) Miske's letter reports a trial trench next to Szentkút Spring; (b) Szilveszter Katona confirmed this during our inspection of the site, noting that the owner of the neighbouring land was called Bónya. Since then, we know from the countless studies devoted to this subject[55] that wet environments, the proximity of a river or spring, were highly preferred locations to the peoples of the European Bronze Age for presenting sacrifices (see Chapter 11, below).

In the light of the above, it is hardly surprising to find two pits, each roughly one meter deep (*Fig. 10. 5*), perhaps dug by treasure hunters, about 15–25 meters from the spring and the ruins of the scout camp, south-southwest of the aforementioned path. It is impossible to tell whether they were dug before 1929, after the discovery of the golden treasure, or no more than a few decades ago. These pits are called "Miske pits" by the locals. However, it is my conviction that (a) Miske did not dig pits, but opened proper trenches (see *Fig. 5* and his cited letter describing the planned excavation over a 30–35 m^2 large area and the trial trenches that cut through the terraces), and (b) he had the necessary foresight to always backfill his trenches to prevent any possibility of subsequent looting – not even the locals would be able to identify them after a few years.

---

[54] Gábor Bándi and Mária Fekete probably knew about this site from the recollections of the locals of Velem because they had opened three of their trenches dug in the assumed area of the golden treasure's findspot.

[55] For two more recent ones, cf. HANSEN 1997, 29–34; FONTIJN 2012, 49–68.

1.3 Investigating the golden treasure: Amália Mozsolics and Gábor Bándi

The first and still the fullest publication of the golden treasure, listing the then known analogies, was the book by Amália Mozsolics (1910–1997), printed in Basel (*Fig. 6. 3*).[56] Funded by the Hungarian National Museum, she had virtually completed the manuscript on the treasure in February 1944. This is attested by her letter addressed to Ágoston Pável, appointed the director of the Szombathely museum after Miske's death[57] (see *Appendix 6*). The publication of the monograph meant that the pieces of the treasure became known to international research.

Amália Mozsolics learnt about the golden treasure in 1940/41 when, employed by the Szombathely museum, she worked as an assistant to Miske, who rarely made the journey to Szombathely from his Kőszeg home due to his advanced age. Her task was to catalogue the museum's prehistoric collection.[58] She defined the diadem as a belt in the inventory book (*Fig. 11. 1*). The first "conservation and restoration" of the folded artefacts had been performed sometime before the inventorying, and it practically involved the partial straightening out of the diadem had been folded thirteen times, which probably caused additional damage and modification to the piece, resulting in some loss of information. Mozsolics glued a photograph of the diadem showing the "restoration" to accompany the description in the inventory book of the modern museum's predecessor (*Fig. 11. 1*). A more thorough conservation, the full straightening out, was performed between April 24 and August 5, 1943, by István Méri,[59] a conservator of the Hungarian National Museum at the time, who later became the leading Hungarian archaeologist of the Middle Ages (*Fig. 11. 2*). Performed in Kolozsvár, a few months after Miske's death,[60] the work itself was funded by the Hungarian

---

[56] Mozsolics 1950.

[57] See the records of the museum's history, SM Deparment of History, inv. no. 1944/13.

[58] Her entries in the inventory book opened by her are enriched by her drawings and the photographs of the treasure. The pieces she did not inventory at the time such as the fragments of the backplates of the treasure'a gold foils have remained uninventoried to this very day. Gyula Nováki did not re-inventory them in 1954, during re-inventorying campaign of the museum's holdings.

[59] Mozsolics 1950, 8. The receipt of the restored artefact is archived among the records of the museum's history. SM Department of History, inv. no. 111/1943 (former inv. no. 119/1943).

[60] Museum director Ágoston Pável recorded it in the list of golden artefacts kept in the museum dated May 11, 1944, which he authenticated (SM Department of Ethnography,

National Museum.[61] Méri had quite certainly mounted the diadem onto a backing (*Fig. 15. 1*) because museum director Ágoston Pável made the following entry in the 1944 gold inventory: "1 (one) gold head ornament (head band) mounted on a circular base".[62] This backing was a crude copper plate (*Fig. 13*, *Fig. 15. 1*; see Katalin T. Bruder's conservation diary, below). This conservation and restoration was undoubtedly performed on Amália Mozsolics's initiative and request, obviously with the consent and knowledge of Ferenc Tompa who had by then become the respected head of a university department. Tompa's tragic death in 1945 ultimately enabled the planned publication of Amália Mozsolics's book. In her excellent monograph,[63] she dated the golden treasure to the Hallstatt B period by associating it with the bronze hoard (Hoard I) from Velem (1896), the lost gold plates of Hoard II from Ság-hegy, the treasure found in Várvölgy (Felsőzsid), and the Rothengrub assemblage. Later, she assigned the finds from Rothengrub, Velem and Felsőzsid to the Gyermely horizon (Mozsolics BVc, Ha A2).[64]

Several decades later, Gábor Bándi (1939–1988; *Fig. 6. 4*) studied the gold foils. He published a short article in the 1976/8 issue of *Művészet*, an art periodical, in which the photograph of the diadem was first published. On the testimony of the photograph on page 29, the copper plate onto which the gold foil had been mounted was covered with cloth/textile. It seems likely that metal conservator Aladár Hesztera,[65] who was employed by the museum and completed his academic studies in those years, performed this work on Gábor Bándi's request. Regrettably, his thesis does not reveal any information relevant to this study because it does not contain any photographs. Gábor Bándi presented the assemblage of jewellery at an international conference on the Amber Road held in Bozsok in 1982.[66] He quoted a few additional analogies in his presentation and

filed under no. 47/1944. in the uninventoried material). Ethnographer Dr. Sándor Horváth called my attention to this uninventoried bundle of documents, for which I am greatly indebted to him. Cf, ILON 2009, Fig. 18.

61 Amália Mozsolics informed museum director Ágoston Pável about this in her letter dated February 21, 1944.

62 See the list of gold artefacts (filed under no. 1944/13) cited above.

63 MOZSOLICS 1950, 24–25, 41.

64 MOZSOLICS 1981, 306; 1985. 59.

65 As suggested by his manuscript, "A Velem Szent-Vidi őstelep aranydiadémája" [The gold diadem from the prehistoric settlement on St. Vid Hill of Velem]. Undated. SM Archaeological Archves, inv. no. 2147-07.

66 BÁNDI 1983.

he also proposed an early date – the beginning of the Urnfield period – compared to the one suggested by Amália Mozsolics.

The diadem mounted onto the bent, textile-covered copper plate (*Fig. 13, Fig. 15. 1*) was displayed at the archaeological exhibition in Szombathely entitled "Regions – Ages – Settlements: the Birth of the Town", opened in October 1982. The exhibition was dismantled in July 2014. It is conceivable that the missing portions of the gold foil were restored by Aladár Hesztera with poor-quality materials in an aesthetically questionable way in 1982 (*Fig. 14. 1, Fig. 15. 2–3*). The domed roundels were glued to plastic sheets (perhaps also by him) rather carelessly (*Fig. 18. 2*). Regretfully, this "restoration" is not attested in any currently known museum records. This, then, was the condition of the treasure's pieces before the new conservation work.

The new conservation project was carried out between 2004 and 2006 by Katalin T. Bruder, the chief conservator of the Hungarian National Museum, who died in 2012.[67] It was my hope that her work would also provide answers to several questions, some archaeometric in nature.

1. What was the original size and shape of the diadem?
2. Do the bronze patina marks on the reverse of the diadem and the thin bronze backplate fragments originate from the backing of the gold foil? (Similarly to Amália Mozsolics,[68] I too believed that the bronze plates were the backplates to the diadem and/or domed roundels).
3. Were the diadem, the four domed roundels, and the gold spirals manufactured in the same workshop? In addition to typological and manufacturing technological observations, it was my intention to resolve this issue by a provenance study.
4. Based on their raw material, is there any connection between the Velem assemblage and a particular group of gold finds analysed in large series by international research?

The chief conservator received the diadem and the four domed roundels in February 2004, and the gold wires, the gold spirals and the bronze backplates in September of the same year.

---

[67] Dombóvári 2012, 293.

[68] Mozsolics 1950, 7, Taf. III. 17–28.

2 Description of the artefacts and the results of the new conservation project

2.1 Description of the artefacts based on Kálmán Miske's incomplete manuscript, our observations[69] and the results of the conservation

Kálmán Miske's recently discovered manuscript dating from 1929 contains the first description of the artefacts of the treasure.[70] I shall cite the relevant passage verbatim because it contains essential information and other important remarks:

> "This gold assemblage, discovered through a stroke of good luck on the St. Vid Hill of Velem, is made up of a folded band of pure gold with a width of ca. 6 cm, whose length, give or take a little, is 80 to 100 cm, and an adornment of hopelessly tangled twisted gold wires to which round gold discs had been attached to form a necklace. The gold band as well as the round discs are decorated with circular and twisted cable motifs. The gold threads of the necklace, as can be concluded from its undamaged parts, were spirally twisted. The pure gold used for its creation indicates three techniques of wire drawing, which are as follows: triangle-shaped Δ, another one that also has D thus ◘ cross-section and a commonly used ○ round cross-section. The total weight of the gold artefact is … grm, of which the belt band's weight is … grm.
> In any case, the manufacturing technique of this gold band and the round gold plates is interesting because these incredibly thin plates are attached to a bronze plate probably for the purpose of their reinforcement, or perhaps merely to enhance the repoussé, seeing that the bronze plates are just as thin. Regrettably, these thin bronze

---

[69] I checked the smaller details together with metal conservator Csaba E. Kiss. In January and February 2008, we examined the earlier gold artefacts from Várvölgy in the Hungarian National Museum and the more recently discovered ones from the same site in the collection of the Balaton Museum of Keszthely. I was assisted in the analysis of the finer details of the goldsmithing techniques used for creating the foils by goldsmith András Radics.

[70] KVM Local History Archives, inv. no. 1942/XXXIX.109.

plates are totally obsolescent [worn?] and were found in a most fragmented condition."

2.1.1 The diadem (*Figs 12–16*)

The thickness of the gold foil varies between 0.41–0.47–0.52 mm owing to the repoussé decoration.[71] The thickness of the folded-over foil at the edge is 0.7 mm. Originally, the gold foil was applied onto a bronze backplate, as shown by folded-over edge and the scraps of the bronze backplates. The remnants of the bronze backplate[72] identified during the new conservation in three spots on the reverse of the foil were not in their original position because the impressions of the ornamental motifs on the corroded backplate do not correspond to the decoration on the diadem in the same area. The flattened drawing of the diadem (*Fig. 12. 2*) shows that it has an elongated, recumbent S shape, with one end curving upward and the other downward. There is a pair of perforations on each end of the foil (*Fig. 16. 2*), a pair under the peak in the middle (*Fig. 16. 1*) and additional ones along the lower edge (*Fig. 15. 2*). The number of the latter cannot be specified accurately owing to the damage caused by earlier folding. The perforations were made with a punch from the reverse towards the obverse bearing the decorative design (*Fig. 16. 2*), a not particularly elegant procedure. The diameters of the perforations vary. The upper amorphous perforation on the left end is 1.8 x 1.2 mm, while the lower one is 1.5 mm. The upper perforation on the right end is pentagonal and measures 2.2 mm, while the one underneath it is oblong shaped and measures 2.2 mm as well (*Fig. 16. 2*). Of the perforations on the top, the one beside the concentric circle is triangular and measures 2 mm, while the one interrupting the cable pattern is round and measures 1.2 mm (*Fig. 16. 1*). The stamped decoration of the diadem is composed of concentric circles combined with bosses in the centre (*Figs 14–16*), zigzag (*Fig. 16. 3*) and cable patterns (see below, for a detailed discussion). The length of the flattened diadem is 403 mm, its greatest height is 97 mm. The greatest diameter of the foil in its "original" form after conservation is 193 mm; its weight is 23.09 g. Inv. no. 54.603.11, sample code: VD and V5. Formerly unavailable essential information

---

[71] The thickness of the gold foil of the cap ornament (*Goldhut*) in the Museum für Vor- und Frühgeschichte in Berlin is 0.06 mm (60 micron), while that of the neck ornament in Berlin is 0.02 mm (BORN 2003b, 89, 95); the median thickness of the gold foil of the cap ornament (*Goldkegel*) from Ezelsdorf is 0.08 mm (KOCH 2003, 99).

[72] Cf. MOZSOLICS 1950, Abb. 1. 1, for a reconstruction drawing of the backplate.

(such as weight) about the diadem and the other pieces of jewellery as well as the first reconstruction of how it was worn appeared in the guide to an exhibition organised in 2008 by the present author in collaboration with Marcella Nagy as well as in the jubilee volume of the Savaria Museum in 2009.[73]

2.1.2 The domed roundels (*Figs 17–20*)

These artefacts have always been referred to as *Scheibe* ("disc") in German publications;[74] however, given that their form is semi-spherical, the term domed roundel seems more appropriate, especially in view of similar artefacts found at Ippensheim–Bullenheimer Berg,[75] Worms[76] and Hammersdorf[77] designated as *Buckel* in German. Like the diadem, they were made of gold foil and similarly mounted on a bronze backplate (*Fig. 23*), over which the gold foil was folded back. A reconstruction of the gold foil and the backplate was published by Amália Mozsolics over half a century ago.[78] The domed roundels are framed by gold wire wound around bronze wire as was observed and recorded by Miske in his letter cited above.

The decoration and colour of each domed roundel pair (before conservation) was identical, but the decoration and colour of the pairs differed. Amália Mozsolics assumed that the lighter-coloured domed roundels (*Figs 19–20*; Mozsolics 1950, Taf. II. 3–4, Pair II according to the current classification) and the diadem of identical colour had been made of electrum using the same tools.[79] Her contention was refuted by Katalin T. Bruder's observations on colour (see below), which has since been confirmed by the metal analysis too. A new theory based on the visually identifiable traits and the assumed colour differences of the treasure[80] can thus be rejected as being entirely groundless.

---

73 Nagy – Ilon – Révész 2008; Ilon – Nagy 2009, 52–53.

74 Mozsolics 1950; Bándi 1983.

75 Gebhard 2003, Abb. 2.

76 David 2003, Abb. 2, 11–12.

77 David 2010, 455–456, Abb. 11.

78 Mozsolics 1950, Abb. 1. 2.

79 Mozsolics 1950, 9.

80 Fekete 2010, 394–398.

Pair I (*Figs 17–18*)

This ornament pair was manufactured from gold foil and a bronze backplate. Its colour, darker than that of the other pair, was caused by the staining of the gold foil (see Katalin T. Bruder's conservation diary, below).

Domed roundel 1[81] (*Fig. 17. 1, 4, Fig. 18. 1*; BÁNDI 1983, Abb. 3. 1 = MOZSOLICS 1950, Taf. II. 1) lacks about one-sixth of its original size, which probably broke off. Gold wire twisted around a bronze wire was set around its edge. Six points of the attachment of the spiral survive. The diameter of the spiral is 1.4 mm. A stamped design of seven concentric circles (*Ringbuckel*) in the centre is framed by stamped cable and zigzag motifs. The diameter of the domed roundel is 56 mm, its thickness is 0.41–0.6 mm. Its weight prior to conservation was 3.16 g and 3.86 g after conservation, together with the Japanese tissue and adhesive. Inv. no. 54.603.9, sample code: V1.

Domed roundel 4 (*Fig. 17. 1, 4, Fig. 18. 2*; BÁNDI 1983, Abb. 3. 2 = MOZSOLICS 1950, Taf. II. 2) lacks about one-half of its original size. It ornamentation is identical to the previous one. The diameter of the spiral placed around its edge is 0.8–1 mm. Five points of its attachment survive. A fragment of the bronze backplate can be seen on the reverse, but it was not placed in its original position during conservation. The diameter of the domed roundel is 56 mm, its thickness is 0.51 mm. Its weight prior to conservation was 1.50 g and 4.87 g after conservation, together with the Japanese tissue and adhesive. Inv. no. 54.603.8, sample code: V4. In 2012. I published a preliminary report on this domed roundel pair earlier.[82]

Pair II (*Figs 19–20*)

This ornament pair was made of gold foil whose colour, prior to conservation, was a slightly lighter yellow than of the previous pair.

Domed roundel 2 (*Fig. 19, Fig. 20 1. 3*; BÁNDI 1983, Abb. 4. 2 = MOZSOLICS 1950, Taf. II. 3) lacks two sections opposite each other. Gold wire twisted around a bronze wire was set around its edge. The diameter of the spiral is 1.2 mm. Six points of its attachment survive. A row of concentric circles was stamped around its edge, followed by cable and zigzag motifs which frame a pattern of seven stamped concentric circles in the centre. The diameter of the domed roundel is

[81] The numbering was determined by the sequence of the artefact as a belt reconstruction displayed at the permanent exhibition opened in October 1982; after its dismantling, the conservator numbered them according to that sequence.

[82] ILON 2012a.

56 mm, its thickness is 0.8 mm. Its weight prior to conservation was 2.05 g and 3.56 g after conservation, together with the Japanese tissue and adhesive. Inv. no. 54.603.6, sample code: V2.

Domed roundel 3 (*Fig. 19*, *Fig. 20. 2, 4*; BÁNDI 1983, Abb. 4. 1 = MOZSOLICS 1950, Taf. II. 4) is identical with previous piece as regards its decoration. However, a part has broken off and it has radial cracks on its surface. The diameter of the gold spiral is 1 mm. Seven points of its attachment survive. The diameter of the domed roundel is 56 mm, its thickness is 0.44 mm. Its weight prior to conservation was 2.46 g and 3.93 g after conservation, together with the Japanese tissue and adhesive. Inv. no. 54.603.7, sample code: V3. In 2013, I published a preliminary report on this domed roundel pair.[83]

2.1.3 The bronze backplates (*Fig. 23*)

The bronze backplates served as reinforcements to both the diadem and the gold foils of the domed roundels.[84] Their total weight is 17.9 g, without the fragments that were earlier glued to the plastic plates, making them irremovable and immeasurable. Inv. no. 54.603.12.

2.1.4 The gold spirals (*Figs 21–22*)

A smaller portion are still spirals, but the majority was carelessly straightened out either before the deposition and/or after their discovery,[85] which, regrettably, makes any interpretation of their function much more difficult or downright impossible. They were attached to polystyrene plates and stored in a box, a rather lamentable . Each piece was numbered and measured during their conservation, and a better storage was also ensured.[86] The total weight of the sixty-six gold spirals is 49 g (*Table 1*). Inv. no. 54.603.10, sample code of the pieces selected for analysis: Vel4, Vel5, Vel6.

---

83 ILON 2013b.

84 The mode of attachment of the backplates to the golden foils could be analysed by modern technology (e.g. 3D scanning), but I had no means of using an instrument of this type.

85 When Amália Mozsolics inventoried the pieces of the treasure in 1941, the spirals were still entangled.

86 Their weight was not published earlier.

Table 1: The weight of the gold wires

Number	Weight (g)	Number	Weight (g)	Number	Weight (g)
1	9.3	23	<0.1	45	0.8
2	1.8	24	2.1	46	0.8
3	0.2	25	0.8	47	0.8
4	1.3	26	0.8	48	1.0
5	0.6	27	1.4	49	0.8
6	0.2	28	0.4	50	0.9
7	1.6	29	0.6	51	0.7
8	0.2	30	0.5	52	0.1
9	0.4	31	0.5	53	0.2
10	0.4	32	0.9	54	0.5
11	0.1	33	1.1	55	0.4
12	0.2	34	0.3	56	0.4
13	1.0	35	0.6	57	0.3
14.	0.6	36	0.4	58	0.2
15	0.5	37	0.5	59	0.4
16	0.4	38	0.4	60	0.4
17	0.2	39	0.4	61	0.2
18	0.2	40	0.1	62	0.2
19	2.1	41	0.7	63	0.2
20	0.4	42	1.2	64	0.1
21	2.3	43	0.7	65	0.1
22	0.2	44	0.8	66	0.1
Total	**49.0**				

2.1.5 The weight of the treasure

The total weight of the surviving gold foils prior to conservation was 82.07 g.[87] Can the original weight of the artefacts be estimated somehow? Yes, it can, although we have to proceed very cautiously.

The weight of the diadem is 23.09 g. A piece of foil the size of a domed roundel is missing from the diadem on its right side if viewed frontally and on its left side if viewed according to how it was worn (*Fig. 12, Fig. 14. 1, Fig. 15. 3*),

[87] Amounting to one-sixth of the total weight of the treasure mae up of thirteen gold vessels found in Villena (Alicante, Spain). Cf. ARMBRUSTER 2012, 371.

disregarding now the other minor damages (*Fig. 15. 6*). Based on the weight of the light domed roundels, this missing portion must be at least 2.5 g. Therefore, the original weight of the foil can be estimated as roughly 25.59 g.

Some of the domed roundels are also incomplete. In the case of Pair I (*Fig. 17*), the average weight of each piece is *ca.* 3 g (V1: 3.16 g; V4: 1.50 g, but the latter barely exceeds a half fragment). Their damage and missing portions suggest a gold foil that must have been slightly heavier originally. The domed roundels of Pair II (*Fig. 19*; V2: 2.05 g, V3: 2.46 g) suggest gold foils that had an original average weight of *ca.* 2.5 g, but certainly below 3 g. In other words, the weight of these four jewellery foils must have been 2 x 3 g or 2 x 2.5 g, totalling roughly 11 g. It must be borne in mind that this figure does not represent the pure gold weight because the gold spirals had been wound around a bronze wire core. As far as the almost completely unravelled gold tangle weighing 49 g in all is concerned (*Fig. 21*; some of the spiral fragments also contained bronze wire cores!), its weight remains wholly uncertain because there is no information about how much of it disappeared since its discovery in 1929.

Therefore, the reconstructed minimum total weight of the gold foils and the surviving spiral wires is 85.59 g + x g, the latter representing the spirals presumably lost.

2.2 Extract from Katalin T. Bruder's conservation diary[88]

2.2.1 The first phase of the conservation project: assessment of the condition of the artefacts

Diadem (sample code: VD and V5)

The gold foil of the diadem originally overlay the bronze backplate. The foil was mounted onto the backplate by folding over an approximately 2 mm wide strip along the edges. In our opinion, there must have been some organic adhesive or filling between the bronze and gold plates, similarly to the "discs"; this adhesive naturally broke down as time passed. Regrettably, the folded-over part was carelessly flattened during previous conservation – the bronze remains

[88] Together with chief conservator Csaba E. Kiss, we checked all the measurements specified in the conservation diary on March 5, 2012.

were perhaps destroyed at this time. Its restoration into its assumed original state cannot be performed without damage.

During one of the conservation projects, the gold overlay was glued to a crude copper plate having a thickness of 1 mm (359 g) (*Fig. 15. 1*). The missing portions of the gold foil were filled with dental plastic (Kalloplaszt, Duracryl, or some similar material). Acetone was used to remove this plastic, after which we found that the gold foil had broken into several fragments at certain points. Traces of iron corrosion were noted in the grooves of the design covering the surface of the diadem.

There are two perforations on either end of the diadem, and two others underneath the peak on top; additional perforations could be identified at four points along the lower edge. It seems likely that the fractures occurred exactly where there were perforations originally. The perforations were probably made to fasten the diadem to a cap-like headwear, or to attach the bronze backplate and the gold overlay to each other. The form of the perforations differs from those on the "discs".

Domed roundels (sample codes: V1, V2, V3, V4)

Acetone was used to detach the gold foils from the transparent, green plastic plates (*Fig. 18. 3*; the adhesive was some sort of soluble and colourless lacquer). The "discs" are not only incomplete, but were also fragmented when attached. The adhesive could be removed with acetone and alcohol, but an unidentifiable staining could only be removed by hand. Sodium hexametaphosphate was used for the treatment of the stained and lacklustre surface of the gold foil. "Discs" 1 and 4 were stained brown,[89] and the staining from these discs could be removed for the greater part.

There was a round, bronze backplate underneath the gold foils, which was almost completely destroyed, presumably due to previous treatments and during the time they lay buried. The edge of the gold foil is wavy, has a fairly irregular line, and is folded over the round bronze backplate along a 0.2 mm wide strip. The twisted cable around the edge of the obverse of the gold-covered bronze backplate was created by tightly winding a 1 mm wide gold strip around 1 mm wide bronze wire without leaving any space (*Fig. 21. 2–3*). The twisted cable thus created was attached by means of two, or perhaps three, bands laced through a rectangular perforation cut into each "disc" (*Fig. 17. 3*). The distance between

[89] Amália Mozsolics noted their darker colour. MOZSOLICS 1950, 8–9.

the attachment points varies. The use of solvents for removing the "discs" from the green plastic plates resulted in the gold overlay falling into many small fragments, especially in the case of the two "discs" decorated with two concentric circles (Pair II). We confirmed what had been merely an impression earlier, namely that their previous refitting was rather erratic. The removal of many kinds of adhesives[90] was followed by the sorting of the fragments and their temporary refitting to each other. We found that if the fragments were refitted accurately, the restored object would be semi-spherical with a convex surface,[91] instead of being a flat and round object (*Fig. 17. 4*, *Fig. 19. 2*). The final refitting was made using Japanese tissue coloured golden yellow in order to reinforce the artefact (with the use of Planatol).

Gold spirals

They vary in size (the following figures are approximate because these spirals are deformed in many cases).

– Spirals with round cross-section and a diameter of 1.09–1.12–1.25 mm, made from a gold band of triangular cross-section wound tightly around a 1 mm thick bronze wire. The width of the latter is 0.5 mm. Sample code: Vel4. These spirals were used for creating three-lobed passmanterie-like patterns connected by a gold band (*Fig. 21. 2–3*).

– Spirals with round cross-section and a thickness of 2.38–2.6 mm, made from a gold band of triangular cross-section wound tightly around a bronze wire. The latter did not include any that could be measured. Sample code: Vel 5.

– Spiral with flattened circle (rounded rectangle) cross-section, made from gold band of triangular cross section. The width of the spiral at each end is 3.7 mm and 4.7 mm, and 2.4 mm, respectively. An additional similar piece, measuring 5.8 x 4.9 mm (*Fig. 21. 2*; MOZSOLICS 1950, Abb. 5. 1), made from a gold band with triangular cross-section. Sample code: Vel6 (*Fig. 21. 4*). In our opinion, these might have been wound around some sort of organic material such as a textile

90 Perhaps added by István Méri and Aladár Hesztera during their conservation work.

91 The same phenomenon, i.e. an earlier flattening and straightening of the "*Buckel*", reflected by the radial cracks, fractures and creases, has been noted in the case of several similar artefacts, e.g. Óbuda: MOZSOLICS 1950, Abb. 7. 1–2; Felsőzsid: MOZSOLICS 1950, Taf. VII. 8–10; Cófalva: MOZSOLICS 1950, Taf. VIII. 1–9, 11–12; Moordorf: GOLD UND KULT 2003, Kat. Nr. 12.

ribbon or leather strap because no remnants of a bronze backplate were found on them. Comparable objects are known from the assemblage from Óbuda.[92]

Bronze plate fragments (Fig. 23; Mozsolics 1950, Taf. III, 17–28)

One part of the corroded bronze fragments was stored in a little plastic box (once used to store typewriter ribbons) which was kept in the vault of the museum. These fragments were the few entirely corroded scraps of the bronze backplates reinforcing the reverse of the decorated gold overlay. These were corroded to the gold overlay due to the nature of the material, although they did preserve its pattern. Regrettably, the number of fragments is negligible compared to the size of the gold overlay. In general, it is impossible to determine with any certainty whether these fragments were attached to the diadem or the "discs" (and, more specifically, to which of the latter), they are unsuitable for comparative metal analyses or for far-reaching conclusions in this respect. The following could be noted during their examination:

- One fragment, the largest of all, from the inner part of one of the "discs", is strongly deformed. Since the bronze is wholly corroded, this deformation could only have occurred when the piece was still an intact, i.e. at the time of its deposition at the latest.
- Relatively larger fragments (¼–½ cm^2), most likely from the domed roundel(s) have a domed surface, confirming that they were not flat discs, but had a semi-spherical form typical of domed roundels.
- The fragments included a granule, a tiny spherule with a diameter of *ca.* 1 mm. Its colour is white and metallic, but black staining (corrosion) covers its surface. It is possible that it was added to the original fragments during previous work. These fragments were previously neglected because there were plant root fragments and soil among them.
- The careful examination indicated that there were bent fragments as well, which had been deformed in their original state. It seems to me that they were parts of the diadem's bronze backplate[93] and that they became deformed when the gold foil was folded, and became corroded afterwards. When the gold overlay was straightened out,[94] these corroded bronze backplates fell out.

---

[92] Barth 1988/1989, 156, Taf. 1–8.

[93] Kálmán Miske recognised the "backing" function of the bronze plates and described it in the draught of his letter from 1929, cited in the above.

[94] Between 1929 and 1943, and in 1943.

2.2.2 The second phase of the conservation project: the reconstruction of the artefacts

The extremely thin gold foil and fragments were sorted after cleaning. Refitting was first temporary and the final refitting was made using Japanese tissue coloured golden for reinforcement and Planatol (a water based, neutral adhesive that can be removed easily after drying by solvents). The artefacts were doubly reinforced at the gaps. The accurate refitting revealed that the "discs" had a convex surface and that the diadem too was slightly convex in its centre.

It became clear that the planned galvanoplastic restoration could not be performed; the gold foil was thinner than assumed during the preliminary examination, and the galvanoplastic restoration would in this case have been a rough and heavy solution, making refitting much more difficult.

2.2.3 Summary of the results of the conservation project

First of all, it must be highlighted that the general condition of the assemblage called for extraordinary care owing to its significance, which meant a fairly slow pace of conservation work. Immediately upon beginning our work, one of the encountered difficulties was that the gold foils had been carelessly attached to crude backplates (*Fig. 14. 3*), namely coarse copper and plastic plates (*Fig. 14, Fig. 15. 1*), by gluing and that both the diadem and the "discs" were "cobbled together" erratically. Moreover, the original shape of these artefacts was further deformed before they were displayed.[95]

The meticulous and slow conservation calling for immense care could only be begun after the assessment of these problems.

1. The diadem and the "discs" (four pieces) were detached from the copper and plastic plates and their original form was restored.

2. We established that the diadem had been mounted on a thin bronze backplate (*Fig. 23*) whose fragments survived, and a few of these could be preserved on the gold plate.[96]

---

[95] Deformation did not occur at that time, but before the deposition of the objects.

[96] Although not in their original position. Microscopic observation made together with conservator Csaba E. Kiss on March 5, 2012.

3. We found that the circumference of the diadem was greater than presented prior to the conservation. We established that there were four perforations made by the goldsmith on the lower part of the diadem.[97]

4. We established that the planned galvanoplastic restoration could not be performed owing to the thickness (or, rather, the thinness) of the gold foil.

5. After cleaning, the thin gold foils were mounted onto Japanese tissue and refitted. The Japanese tissue allows the study of the reverse, and its subsequent removal, if necessary, can be performed without damage. It is a neutral material that does not react with the metal, but it is, at the same time, a flexible medium that moves along with the original. We therefore experimented with creating a durable restoration. Knowing that any substitute applied next to gold can be immediately recognised, the surface was coated with real gold.

6. We found that the "discs" had a semi-spherical form, which was confirmed by the remnants of the bronze backplates onto which they had been mounted. The restoration was performed accordingly. Three of the domed roundels were reconstructed using the procedure described above, while the restoration of the fourth called for the application of a stronger material which would meet the above requirements. The reason for this was that a weaker material would not maintain its shape in the case of such a significant degree of restoration.

7. The creation of replicas. A replica of the diadem was also produced; however, a negative could only be made with the utmost care because of its dimensions and the thinness of its material. It first had to be reinforced in order to prevent any damage or deformation. After careful isolation, this was performed with foam, which would take up the shape, while its weight would be negligible, and also because it was neutral, it would not emit contaminants and would guarantee appropriate stability. The replica was produced by galvanoplasty (galvano-gilding). Manufacturing the replicas of the domed roundels was also difficult because of their poor condition and because of the decorative gold spirals attached to them. Therefore, creating their negative by the conventional technique was impossible; instead, we used a somewhat modified material and technique for the purpose of siliconing. Their replicas were produced in a similar manner as that of the diadem.

8. The spiral decoration. The bronze wire wound tightly with a gold band encircling the domed roundels had at least one eyelet or loop on the domed roundels (except for domed roundel 1, on which it could not be identified). The

[97] Or perhaps only two.

width of the spiral band was about 1.5 mm, although the width and thickness of these bands varied, probably owing to their manufacturing technique and, also. because of elongation when winding. Regrettably, the spirals lacking a bronze wire core had been straightened out earlier (*Fig. 21. 3*), and they had thus not only lost their original shape, but the band itself had an occasional twist in it, which also involved the elongation of the material. These had to be straightened out carefully and painstakingly before they were rewound again. They were rewound clockwise.

The size of the gold spirals varied (see below, in Chapter 3).

9. Before the start of conservation work, digital photographs of the artefacts were taken by Gábor Papp in Szombathely on September 13, 2002 (*Fig. 14*). Additional photos were made by Katalin T. Bruder in Budapest on April 14 and 17, July 14, September 1, 2, 17 and 23, and October 1, 2004 (*Fig. 15*, etc.) during the work. Other photos were taken by Tamás Tárczy in Szombathely on April 29, 2008 (*Fig. 24*, etc.) and by Tibor Takács, also in Szombathely, on July 11, 2013 (*Fig. 16*, etc.).

3 The results of the archaeometric analysis of the golden treasure

3.1 The results of the scanning electron microscopy with X-ray microanalysis (SEM-EMA) and their evaluation

These analyses were performed by physicist Attila L. Tóth. The first series of measurements focusing on the gold foils (diadem, domed roundels) was completed on August 15, 2004. The samples were the tiny, apparently gold metal scraps that could not be refitted during restoration originating from the diadem (VD/V5) and the domed roundels (V1-4). The qualitative and semi-quantitative analyses (i.e. slightly inaccurate because of the unevenness of the surface owing to the decorative designs) were performed on the fracture surfaces of the samples.

Domed roundels, Pair I:

- Domed roundel 1, having a weight of 3.16 g, sample code: V1 (*Fig. 17. 1, 4, Fig. 18. 1*; BÁNDI 1983, Abb. 3. 1 = MOZSOLICS 1950, Taf. II. 1);
- Domed roundel 4, having a weight of 1.50 g, sample code: V4 (*Fig. 17. 1, 4, Fig. 18. 2*; BÁNDI 1983, Abb. 3. 2 = MOZSOLICS 1950, Taf. II. 2).

Domed roundels, Pair II:

- Domed roundel 2, having a weight of 2.05 g, sample code: V2 (*Fig. 19, Fig. 20. 1, 3*; BÁNDI 1983, Abb. 4. 2 = MOZSOLICS 1950, Taf. II. 3);
- Domed roundel 3, having a weight of 2.46 g, sample code: V3 (*Fig. 19, Fig. 20. 2, 4*; BÁNDI 1983, Abb. 4. 1 = MOZSOLICS 1950, Taf. II. 4).

The measurements were assessed by chemist Márta Járó,[98] who noted that all the five samples of Series I were gold alloys with a similar composition. The diadem (sample V5/VD; *Fig. 25*) and domed roundels 1 and 5 (samples V1 and V4; *Fig. 26*) had a virtually identical composition. The composition of domed roundel 2 (sample V2; *Fig. 27. 1*) differed slightly. Nonetheless, the composition of the four samples could be regarded as identical within the margin of error of the semi-quantitative analysis: ≈ 79–82% gold, ≈ 15–18% silver, and ≈ 2–3% copper. The composition of domed roundel 3 (sample V3; *Fig. 27. 2*) was ≈ 86% gold, ≈ 11% silver, and ≈ 3% copper and it differed but slightly from that of the other four artefacts, although this difference does not necessarily suggest another

[98] SM Archaeological Archives, Márta Járó's report dated August 21.

provenance or alloy. According to Márta Járó, the alloys could originate from both primary or secondary sources of native gold[99] (gold mines, or alluvial gold washed from rivers such as the nearby Danube,[100] which has the second highest gold content after the Rhine).

Thus, we may reasonably conclude that the diadem (VD) and one pair of domed roundels (Pair I: V1 and V4) were made of identical raw material in the same workshop, as I had earlier suggested. In my view, the key evidence for manufacture in the same workshop is provided by domed roundel 2 of pair II (V2: *Fig. 19*, *Fig. 20. 1, 3*, *Fig. 27. 1*; BÁNDI 1983, Abb. 4. 2 = MOZSOLICS 1950, Taf. II. 3) because despite its different colour prior to conservation, its metal composition links pairs I and II with the diadem. In other words, it is possible that all five objects had been produced in the same workshop, despite the slight divergences in the combinations of decorative motifs and the sizes of the punched and stamped designs.

A brief detour must here be made regarding the relationship between the domed roundel pairs. Another difference between them, aside from the combination of decorative motifs, is their weight. The most recent measurements made using digital scales, for the first time since the treasure has been studied, gave the following data: the average weight of the two domed roundels of Pair I (V1: 3.16 g; V4: 1.50 g, but only about one-half of the latter survived) suggests that the original gold foil had an approximate weight of 3 g or slightly more, while the domed roundels of Pair II (V2: 2.05 g; V3: 2.46 g) suggest an original gold foil weighing approximately 2.5 g, but certainly less than 3 g. This difference is negligible considering prehistoric measuring techniques and irrelevant in terms of identifying workshops. This is also confirmed by the slightly differing weight of the virtually undamaged pair of gold domed roundels allegedly found in Óbuda (2.4 g and 2.9 g, respectively).[101] Regrettably, the weight of the six heavily fragmented domed roundels (all weighing less than 1 g) of gold hoard 1 found in Várvölgy in 1926[102] are unsuitable for a similar comparison. At the same time, the weight data of the domed roundels from Velem and Óbuda are very instructive because they suggest the use of a standard weight system.

---

[99] LEHRBERGER 1995, 115–144.

[100] UZSOKI 1984, 73–81; UZSOKI 1985, 285–303; UZSOKI 2004; CZAJLIK 2012, 39–40, Abb. 1B.

[101] BARTH 1988/1989, 158, Taf. I. 12–13.

[102] MOZSOLICS 1981, 300, Taf. 7–12.

It seems to me that the similarities and divergences described here wholly confirm that the gold foils of the five artefacts (the diadem and the four domed roundels) were crafted at the same time from almost identical raw material in the same workshop. It is possible that domed roundel 3 of Pair II was manufactured from a gold foil with a different composition or was made somewhat later as a replacement, but with the same tools and in the same workshop. Moreover, we could equally well ask why the four domed roundels should represent artefacts of the same category regarding their decoration and weight. We could conceptualise a construct that is both asymmetric, with the domed roundels differing in terms of their ornamentation and weight, and symmetric, with the two domed roundels of each pair being identical. It must be borne in mind that we have no way of telling whether the artefacts of a treasure represent a functional assemblage, or whether they were simply deposited together. Nevertheless, the symbolism of the gold foils too points towards their being related (see below, in Chapter 4).

The second series of analyses focused on the bronze backplate fragments and the gold spirals.[103] They were analysed on October 7, 2004. We found that the uninventoried gold spirals (originally the elements of the breast ornament/pectoral and the framing of the domed roundels) were gold alloys containing silver and copper. Similarly to the gold foils of the treasure, the material of the alloys could equally have originated from primary (gold mine) or secondary (alluvial gold) sources of native gold.

Thin spiral (sample code: Vel4). Round cross-section, width: 1.25 mm, made of a gold band with triangular cross- section.[104] The sample indicated an alloy of 88.5% gold, 10.5% silver and 1% copper (*Fig. 28*), a near-identical composition to domed roundel 3 (sample V3; *Fig. 27. 2*). Medium-thick spiral (sample code: Vel5). Round cross-section, width: 2.5 mm, made of a gold band of triangular cross-section. The sample indicated an alloy of 98% gold, 1% silver and 1% copper (*Fig. 28. 2*). Thick spiral (sample code: Vel6). Flattened circular cross-section, thickness: 6 x 4 and 7 x 5 mm, made of a gold band of triangular cross-section. The sample indicated an alloy of 78% gold, 19% silver and 3% copper (*Fig. 29. 1*), a near-identical composition to the diadem (*Fig. 25*) and domed roundels 1 and 4 (*Fig. 26*).

As we can see, the composition of the medium-thick spiral (Vel5) with a high (almost totally pure) gold content differs significantly from the thinner spiral

[103] SM Archaeological Archives, Márta Járó's report dated October 25, 2004.

[104] Miske had correctly noted and described cross-sections of this type in his letter cited above.

(Vel4, ≈ –10% Au), and from the thicker spiral (Vel6, ≈ –20% Au). At the same time, the three bands from which the spirals were twisted are morphologically identical (triangular cross-section), meaning that they were made using the same technique. The composition of the medium-thick spiral (Vel5) differs from all the other gold artefacts in the treasure: it is the purest and the softest.

I was also curious to know whether the gold foils had been attached to the bronze backplates in the same workshop and whether they had the same raw material.

The remnants of the backplate from domed roundel 1 (3.16 g; BÁNDI 1983, Abb. 3. 1 = MOZSOLICS 1950, Taf. II. 1; sample code: Vel3, Vel3a) were corrosion products and had no metal core. Its composition was 12% copper, 66% tin and 19% lead (*Fig. 30. 2*). The same was found for the residue from the reverse of domed roundel 3 (2.46 g; BÁNDI 1983, Abb. 4. 1 = MOZSOLICS 1950, Taf. II. 4; sample code: Vel2), whose composition was *ca.* 74% copper, 22% tin and 3% lead (*Fig. 30. 1*). Regrettably, the same held true for the sample taken from the reverse of the diadem as well (sample code: Vel1; *Fig. 29. 2*). The corrosion contained *ca.* 46% copper, 48% tin and 5% lead. In sum, all three samples were the corrosion products of copper-tin-lead alloys and in the lack of the original metal of the backplate, they were unsuitable for drawing any conclusions regarding workshops.

The results of the metal analyses can be summed up as follows:

1. All artefacts of the treasure are gold alloys, but none is white gold (i.e. electrum that is composed of three parts gold and one part silver).

2. One spiral (Vel5) is nearly 100% pure gold (*Fig. 28. 2*).

3. Domed roundel 3 (V3; *Fig. 27. 2*) and one spiral (Vel4; *Fig. 28. 1*) have the next highest gold content: ≈ 86% and 88.5%, respectively.

4. The composition of the diadem (VD/V5) and domed roundels 1, 2 and 4 (V1, V2, V4) as well as one spiral (Vel6) is as follows: ≈ 79–82% gold, ≈ 15–18% silver, and ≈ 2–3% copper.

5. The composition of Pair I of domed roundels (V1, V4) (*Fig. 26*) is closest to and practically identical with that of the diadem (V5; *Fig. 25*), refuting Amália Mozsolics and Mária Fekete's contentions – based on the colour of the artefacts – that they had been replacements made at a later date. In other words, the diadem and Pair I were presumably manufactured at the same time from the same material.

6. The presence of tin (Sn) was not indicated by this analysis, and thus the origin of the gold, whether it was alluvial or mined, remains open.

7. The bronze backplates to the gold foils (samples from the diadem and domed roundels 1 and 3 were submitted to analyses) were heavily corroded and had no metal cores (*Fig. 23*, *Fig. 29. 2*). The corrosion product is an alloy of copper, tin and lead, in which tin is a contaminant and might indicate the ore type. The high lead content could be the result of slow solubility and of its accumulation at the point selected for sampling.[105] The bronze backplates of the gold foils interpreted as necklaces (*Halskragen*) or collars (*Halsbergen*)[106] housed in the Museum für Vor- und Frühgeschichte in Berlin were also heavily corroded. They had a high copper, but no tin content.[107] Therefore, the metal analyses did not is as any clues regarding the raw material of the backplates.

3.2 Metal provenance studies in a European context

The provenancing of the metal raw material of European gold objects was begun in 1952 under the direction of Siegfried Junghans (1915–1999), who conducted systematic analyses (Studien zu den Anfängen der Metallurgie, SAM), still a basic reference series, in collaboration with the Württemberg State Museum in Stuttgart, the Römisch-Germanisches Zentralmuseum and researchers from various other countries.[108] The results were published by Axel Hartmann in 1970 and 1982.[109] Gold artefacts found in Spain were analysed with more modern instruments as part of the so-called "Proyecto-Au" project of the past decade.[110]

The analyses conducted by Axel Hartmann were performed by neutron activation, X-ray fluorescence and spectral analysis.[111] These analyses required at least 5 mm² large samples weighing 5–10 mg. Groups were distinguished according the ratio of gold (Au), silver (Ag) and copper (Cu). Because the presence of tin (Sn) and of other trace elements could not be accurately determined, the fundamental question of the origin of the gold, whether it had been washed or mined, remained unanswered, and thus a reliable provenancing could not be

[105] I am grateful to Géza Szabó for calling my attention to certain problems related to lead in his review of the manuscript. SZABÓ 1998, 161, Fig. 4.
[106] HÄNSEL 2003, 158, Abb. 2c, 161, Abb. 7, 163, Abb. 9.
[107] BORN 2003a, 179, note 7.
[108] HARTMANN 1982, XII.
[109] HARTMANN 1970, 1982.
[110] ARMBRUSTER 2013, 456.
[111] HARTMANN 1970, 16–17.

performed either. The series of measurements only enabled the chronological and spatial classification of the gold artefacts.[112]

Similarly to the SAM measurements, we could not measure the amounts of tin and trace elements in the case of the Velem gold foils, but we can compare the analytical results with the SAM data. The copper content of these foils ranges between 2–4%. The "alloys" could equally well originate from primary (mined deposits) or secondary (washed, alluvial gold) sources. The absence of tin[113] too reflects this duality. Based on their composition, the Velem gold finds share a partial similarity with the Danubian groups as identified by Axel Hartmann:[114] (a) with Group A_3,[115] insofar as some samples do not contain tin; (b) within this group, with the sub-group with a higher copper content, of which two samples (1437: Armeniş, 1445: Slatina)[116] had a copper content exceeding 3% and a tin content of only 0.005 and 0.006%, respectively. However, the majority of artefacts assigned here had a silver content that was twice as high as that of the domed roundels from Velem; (c) the gold foils can be best compared with Group A_1/N in terms of their Au, Ag and Cu contents, although a minimum amount of tin was also detected in the case of the pieces assigned to this group.[117] It must here be recalled that Hartmann assigned the gold foil jewellery from Óbuda[118] and Rothengrub[119] in the Museum of Natural History in Vienna, the best typological analogies to the above domed roundels, to this group. The composition of these more or less contemporaneous gold artefacts from sites lying closest to Velem are as follows:[120] the domed roundel from Óbuda (sample. no. 51 299) contained ≈ 20% silver and 2% copper, while the spiral contained ≈ 18.5% silver and 1.5% copper; the "belt mount" from Rothengrub (sample no. 72 475) contained 18% silver and 3% copper; the "disc" (sample no. 72 474) had 29% silver and 2.5%

[112] Hartmann 1982, 4–43.

[113] Hartmann 1970, 11.

[114] The groups defined by him have withstood the test of time; while the results of the control measurements performed with more modern analytical methods (PIXE) on the finds from Lebrija (Seville, Spain) are more accurate, the ratios of the components are basically the same. A difference of 1–3% for Ag and of 0.05–0.2% for Cu has been determined. Cf. Perea – Armbruster – Demortier – Montero 2003, 99–114, Taf. 3.

[115] Hartmann 1970, 39–40, Abb. 3; Hartmann 1982, 10–11, Abb. 4.

[116] Hartmann 1970, 41, Tab. 16a.

[117] Hartmann 1970, 42–43, Tab. 18.

[118] Mozsolics 1950, 14, Abb. 7

[119] Pittioni 1952.

[120] Hartmann 1970, Tab. 18.

copper, while a spiral (sample no. 72 476) contained ≈ 15% silver and 2.1% copper.

Axel Hartmann assigned the gold plate from Binningen (Ag: ≈ 18%, Cu: 3.6%) and the gold disc from Worms (Ag: 10–12%, Cu: 4.9–5%)[121] to the N/NC Central European Group and the pieces from Óbuda, Székesfehérvár, Felsőzsid and Rothengrub to the A1/N, i.e. the Danubian Group.[122]

The gold artefacts from Arikogel and Koppental by Lake Hallstatt contained 16–22% and 12–23% silver, as well as 0.9–2.7 and 0.2–4% copper, respectively. These gold treasures were assigned to Group A_3 (gold of the Hajdúsámson horizon) in Hartmann's classification, with the remark that the identification of the provenance of this group is uncertain.[123] Although near-forgotten by research, two artefacts from Féregyháza,[124] a site lying farther and more eastward (Mozsolics's BIVb, Bz D1, Ópályi horizon), were analysed with destructive wet testing by József Loczka, revealing that one of the bracelets contained 81.18% gold and 18.19% silver as well as copper and iron. The composition of one of the wires of the treasure is as follows: 85.62% Au, 14.64% Ag, 0.21% Cu and 0.16% Fe. The gold artefacts of the Tumulus culture and of the Urnfield culture in Moravia contained silver up to 9–20%.[125]

The margin of error of the analyses (or perhaps better said, the uncertainty factor) of the SEM-EMA measurements by Attila L. Tóth does not exceed that of the similarly dated gold cap ornament (*Goldhut*) in the Museum für Vor- und Frühgeschichte in Berlin[126] (Urnfield, Ha A–B, 11th–9th centuries BC) as shown by analytical measurements performed in Berlin (microsondage) and in Paris (PIXE) in 1996. The silver content measured by the two laboratories differed by 5–6%, a figure that specialist Hermann Born regarded as being within the margin of error.[127] Similarly, the semi-quantitative XRF analyses of six lockrings and their fragments from Berwick-upon-Tweed (Northumberland, northern England)

---

[121] HARTMANN 1970, 35, 106, Tab. 13. The origin of the gold disc from Worms – whether it had been produced in the north, in southern Germany, in Transdanubia or in Italy – was the subject of heated debates for many decades; cf. GERLOFF 1995, 170.

[122] HARTMANN 1970, 43, 116, Tab. 18, Taf. 48. 193–195, 255, 301.

[123] PERNICKA – BÜHLER – LEUSCH – MEHOFER 2008, 79.

[124] MÁRTON 1907, 68.

[125] DAS PRÄHISTORISCHE GOLD 1997, I: 192.

[126] GOLD UND KULT 2003, 303–304, Kat. Nr. 35.

[127] BORN 2003b, 87. According to the analysis performed in Berlin, the Ag content is 9.77–9.85%, while according to that in Paris, it is 14.26–15.51%.

dated to the Late Bronze Age[128] gave a broader range: 79–83% gold, 14–16% silver and 3–6% copper. The composition of two beads of the gold bead (neck or breast) ornament from Blanot according to PIXE measurements is as follows: Au: 85 and 84%, Ag: 8.6 and 10.2%, Cu: 3.5 and 3.2%, Ca: 1.3 and 0.6%, with traces of Ba, Zn, Ni, Fe, Mn, Cr and Ti.[129] The jewellery foils of the Bernstorf treasure dating to the late Tumulus culture (Bz C2–D; 15th–13th centuries BC) are extremely pure and were most likely refined artificially, because they contain 99.7% gold.[130] With its 98% gold content, the medium-thick gold spiral of the Velem treasure (Vel5; *Fig. 28. 2*) can be assigned to this class of refined gold.

Among the many possible gold deposits in Europe (*Fig. 32*),[131] the nearest gold mining sites for the gold artefacts of Velem are located in Austria's Eastern Alps, the Eisenerzer Alps in Styria and the Rax Alps on the boundary of Styria and Lower Austria,[132] and the High Tauern region.[133] These are located within 80–130 km and 300–350 km from Velem. As already suggested by Hungarian research,[134] gold was most likely transported on routes along river valleys or shipped on water,[135] or possibly by a combination of the two. The other gold mining sites in the Little Carpathians[136] lie roughly 100–120 km away (Banská Štiavnica/Selmecbánya and its broader area),[137] whence raw material could be transported via the Morava–Danube–Répce river route, or by combining water and overland routes via the Gyöngyös Valley and the Amber Road passing near St. Vid. However, the use of gold washed in the Csallóköz and Szigetköz regions and from the Mura and Dráva Rivers (in the Radkersburg and Maribor areas, *Fig. 32*) is also feasible. Of course, we cannot preclude the possibility that the jewellery reached Velem as finished products (see below). The distant gold mining sites in Transylvania characterised by gold with an extremely high silver content (18.7–31%), with only one exception (10%), can be excluded as possible sources.[138]

---

128 La Niece – Cartwright 2009, 307–312.
129 Pernot 1991, 134.
130 Bähr – Krause – Gebhard – Lühr – Herbig 2012, 29, Abb. 23–24.
131 Bartelheim 2009, 181.
132 Krause 2003, 36, Abb. 11.
133 Lehrberger 1995, 127–128, Fig. 8; Czajlik 2012, 37, Abb. 1, 1.
134 Tompa 1937, 49–56; Bácskay 1985, 566.
135 For the boat model from Dárda, cf. Kiss 2007, 119–128, Pl. XXIV. d, g.
136 Krause 2003, 41, Abb. 15.
137 Lehrberger 1995, 133–134, Fig. 11; Czajlik 2012, 38, Abb. 1. 2.
138 Hartmann 1968, 72, Tab. 2.

4 The ornament of the jewellery and the craftsmanship of the diadem

4.1 Decorative motifs and the goldsmith's tools used for their creation

Each concentric circle that decorates the diadem was impressed by one or the other of two stamps/patterned punches (*Stempel*) of different sizes. This is borne out by the errors in the line of the designs such as the misplaced impression underneath the peak in the centre of the diadem (*Fig. 16*). The depths of the impression also differ.

The diameter of Stamp I, which was larger, was 7 mm. It left an impression of five concentric cordons and a boss in the centre. A total of 109 (+1)[139] impressions were stamped along the edge, 94 (+3) slightly farther from the edge, and four in the peak, totalling 211 impressions. The diameter of Stamp II, which was smaller, was 5 mm. It produced three concentric cordons and a boss in the centre. It was used for eight impressions arranged in two vertical rows underneath the peak, with four in each row. A total of 219 concentric circles stamped with the two stamps of differing diameter can be identified on the foil. The central field of the diadem bears bundles of vertical zigzag motifs set in eight panels of various sizes. These were produced with different stamps (*Fig. 14. 2*, *Fig. 15. 4*, *Fig. 16. 3*). If viewed frontally, it can be seen that each row of the vertical zigzag motif arranged in the three vertical bundles running on the right side from the missing part toward the top was made with the same stamp (*Fig. 12. 2, Fig. 16. 3*). The length of the stamp was 11.5 mm, its width was 2.6 mm.

The design is arranged in zones separated by a cable pattern, which also frames the diadem. The width of the impression made by the tool that produced this cable pattern is 1.2 mm.

4.1.1 Domed roundels, Pair I

Decorated with seven concentric circles that were produced with a stamp having a diameter of 6 mm, leaving an impression of five concentric cordons and a boss in the centre. Although one domed roundel is very fragmented, its design can

[139] The numbers in parentheses are based on the reconstruction because they are no longer visible owing to damage (folding, gaps).

similarly be best reconstructed as made up of seven concentric circles. Zigzag motifs (double row + single row variants) + grooving/cable pattern (outward 3 + 3 + 2) can be identified on both domed roundels that, based on their decoration, make up the pair. According to the current numbering, these are domed roundels 1 (*Fig. 18. 1*; inv. no. 54.603.9; Bándi 1983, Abb. 3. 1 = Mozsolics 1950, Taf. II. 1) and 4 (*Fig. 18. 2*; inv. no. 54.603.8; Bándi 1983, Abb. 3. 2 = Mozsolics 1950, Taf. II. 2).

4.1.2 Domed roundels, Pair II

There are seven concentric circles in the centre. The central one was produced with a stamp having a diameter of 6.8 mm, which left an impression of five cordons and a boss in the centre. It is enclosed by six concentric circles made up of three cordons and a boss in the centre. The stamp producing the latter had a diameter of 4.8 mm. Zigzag ornamentation (double row variant) + grooving/cable pattern (outward 3 + 2 + 1) can be identified on both domed roundels that make up the pair. According to current numbering, these are domed roundels 2 (*Fig. 20. 1*; inv. no. 54.603.6; Bándi 1983, Abb. 4. 2 = Mozsolics 1950, Taf. II. 3) and 3 (*Fig. 20. 2*; inv. no. 54.603.7; Bándi 1983, Abb. 4. 1 = Mozsolics 1950, Taf. II. 4).

Therefore, the domed roundel pairs are connected by the similarity of their ornamentation, its arrangement in zones and the impressions made with stamps producing concentric circle motifs of identical diameter during their manufacturing process. The near-identical dimensions of Stamp I of the diadem (larger, 7 mm) and the central stamp of Pair II (larger, 6.8 mm) as well as of Stamp II of the diadem (smaller, 5 mm) and the impression of six concentric circles of Pair II (4.8 mm), are quite noteworthy. The diameter of all the impressions produced by stamps on Pair I is 6 mm. Were these minimal deviations caused by damage during the decades before the gold foils were buried, or during the decades after their discovery? Are they a consequence of deformation/stretching/squeezing in the course of modern conservation? Alternately, can they be ascribed to the use of stamps of different sizes, which were available in the workshop? Or did the goldsmith strike the punch with varying force, explaining the difference of 0.2 mm in the diameters of the motifs? Whichever the case, we may reasonably assume in view of the above that the diadem and the domed roundels were crafted with the same tools and probably in the same workshop.

The decoration on the diadem's peak (*Fig. 16. 1*) and on Pair I of domed roundels, the design of seven concentric circles (*Figs 17–18* = BÁNDI 1983, Abb. 3. 1–2; MOZSOLICS 1950, Taf. II. 1–2) is best matched by the triple gold foil discs mounted on bronze backplates attached to a reconstructed textile belt and the gold foil of the domed roundel with bronze backplate of the Rothengrub treasure, dated to the Ha A (more recently to the Ha B2–3) period, whose findspot lies geographically closest to Velem.[140] Another good parallel is the pair of domed roundels of the Bullenheimer Berg treasure dated to the Ha A–B period, lying somewhat farther.[141] A similar design of seven concentric circles can be seen in the centre of a gold disc found at Zelené (near Plzeň, Czech Republic)[142] dated to the Bz B2/C period. It is noteworthy that the decoration of concentric circles connected to form S motifs[143] on the female diadem (or breast ornament) from Binningen (Basel-Landschaft Canton, Switzerland)[144] can be derived from earlier pieces;[145] it was probably made for a high-ranking person of the Urnfield culture (Bz D2).[146] For example, there are seven concentric circles between the (boxing) heroes engaged in what was perhaps a ritual ceremony depicted on Bucket XI found at Kleinklein–Kröllkogel.[147] This would suggest that the number seven probably had a special meaning for many centuries. However, I will not discuss the symbolism of numbers here, but merely touch upon this issue below.

The primary decorative element of the Velem golden adornments is the concentric circle (*Kreisbuckelmuster/konzentrische Kreisaugenmuster*) that, to the best of my knowledge, is first attested on a gold plate of the European Bronze Age in the material of Periods I and II of the Nordic Bronze Age.[148] This motif was made by stamping (*Stempelverzierung*), the same technique that was used to create the design of the Trundholm sun chariot (*Kultwagen*, 1350 BC),[149]

---

140 PITTIONI 1952, 96, Abb. 1, Taf. II. 4a-b, 5–8, Taf. III. 1–8, Taf. IV. 1–7; GLEIRSCHER 2014, 141, quotes Anton Kern's new dating.

141 GEBHARD 2003, 150–151, Abb. 2, Kat. Nr. 40/c; DAVID 2007, 422.

142 DAS PRÄHISTORISCHE GOLD 1997, II: 268, Taf. 5.

143 A similar design adorns the diadem from Hoard I of Medvedevcy, dated to the Ha A1. KOBAL' 2000, 87, Taf. 60. 6, 61. 10.

144 MOZSOLICS 1950, Taf. XVI. 2; BÁNDI 1983, Abb. 6. 1; PRIMAS 1998, 344, 374, Abb. 198.

145 DAVID 2001, esp. Abb. 1–3, 6, 8, Abb. 6. 1.

146 DELLA CASA – FISCHER 1997, 205, 228, Abb 4. T85.

147 EGG – KRAMER 2005, Abb. 22.1.

148 JOCKENHÖVEL 2003, 110; PRIMAS 2008, 134–135, Abb. 5. 12.

149 KAUL 2003, 39, Abb. 1.

the perhaps most renowned object assigned to Period II of the Nordic Bronze Age (Bz B–C, 1550–1300 BC), and the ornamentation on one group of sheet neck jewellery (*Halskragen*) of the Sonnerup type,[150] dating to the same period, reflecting its popularity in the late Tumulus culture and later, until the late Urnfield culture (9th–8th centuries BC).[151] This decorative motif was widely used across an immense territory from England and Ireland through Sweden, Denmark, Spain, France, Italy and Germany to the Carpathian Basin on a wide range of artefact types such as vessels, shields, cones (*Kegel*), caps (*Hut*), the upper part of helmets (*Kalotte*), "collars" (*Halskragen*) and other costume jewellery (belt plates, bracelets, pendants, pins, etc.)[152] as well as on tools, for example on axes.[153] Its true *floruit* was the so-called gold diadem style (*Gold-Diademstyl*). In the north, it was a popular motif on the bronze and gold vessels of the late Urnfield culture and the Hallstatt period,[154] while in the south, it appears on the plate pendants from the Cerveteri burial[155] dating to the later 7th century BC.

Owing to the extraordinary popularity of this motif, patterned punches/stamps producing concentric circles were widely used; I shall here only cite a few artefact types such as the defensive armour of the Urnfield culture, for example a group of helmets (two unprovenanced pieces from Hungary, the specimens from Nagyvejke, Pamuk, Poljanci and Privina Glava)[156] and a shield from Nadap.[157]

This decorative motif is attested on vessels too, as will be shown below. A design identical to the one on the domed roundels of Velem can be found on the base of a vessel recovered from a grave in Löptin (Schleswig-Holstein), the only difference being that the latter has an extra circle and that the circles are

---

150 NØRGAARD 2011, 13, 87, Abb. 52, Taf. 55/436–439.

151 GERLOFF 1995, 165, Abb. 4, 6–7; DAVID 2003, 35; HÄNSEL 2003, 165–166, 168.

152 KILIAN-DIRLMEIER 1975, 110, Taf. 46. 454 (actually Palotabozsok, Baranya County), Taf. 47. 460, Abb. 4, 6–7; GRIMMER-DEHN 1991, 50, Abb. 3, Taf. 109. 1, Taf. 122. 1; HAGBERG 1998, 507–508, Abb. 3; ARMBRUSTER 2000, Taf. 86; DAVID 2002b, Abb. 4. 3; GOLD UND KULT 2003, Kat. Nr. 32, 21, 31, 30, 34, 25; L' EUROPE AU TEMPS D' ULYSSE. 1999, 169, Cat. no. 230; VERGER 1998, Figs 3–4; NØRGAARD 2009, 95–114; LEITSCHUH-WEBER 1996, 281–291; JOCKENHÖVEL 1975, 134–181, Abb. 15. E/3; MÜLLER-KARPE 1959, Taf. 103. 27; SALAŠ 2005, Tab. 13. 123.

153 MÜLLER-KARPE 1959, Taf. 199. B/12.

154 SPROCKHOFF – HÖCKMANN 1979, 26, Abb. 2, Abb. 3. XXII C.

155 HASE 1995, 535, Fig. 13. 4, 6.

156 CLAUSING 2001, 208–215, Abb. 7–8, 11.

157 MAKKAY 2006, 139, Pl. V. 7. The hoard was probaby buried during the Ha A1 (cf. MOZSOLICS 1981, 304) or the Ha A2 period; for the latter, cf. PETRES 1990, 93.

connected with a line. This vessel has been dated to the onset of Period III of the Nordic Bronze Age.[158] Concentric circles adorn the neck and shoulder of a footed bowl dated to the end of the Urnfield period found in one of the burials at Gevelinghausen (Lower Saxony).[159] Concentric circles decorate a jug deposited in a burial uncovered in Grevenkrug (Period VI) and the high-swung handle of a vessel placed in a burial in Ettin (Bavaria), dating to the Early Iron Age (Ha D1).[160] The same motif, arranged in three rows, recurs on a vessel of a hoard (Period V) found in Broock (Mecklenburg-Vorpommern, Germany),[161] and on every vessel of the gold treasure from Brandenburg (Period VI).[162] Double concentric circles were punched onto the cross-shaped handles of the cauldron from the hoard from Biesenbrow (Period V, Ha B3)[163] and on two gold vessels from Unterglauheim (Bavaria); the use of these vessel types spanned the entire Urnfield period.[164] A design of concentric circles arranged in several rows adorns a gold vessel found in the Early Iron Age (Ha C) tumulus burial in Wehringen.[165] The cross-shaped handles of the cauldron from Glowińsk each bear seven concentric circle motifs; this vessel type was popular from the turn of the Ha B1–2 to the Ha B2–3.[166] A similar decoration adorns the body of a cauldron found in Dzwonowo; this type of vessel remained in use until Phases IV–VI of the Nordic Bronze Age.[167] From his meticulous analysis of concentric circles on the base of the bronze buckets from Kurd (fourteen so-called *cista a cordoni*) and their comparison with other similar pieces (among them the ones from Vaskeresztes and Debrecen) dating to the Early Iron Age, Géza Szabó demonstrated that they had been produced in the same workshop.[168]

Of the belt plates decorated with repoussé concentric circles, suffice it here to mention the pieces from Augsdorf (Austria), Přestavlky (Moravia), Budinščina (Croatia) and Bingula–Divoš (Serbia), the early Urnfield hoard horizon hallmarked by Kisapáti–Lengyeltóti–Uriu–Domăneşti and the later one (Ha B1) represented

158 Jacob 1995, 11, Taf. 1. 1.
159 Jacob 1995, 112–113, Taf. 62–63.
160 Jacob 1995, 41–42, 53, Taf. 9. 50, Taf. 14. 108.
161 Martin 2009, 73, Taf. 25. 97.
162 Jens 2009, 133–134, Taf. 52. 212–213, Taf. 53. 214–219.
163 Jens 2009, 92–94, Taf. 35. 128.
164 Jacob 1995, 124, Taf. 77. 408–409.
165 Jacob 1995, 127, Taf. 78. 417.
166 Gedl 2001, 31–32, Taf. 12. 35.
167 Gedl 2001 52–55, Taf. 37. 81.
168 Szabó 2012, 83–85, Figs 2–3; Szabó 2013a, 297–298, Pl. 7.

by Blanot (France, Burgundy), containing repoussé-decorated belt plates.[169] The fragments from Pamuk (Somogy County), Slavonski Brod (Croatia) and Jurka Vas (Slovenia) too came from similar belt plates.[170] The motif was well-crafted on all.

On the western fringes of the Carpathian Basin, this decorative motif appears in Grave 95 of the Hainburg cemetery, dating to the Middle Bronze Age.[171] Its local forerunners in the Carpathian Basin[172] can be found on several artefacts of the Ţafalău (Cófalva) treasure (Bz A2b–B1)[173] as well as on the Ráks type pendants,[174] the base of the golden kantharos from Bia (Magyarbénye/ Bendendorf),[175] the diadem from Lovasberény[176] and on the head of the bronze pin (*Spundkopfnadel*) from Plevník–Drienové near the Váh River dating to the Tumulus period.[177] Finally, the concentric circles adorning the belt plates of the Tumulus culture must also be mentioned.[178] In addition to the artefacts listed above, concentric circles adorn the belt plate of the Palotabozsok treasure[179] and the bronze diadem from Pamuk, both dating to the Ha A1 period (Mozsolics BVb, Kurd horizon).[180] The motif retained its popularity in Mozsolics's BVc, Gyermely horizon (Ha A2), as shown by the large disc (no. II) of the Pötréte hoard (Zalaszentmihály).[181]

Wooden, bone,[182] and bronze[183] patterned punches/stamps (*Ringpunzen*, *Kreisaugenpunze*, *Stempel*, *Matrize*) were used to create the decorative patterns. The punches published from Génelard, France (*Fig. 31. 1*; Ha A1, 13th–12th

---

169 MÜLLER-KARPE 1959, 278, Taf. 129. 22; KILIAN-DIRLMEIER 1975, 113, Taf. 46/47, 460, Taf. 49. 470; SALAŠ 2005, I: 386; II: Tab. 264. 150; THEVENOT 1991, Fig. 32.

170 MOZSOLICS 1985, 169, Taf. 106. 22; CLAUSING 2003, 131–132, Abb. 40. 130; ČERČE – ŠINKOVEC 1995, 203, Pl. 91. 51, Pl. 160. 10.

171 RUTTKAY 1988/1989, 136–139, 143, 147, Abb. 1. 2, 2. 5.

172 KEMENCZEI 1996a, 105.

173 DAVID 2010, 449, Abb. 6. 10–22.

174 WELS-WEYRAUCH 2008, 275–289.

175 MOZSOLICS 1968, 48, 54, Taf. 2–3, Taf. 12.

176 BÓNA 1959, 56, Abb. 17; BÓNA 1975, 71, Taf. 52. 3.

177 BARTÍK 2009, 49, Abb. 7. 2.

178 KEMENCZEI 1991b, 40, Fig. 2, 1, Fig. 3, 1.

179 MOZSOLICS 1985, 168, Taf. 75. 25; KILIAN-DIERLMEIER 1975, Taf. 46. 454.

180 MOZSOLICS 1985, 168, Taf. 106. 20.

181 MÜLLER 1972, 60–61, Fig. 6, 1, Fig. 7, 1; MOZSOLICS 1985, 216.

182 JOCKENHÖVEL 2003, Abb. 5. 7.

183 JOCKENHÖVEL 2003, Abb. 5. 1–6, 8–11; ARMBRUSTER 2003, Abb. 15–16.

centuries BC)[184] and Hauterive-Champréveyres (Switzerland)[185] were made of bronze, while the ones from Arbois[186] of bone. An assemblage of twenty-seven artefacts, a set of metalsmith's tools (14th–9th centuries BC) that included two patterned punches suitable for creating two, four, or five concentric circles (*Fig. 31. 2*) probably comes from Marnau (Bavaria).[187] Bronze punches were among the items of the hoards discovered at Stockheim (Bz D)[188] and Nürnberg–Mögeldorf (Ha A1).[189] A bronze patterned punch creating an impression of double concentric circles has been reported from Přestavlký (Moravia; Lausitz culture, Ha A1).[190] A bronze patterned punch of the Lausitz culture dated to the 13th–8th centuries BC in the Museum of Natural History in Nuremberg[191] has a diameter of 24 mm and could be used for creating a motif of three concentric circles with a central boss.[192] A patterned punch was probably found on the St. Vid Hill of Velem too.[193] In sum, the punches quoted in the foregoing have all been dated to the Urnfield period, with the earliest specimen being the one from Stockheim (Bz D).

In her study on the collars (*Halskragen*) from the Thaya region (northern Lower Austria/southern Moravia; *Fig. 39. 1*) in the Museum für Vor- und Frühgeschichte of Berlin made of decorated gold foil mounted onto bronze backplates, dated to the Ha B period (10th–9th centuries BC), Alix Hänsel described the sizes of the impressions made with the punches.[194] In her view, two stamps/patterned punches were used: the diameter of Type I was 8.5 mm and created a pattern of seven concentric circles with a boss in the centre, while Type II had a diameter of 5 mm and produced four concentric circles with a boss in the centre.[195] The latter is identical in size with the smaller stamp/punch (Stamp II) used for decorating the Velem diadem, although the latter produced three concentric cordons and a boss in the centre.

---

184 THEVENOT 1998, 129, Fig. 5. 9–13.
185 RYCHNER-FARAGGI 1993, 43, Fig. 40, Pl. 41/35; JOCKENHÖVEL 2003, Abb. 5. 10.
186 JOCKENHÖVEL 2003, Abb. 5. 7.
187 GOLD UND KULT 2003, Kat. Nr. 7a.
188 MÜLLER-KARPE 1959, 148–149, 288, Taf. 156. 52; JOCKENHÖVEL 2003, 111, Abb. 5. 8.
189 JOCKENHÖVEL 2003, 283, Abb. 5. 11, Kat. Nr. 10.
190 JOCKENHÖVEL 2003, Abb. 5. 6; SALAŠ 2005, I: 381–382, 386, II: Tab. 256. 25.
191 GOLD UND KULT 2003, 281, Kat. Nr. 8a.
192 ARMBRUSTER 2000, Taf. 6. 2.
193 MISKE 1908, Taf. XXXVI. 45.
194 HÄNSEL 2003, 157–175.
195 HÄNSEL 2003, 159.

In my view, the handled clay stamp[196] from Grave 40 of the Haunstetten I cemetery (Ha B1, 11th–10th centuries BC) creating a circular impression was more suited to decorating soft materials such as clay, wax and dough than metal plates. It could be used for making a motif of five cordons and a boss combined with oblique grooving (cable pattern) in-between. Certain elements of the motif recur on gold artefacts.

One of the goldsmith's tools possibly used to create the cable pattern (*Fig. 12. 2, Figs 14–16, Fig. 23. 4–5; Fig. 13, Fig. 20*)[197] can be identified among the artefacts from Génelard[198] and Murnau (*Fig. 31. 3*).[199] Gold vessels decorated with this design are known from Denmark (Kohave), Germany (Albersdorf) and France (Villeneuve-Saint-Vistre-et-Villevotte)[200] and it also appears on the gold head ornament in Berlin.[201] In the Central European and more easterly regions, this decorative style occurs, for example, on the gold jewellery from Bullenheimer Berg, Hammersdorf, Worms, Rothengrub, Várvölgy, Velem and Tafalău (Cófalva), the latter dated earlier.[202]

A stamp/punch was probably used to create the vertical zigzag motif appearing in two sizes on the Velem diadem (*Fig. 12. 2, Fig. 15. 3–4, Fig. 16. 3*) as well as on the domed roundels (*Fig. 17. 4, Fig. 18, Fig. 19. 2, Fig. 20*). Special instances of the use of zigzag motifs are represented by gold bracelets with lunular terminals, which were popular in the eastern region of the Carpathian Basin in the 16th–15th centuries BC,[203] as well as by the bronze cult objects from Balkåkra and Haschendorf.[204] The former has been dated to around 1500 BC by Swedish archaeologists, while the latter, according to the most recent studies, to the transition between the Late Bronze Age and the Early Iron Age (9th–8th centuries BC). The two objects, variously interpreted as the casing of a drum, a wooden altar, a wooden throne or a "Holy Tree", are virtually identical in terms of their appearance and technical details, including smaller elements such as the presence of barcode-like lines on the reverse of the spoked wheel motif, with the

---

[196] WIRTH 1999, 580, 598, Abb. 9.

[197] The other is described below.

[198] ARMBRUSTER 2003, 75, Abb. 16.

[199] GOLD UND KULT 2003: Kat. Nr. 7b.

[200] ARMBRUSTER 2012, Abb. 10, Abb. 42.

[201] BORN 2003b, 92, Abb. 10.

[202] DAVID 2010, Abb. 6. 6–9, Abb. 11; DAVID 2003, Abb. 2. 1–5, 10–16.

[203] KOVÁCS 1991, 12, Abb. 4–5.

[204] KAUS – KAUS 2012, 316.

one from Haschendorf being larger by a few centimetres. The one from Balkåkra is interpreted as a sun disc not only because of the ten sun symbols (the spoked wheel motif) on its lower part, but also because of the repoussé zigzag motifs arranged in six concentric circles on its upper plate.[205] The upper plate of the Haschendorf cult object is similarly decorated with repoussé zigzag motifs, but in seven concentric circles.[206]

Looking back on a history of over a century, experimental archaeology uses the replicas of punches for exploring ancient goldsmithing techniques.[207] One puzzling observation was that the impressions made by the replicas of the punches from Génelard and Murnau would not enable the creation of perfectly continuous lines like the ones on the gold foils from Velem and other pieces, on which there are no gaps or ill-fitting sections, suggesting that the cable and zigzag patterns were for the greater part created with a tool resembling a pastry wheel cutter. Today, beekeepers use a tool[208] of this type to fasten wax panels to the wire framework. Earlier, similar tools were used, for example, by bookbinders and shoemakers,[209] as well as by Roman and medieval potters. The tool itself has a little rotating disc with a patterned edge set between two hafted prongs. Hermann Born made a reconstruction of the tool used in the Urnfield period as part of his analysis of the gold foil in Berlin.[210] This type of tool can be applied on soft gold sheet, but not on the more rigid bronze backplates, and it could not have been used to imprint the bronze backplates onto which the gold foils were mounted.[211]

The combination of the widely popular concentric circles, zigzag motifs and cable patterns occurs on a wide range of gold objects already during the Middle Bronze Age as shown by the pair of gold vessels of the treasure from Villeneuve-Saint-Vistre et Villevotte (Marne, France).[212] It is attested on the gold domed

---

[205] http://kulturarvsdata.se/shm/object/html/96948

[206] Kaus – Kaus 2012, Abb. 4.

[207] Rychner-Faraggi 1993, 43, Fig. 40; Armbruster 2012, 380–382.

[208] In my childhood, I had the opportunity to familiarise myself with the former while helping my mother in the kitchen, and with the latter when helping my father with his bees; I have personally used both.

[209] Born 2003b, 91, Abb. 11 and note 11.

[210] Born 2003b, 91, Abb. 9.

[211] Géza Szabó noted that caution should be exercised regarding the use of this auxiliary tool. In his view. the pattern could have been made with a punch if it was carefully placed into the end of preceding impression before making a new one. I am grateful for his remark.

[212] Armbruster 2012, 372, Abb. 2.

roundels mounted on leather or textile found beside the deceased in the cist tomb (Grave 3/1973; Bz D) unearthed in Oberrimsingen[213] and on a bronze plate from Grave 15 at Haag (Bavaria) dated to the Rigsee phase.[214] Similarly ornamented bronze plates include the belt plate from Tumulus 6 in Riegerau (Bavaria).[215] The combination of concentric circles and zigzag patterns made with punches appears on a belt plate of the Drslavice I hoard (Moravia, Bz D2–Ha A1).[216] Concentric circles in repoussé adorn the phalera[217] of the Jenišovice hoard (Czech Republic; (Ha B1) and the bracelets in later hoards (Třtěno, Svárov–Rymáň, Hradištko 1; Ha B3).[218] One of the vessels in the Eberswalde treasure (8th–9th centuries BC; Period V) illustrates the late and joint use of these motifs.[219]

The identical decorative elements and manufacturing technique of the diadem and the domed roundels from Velem indicate the close connection between them and that their ornament was conceived in the same spirit, reflected by the presence of concentric circles, the grooved motif imitating cable patterns and the zigzag motif, all of which can be found on the gold foils.

Similarly to the neck adornment in Berlin[220] and the "disc ornaments" from Innsbruck–Wilten,[221] the Velem diadem was a composite costume ornament. The gold foil of the jewellery in Berlin was mounted onto the bronze backplate by the same technique as the one used in the case of the Velem diadem: the gold foil was folded back along its edge. The two perforations on each end of the Velem diadem and the two perforations under the peak may have been used for attaching the gold foil covered bronze plate to an organic backing, most probably textile or leather, or a piece of clothing made from their combination. Still, the ornaments retained a certain measure of flexibility. It seems likely that the two perforations at each end were for threading through a wire for fastening as noted on one of

---

[213] DEHN 1991, 50, 127, Taf. 109. 1, Taf. 122, top. For the dating, cf. *ibid.*, 64–70, Tab. 4 and 6.

[214] KILIAN-DIERLMEIER 1975, 106, Taf. 43. 427.

[215] MÜLLER-KARPE 1959, 308, Taf. 197H/1.

[216] SALAŠ 2005, I: 332, II: Tab. 136. 584, Tab. 137. 590–591, 601.

[217] KYTLICOVÁ 2007, 267, Taf. 103/43.

[218] KYTLICOVÁ 2007, 311, Taf. 144/39–41;307, Taf. 147/4–8; 266, Taf. 187.

[219] MOZSOLICS 1950, 18; MENGHIN – SCHAUER 1983, 98, Abb. 46. Nr. 16d; HIDDE 1997, 128–130; JOCKENHÖVEL 2003, 114.

[220] BORN 2003a, 178.

[221] SPERBER 1992, 67–68.

the neck ornaments in Berlin (*Fig. 39. 1*).[222] The four or two perforations along the diadem's lower edge perhaps served for its attachment to an organic backing as well as for the suspension of the domed roundels with gold spiral suspension loops (see Katalin T. Bruder's report, above).[223]

Being skilled in the use of fire, the metal-working craftsman (goldsmith/smith)[224] who made this prestigious ornament no doubt enjoyed a prominent position in the social hierarchy; he was proficient in bronze and gold working as shown by the diadem's composite structure (bronze backplate + gold foil). In other words, we should visualise a craftsman specialising not in bronze or gold processing only, but one familiar with both metals in the Urnfield period,[225] commanding the necessary skills and blessed with an excellent sense of beauty.[226] The metals, tools and techniques used by the goldsmith-blacksmith are described in the Homeric epics:

> "With that he left her there and made for his bellows,
> turning them on the fire, commanding, "Work – to work!"
> And the bellows, all twenty, blew on the crucibles,
> breathing with all degrees of shooting, fiery heat
> as the god hurried on – a blast for the heavy work,
> a quick breath for the light, all precisely gauged
> to the god of fire's wish and the pace of the work in hand.
> Bronze he flung in the blaze, tough, durable bronze
> and tin and priceless gold and silver, and then,
> planting the huge anvil upon its block, he gripped
> his mighty hammer in one hand, the other gripped his tongs.
> (Homer, *The Iliad*, Book XVIII: 547–558, tr. Robert Fagles)

---

222 HÄNSEL 2003, Abb. 2. The remnants of a cord made from organic material were identified at the end of the backplate's inner side on one of the necklaces during conservation; cf. BORN 2003b, 95–96. The terminals of the necklaces used in Periods I–V of the Nordic Bronze Age were rolled back and thus their clasp mechanism differed too. Cf. NØRGAARD 2009, Taf. 1–4.

223 MOZSOLICS, 1950. 7.

224 ELIADE 2004, 97, 99, 102–103, 107, 120, 130–131.

225 SPERBER 2000, 396–397.

226 ARMBRUSTER 2011, 19.

> "And another tell our goldsmith, skilled Laerces,
> to come and sheathe the heifer's horns in gold. [...]
> The heifer came from the fields, the crewmen came
> from brave Telemachus' ship, and the smith came in
> with all his gear in hand, the tools of his trade,
> the anvil, hammer and well-wrought tongs he used
> for working gold. And Athena came as well
> to attend her sacred rites.
> The old horseman passed the gold to the smith,
> and twining the foil, he sheathed the heifer's horns
> so the goddess' eyes might dazzle, delighted with the gift.
> (Homer, *The Odyssey*, Book III: 475–476, 481–489, tr. Robert Fagles)

In order to gain a better knowledge of the tools once used by metalsmiths,[227] I reviewed the evidence from the Carpathian Basin and its broader area as well as the finds and assemblages of the Central European Urnfield culture (*Fig. 32*), but disregarded Scandinavia[228] and the British Isles. Instead of the tools of casting, I concentrated on assemblages that contained the possible tools used for working sheets/foils,[229] particularly the ones with a relevance for the manufacture of the gold jewellery found in Velem. The artefacts in question are as follows: the highly-valued anvil and hammer[230] as well as stamps/patterned punches/matrices.

Among the tools used by goldsmiths, the presence, spatial distribution and dating of stamps/patterned punches used for creating the concentric circles adorning the foils are the most relevant to this study. The easternmost occurrence of the tools used for producing this popular motif in the Urnfield distribution is marked by the Přestavlký hoard from Moravia (Ha A1; *Fig. 32. 41*)[231] and, possibly, a stray settlement find from the St. Vid Hill of Velem (*Fig. 32. 89*). More closely dated stamps/patterned punches come from the Bz D and Ha A periods. Other tools such as anvils and hammers, essential for working metal

---

[227] For recent comprehensive overviews of the tools and the social status of metalsmiths and goldsmiths, cf. NESSEL 2010; NESSEL 2012a; NESSEL 2012b; NESSEL 2013.

[228] Over two hundred goldsmith's hammers are known from this region alone. Cf. ARMBRUSTER 2012, 396, with the earlier literature.

[229] For the classification of the types of (goldsmith's) hammers and their discussion, with the earlier literature, cf. NESSEL 2008.

[230] ELIADE 2004, 111, 115, 123, 133.

[231] JOCKENHÖVEL 2003, 111, Abb. 5. 6.

sheet, were distributed widely during the entire Urnfield period, meaning that skilled craftsmen equipped with the necessary tools were present in every region. Patterns of concentric circles, zigzags and cable motifs cannot be restricted to a narrow time interval within the Urnfield period. However, the combination of these three motifs on gold foil covered objects such as vessels, cones (*Kegel*) and caps (*Hut*) were more typical in the western Urnfield culture. It also became clear (*Fig. 32*) that one group of gold foil covered objects (vessels, cones, headwear) was typical in the western region of Central Europe during the Late Bronze Age, and that objects of this type do not occur east of the Riegsee. At the same time, gold foil covered jewellery (diadems, domed roundels) was widespread across Central Europe during the entire period, including the region of the eastern Alps and the Alpine foreland (Rothengrub, Velem). The easternmost examples are known from Nyíregyháza and Hinova (Oltenia, Iron Gates, Romania).

4.2 Prehistoric weights and value standards in western Hungary

The very first artefact found in the region that can be assigned to this category is a mould for an oxhide ingot (*Keftiubarren*) discovered in pit "a" of Trench K-6 on the late Urnfield settlement of Gór–Kápolnadomb (Vas County) (*Fig. 33. 1–2*).[232] Accepting Christopher Pare's arguments, the ingots cast in these moulds should more appropriately be interpreted as weights.[233] The estimated weight of the ingot cast in the Gór mould, calculated from the mould's volume and the weight of bronze, is 34.512 g in the case of one-piece casting and 59.024 g in the case of two-piece casting.[234]

The ingot produced by one-piece casting is four times the weight of the basic "Pannonian" unit of 8.78 g (≈ 9 g; Beremend, Birján, Kloštar Ivanić, Lovasberény, Jászdózsa) and nearly eight times higher in the case of two-piece casting.[235] A one-piece cast ingot is roughly 5.6 times, while the two-piece cast ingot is roughly 11.3 times the weight of the Aegean-Minoan unit of "x" (6.1 g),

232 Ilon 1992, 244, 252–258, Fig. 6. 2.

233 Pare 1999, 495, Fig. 10.

234 Ilon 2001b 220.

235 The minimal differences of 1–2 g can be attributed to the calculation of the weight of the one-piece and two-piece cast ingots found in Gór and Vát, based on the size of the moulds and the average bronze alloy (80 % copper + 20 % tin). Obviously, there will be some slight difference between the calculated and the actual weight of the object.

which has been attested in the Terramare culture of northern Italy.[236] Remarkably, the two-piece cast ingot is only 0.422 g heavier than one of the gold bracelets with a rhombic cross-section found in Féregyháza.[237] One typical feature of the ingot is that there are two lenticular depressions (perhaps for two perforations). A similar depression can be noted on one of the incomplete bronze ingots of the Tiszabecs hoard (Mozsolics BIVb, Ópályi horizon, Bz D1) in the European Urnfield distribution.[238] It can probably be interpreted as a possibly functional feature (perhaps applied for threading / storing / stacking weights) or as a special feature of the Carpathian Basin. A conclusive answer calls for further studies.

Csilla Farkas found a virtually identical piece during a rescue excavation preceding road construction at Vát–Bodon-tábla (Vas County) in autumn 2006.[239] It was recovered from Pit 199 of the Urnfield settlement. Its description is as follows: Ingot mould. The narrower end of the prismatic mould is irregular owing to the fracture of the original rock. The mould was used for producing rectangular ingots and it has an opening where the molten metal would be poured in. One of the edges of the negative of the ingot is damaged: it was perhaps chipped during carving. The flat face of the negative is pitted and coarse, and a regular perforation has been bored through the stone beside one end. There is a fitting mark on one side of the mould. Its fabric is compact, graphitic greenschist. There are no use-wear traces from heat. Its length is 87 mm, its width 30–35 mm, its thickness 23–25 mm. The size of the cast ingot produced would be 40 x 25 x 5 mm. The diameter of the perforation is 5 mm, its depth 11 mm. Assuming an alloy of 80% copper (Cu) and 20% tin (Sn), as was calculated in the case of the Gór mould,[240] the estimated weight of the ingot would be ≈ 43.16 g + projection (≈ 1.86 g), totalling ≈ 45 g. The fitting mark suggests two-piece casting, meaning that the weight of the cast ingot would be ≈ 90 g. SM inv. no. Ő. 2007.55.273 (*Fig. 33. 3–4*). The weight of a one-piece cast ingot (≈ 45 g) from the Vát mould would be the same, with a slight difference of 2 g, meaning that it is also tied to the Near Eastern standard and the "Pannonian–Aegean" unit (9 g), being five

[236] PARE 2013, 512, Fig. 29.1.

[237] MOZSOLICS 1963, 74.

[238] MOZSOLICS 1973, 182, Taf. 53. 6a; PARE 1999, 434, Fig. 19. 8.

[239] I am greatly indebted to Csilla Farkas and Marcella Nagy, who will publish the report on the Late Bronze Age material, for kindly permitting me to publish this artefact. For the site, cf. KŐSZEGI – FARKAS 2007, 263–278.

[240] My calculations were correct because the period's ingots contained tin in a ratio of 16–25%, according to metal analyses. PARE 2013, 518.

times the latter.[241] It is possible that the ingot's cylindrical projection was used to fit it into another weight (cf. the two perforations on the ingot found in Gór), i.e. its function was perhaps to stack two weights onto each other stably. The size of scale pans is finite.[242] It seems to me that the rectangular shape of the ingots produced by the moulds and the marks on them can be associated with the ingots found across the Urnfield distribution.[243]

A unique artefact of this period shedding light on weights and value standards, the first of its kind in Hungary, was discovered in 2011 during the rescue excavation conducted at Ménfőcsanak–Széles-földek by the present author. Description: lead scale weight with iron handle attached by a peg.[244] Its height is 55 mm, its diameter 44 mm, its weight 384.82 g. It was found at a depth of 40 cm during metal detectoring after the mechanic removal of the humus in Trench JD-24. It was submitted to XRF analysis (*Fig. 34*).[245] HNM temporary inv. no. 1.34305.1.163 (*Fig. 33. 5–6*).

Two burials (Graves 10 and 11) of an Urnfield cemetery of twelve graves were uncovered in the same 20 m by 20 m trench. Grave 10 contained the ashes of a 20 to 30-year-old adult (perhaps a female) that was in part disturbed by ploughing. A part of the bowl used for covering the urn was found inside the urn. The lead weight perhaps came from this grave, dated to the mid-Ha A1–Ha B.

In their recent study on Iron Age weights, Lorenz Rahmstorf and Christopher Pare discussed the forerunners of the period's weights. Two analogous finds are relevant to the Ménfőcsanak piece. One (≈ 390 g) was found at Colombier (Switzerland), the other (71 g) at Forbach (France);[246] both are biconical lead weights[247] resembling the one found at Ménfőcsanak. The piece from Forbach was recovered from a securely dated late Urnfield (Ha A2–B3) context. The weight of the piece found at Bismantova (Italy), assigned to the Terramare culture, is close

[241] ALBERTI 2003, Taf. LVIIIa; PARE 1999, 496.

[242] I wish to thank Marcella Nagy for calling my the attention to this possibility.

[243] PARE 2013, Fig. 29. 6. 8–11, Fig. 29. 2.

[244] Other examples include the hematite balls found in Grave 3 at Büchelberg, dated to the Bz D period, probably used as weights. PARE 1999, 454–456, Fig. 24. 4–5.

[245] I would here like to thank metal conservator Szilvia Döbröntey-David (managing director of Archeolore Kft., Budapest) for her kindness.

[246] RAHMSTORF – PARE 2007, 274, Abb. 5. 3–4.

[247] The use of lead weights across continental Europe during this period has been confirmed by a dozen finds as well as by eight pieces from the shipwreck at Uluburun. PARE 1999, 500–505, Fig. 15; PULAK 2000, Tab. 17.

to that of the specimen from Ménfőcsanak (390–392 g).[248] The Ménfőcsanak weight conforms to the basic unit of *ca.* 63 g (B1) among the four pre-monetary weight and value standards assumed to have been used in Bronze Age Europe by Renato Peroni;[249] the weight is six times a certain basic unit (B6). The B1 basic unit of 62.720 grams conforms to one of the eight river pebble weights (no. 5) found beside a bone scales balance beam in a pit at Bordjoš (Borjas, Banat, Serbia) dated to the Ha A1 period.[250]

In a 1999 study, Christopher Pare argued that the use of weighted metals as commodity money (*Gewichtsgeldwirtschaft*) was typical of the Bronze Age, and thus of the Urnfield culture too, and that it was a practice widespread in the Eastern Mediterranean-Aegean-Italian-Central and Northern European *koine* through the trade of gold, copper, tin, amber and salt. Pare assumed that the weight system, a "common language" used by the local elites controlling the trade in these commodities, could be derived from the Eastern Mediterranean *shekel* (≈ 9 g) as a basic unit.[251] The weight found at Ménfőcsanak is 42¾ times the latter and 6¼ times the assumed Aegean basic unit (≈ 61 g) of the Late Bronze Age.[252]

The uniqueness of the weight found at Ménfőcsanak is enhanced by the stone ball (*Fig. 33. 7*) found in the urn of Grave 11. The urn contained the calcinated remains of a 20–x-year old adult, who was probably a high-ranking woman judging from her grave goods (a Röschitz-Sanislău type brooch and the hilt fragment of a Pfatten, Baierdorf, Malbostovice or Pustiměř type grip-tongue knife). Her burial can be dated to the late Ha A1 or early Ha A2 period. The description of the relevant find is as follows: burnt "stone ball" of quartzite pebble. Light grey in colour, smooth surface, without marks of use-wear, with a single crack. Found in the deep bowl used as an urn, grave good no. 8. Size: 30 x 29 x 18 mm. Weight: 23.38 g. HNM temporary inv. no. 1.34305.7942.8 (*Fig. 33. 7*).

Predrag Medović addressed the subject of quartzite pebble weights in connection with the pieces found in one of the pits of the Bordjoš settlement (weighing 16.950 g, 51.180 g, 54.370 g, 55.700 g, 62.720 g, 86.720 g, 122.170 g and 183.700 g, respectively).[253] It seems likely that the piece from the

---

[248] RAHMSTORF – PARE 2007, 273–274, 277, Abb. 5. 8.
[249] PERONI 1998, 217–218, Abb. 1; 3; 7.
[250] MEDOVIĆ 1995, 211, Abb. 2. 5, Abb. 3. 5.
[251] PARE 1999, 505–513.
[252] PARE 2013, 519.
[253] MEDOVIĆ 1995, 209–218.

Ménfőcsanak burial was a local weight of the A1 standard (≈ 26 g) as defined by Renato Peroni.[254] The association between the bone balance beam and the eight river pebble weights found in Bordjoš is undeniable. The two bronze scale pans found in Hungary, which the Association of Antiquities Collectors of Zurich donated to the Römisch-Germanisches Zentralmuseum in Mainz[255] complements the relics of weights and value standards of the Carpathian Basin.

The above offered new evidence regarding the distribution and boundaries of pebble, stone and metal weights.[256] Current archaeological scholarship holds that pebble and stone weights point to the East, while metal weights to the West. The Carpathian Basin can be seen as a transitional region/boundary between the two, as shown by the examples described in the above.

Due to limitations of space, I shall not review the ample Hungarian[257] and foreign studies on this subject,[258] or the recent research findings. Neither will I discuss the re-interpretation of the ingots – assumed weights – from Gór and Vát, which I have published elsewhere.[259] Still, it must be noted that the virtually identical form of the two ingots/weights is more than mere coincidence[260] or a general similarity of form.

Regarding the Velem treasure, the following comparisons can be made in terms of weight. The weight of the diadem (23.09 g, probably missing a small part of roughly 2.5–3 g) is close to Peroni's A1 standard (*ca.* 27 g), and is nearly identical with the weight of the sandstone ball (23.3 g) found in Grave 11 at Ménfőcsanak. It is approximately six times the unit calculated by Christopher Pare (3.83 g, corresponding to 1/16th of the 61.3 g standard).[261] While the median value of the gold standard of the treasure found at Lovas (Slavonia) is 6.85 g, that of the gold spirals from Dyrotz (Brandenburg) is 16.62 g.[262] The latter is nearly

254 PERONI 1998, 217–218, Abb. 7; PARE 1999, 479.

255 PARE 1999, 454, Fig. 23. 6–7.

256 RAHMSTORF 2011, 111–112, Fig. 9. 3.

257 KISS 1859, 174–215; HAMPEL 1864, 29–32; MÁRTON 1907, 64–68; HAMPEL 1896, 186; MISKE 1928, 81–94; MOZSOLICS 1963, 68–77; MOZSOLICS 1984, 31–34; MOZSOLICS 1985, 63–66; SZABÓ 1995, 49–56; SZABÓ 1996, 207–230.

258 BUCHHOLZ 1959; EIWANGER 1989; LENERZ-DE WILDE 1995; SOMMERFELD 1994; PRIMAS 1997, 287–296; PRIMAS – PERNICKA 1998; PARE 1999, 421–514; TERŽAN 2004, 161–202; RAHMSTORF – PARE 2007, 265–295; HÄNSEL 2009; PARE 2013.

259 ILON 1992.

260 KALLA 2000, 86.

261 PARE 1999, 467, 488–490.

262 HÄNSEL 2009, 32.

identical with the weight of one of the quartzite pebbles (no. 1) from Bordjoš and is only 1.02 g more than one-third of the Late Bronze Age unit (48.8 g) calculated for France and Switzerland.[263]

The total weight of the four domed roundels from Velem was roughly ≈ 11–12 g, about one-half of the total weight of the diadem. The reconstructed minimal total weight of the treasure's gold foils is 85.59 g + x g of the spirals assumed to have been lost. This is nearly four times the weight of the sandstone ball (23.3 g) recovered from Grave 11 at Ménfőcsanak, two and a half times the weight of the ingot (34.51 g) produced by one-piece casting from the Gór mould, almost identical with the weight of the ingot (≈ 90 g) produced by two-piece casting in the Vát mould, and twelve and a half times (originally perhaps thirteen times) the weight of the standard of Lovas, meaning that its weight must have been roughly 89.05 g (with roughly 3.5 g missing in the latter case). It is 5.14 times the average weight of the gold artefacts from Dyrotz, indicating an "excess" of 2.2 g, i.e. this is the degree of "mismeasurement/inaccuracy" we are dealing with; it is 12 ¾ times the *shekel* of the Aegean (6.7 g).[264] Regrettably, there are no data on the treasure's original weight because it was not measured either by Kálmán Miske in 1939, by Amália Mozsolics in 1940, or by Gábor Bándi subsequently. Therefore, we know nothing about the possible difference between its original and current weight.

In sum, specific weight units could be reconstructed for the Ancient Near East and the Aegean[265] as well as for Continental Europe during the Urnfield period (Bz D–Ha B),[266] alongside the correlations and common, shared units between them.[267] These value standards were of utmost importance in view of the trade in valuable commodities such amber, dyes, spices/salt, gold and silver. The system used in the Aegean was first introduced in Italy (Terramare) during the Bz D period, whence it spread to the regions north of the Alps.[268] Although studies in this field have already begun, a meticulous analysis of the system used in the Carpathian Basin remains the task of future research. One good springboard in

[263] Pare 2013, 520–521, Fig. 29. 3.
[264] Ruiz-Gálvez 2000, 267–268, Fig. 18.1.
[265] Petruso 1978; Alberti 1998; Lassen 2000; Pulak 2000, 261–264.
[266] Eiwanger 1989; Sperber 1993, 613–619; Sommerfeld 1994; Peroni 1998; Pare 1999, 2013; Ruiz-Gálvez 2000, 267–279; Rahmstorf – Pare 2007; Hänsel 2009.
[267] Pare 1999, 490–493, 497, Fig. 6, Fig. 13; Pare 2013, 519; Vargyas 2010, 202–204.
[268] Pare 1999, 493, Fig. 3; Pare 2013, 517.

this respect[269] seems to be an awareness of the multiples of a unit of roughly 9 g in relation to the Aegean, Italy and the Carpathian Basin – in the Riegsee period or slightly later (Ha A) – and the consideration of other possible source regions (Cyprus) and routes (Caput Adriae) to the Carpathian Basin,[270] as well as the search for connections between smaller regions, as posited earlier by Amália Mozsolics[271] and myself.[272] Thus, we can certainly speak of uniform weight and value standards in Bronze Age Europe that enabled the trade in valuable commodities, a system that only disintegrated in the Iron Age.[273]

4.3 Goldsmithing (blacksmithing) tools from Vas County in relation to the golden treasure and the manufacturing of the foils

Let us now review briefly what we know about the tools of the metalsmiths who worked in the broader Velem area. The following finds can be mentioned in this respect:

1. A bronze embossing hammer, marked IIX on one of its working surfaces,[274] from the Szombathely area, in the collection of the Hungarian National Museum (*Fig. 35. 1*).[275]
2. Bronze socketed hammers in the material collected by Baron Miske in Velem (*Fig. 35. 3, 6*).[276]
3. Mould for an embossing hammer (?) found at Gór–Kápolnadomb (*Fig. 35. 2*).[277]
4. Stray finds of hammers from Celldömölk–Ság-hegy in the Lázár Collection of the Hungarian National Museum.[278]

---

[269] MÁRTON 1907, 65; MOZSOLICS 1963, 68–69; MOZSOLICS 1973, 86; ILON 1992, 252–256; PARE 1999, 493–497, 506–508.

[270] MOZSOLICS 1963, 80–82; JUNG 2005, 57–58.

[271] MOZSOLICS 1963, Egyptian *k.dt* = 9.1 g

[272] ILON 1992; ILON 2001a, 2001b

[273] PERONI 1998, 223; PARE 1999, 509–510.

[274] FEKETE 2008, 531, upper left.

[275] ILON 2004, Taf. LI. 1.

[276] MISKE 1908, 23, Taf. XXIX. 1–4. He proposed the first classification of this tool type in Europe, distinguishing four main types.

[277] ILON 1996a, 177, Taf. 3. 15.

[278] LÁZÁR 1943, 280–287, Taf. VII. 70–71.

5. Mould of a horned anvil and its bronze cast (*Fig. 35. 5*) found on St. Vid Hill in the prehistoric collection of the Savaria Museum.[279]
6. A bronze cutting anvil, from the same site (*Fig. 35. 4*).[280]
7. A bronze stamp/patterned punch (*Stempel*) from Velem, identified as a button by Baron Miske.[281] The artefact can no longer be found in the collection of the Savaria Museum, and thus this find remains uncertain.

There are some metal finds from Velem, described by Baron Miske as "plundered" (i.e. stray finds without a context), whose decoration resembles that on the artefacts of the golden treasure:

1. Bronze ornamental disc. Round, perforated in the centre. Ornamentation: the second row from its edge was created with a stamp/punch making a cable pattern. Incomplete.[282] Weight: 3.3 g, SM inv. no. 54.512.558 (*Fig. 35. 8*).

2. Bronze ornamental disc. Round, a large portion is missing. There are three punch-impressed concentric circle motifs, each with a diameter of 11 mm, along the cordon toward the centre.[283] Weight: 2.7 g, SM inv no.: 54.512.566 (*Fig. 35. 7*).

3. Bronze ornament. Its form resembles a domed roundel, a small portion is missing. Decorated with seven evenly spaced concentric circles and two smaller ones around a larger, central concentric circle. Height: 15 mm, diameter: 57 mm. In the collection of the Museum of Natural History in Vienna.[284]

In the light of the above and the results of the metal analysis of the bronze artefacts found at Velem and of the bronze objects in the Szombathely–Jáki út hoard,[285] according to which the bronze objects found at Szombathely were most likely manufactured on the St. Vid Hill, and essentially in agreement with Kálmán Miske's contention,[286] we may certainly claim that the craftsmen working on the St. Vid Hill of Velem and its broader area had the technical background (tools) and expertise for crafting the ornamented gold foils and composite (bronze, gold) jewellery. Still, we cannot exclude the possibility that the jewellery of the treasure was manufactured in another distant settlement of the Central or Western

---

279 Miske 1908, Taf. XXII. 3, Taf. XXIX. 8.
280 Miske 1908, Taf. XXIX. 7.
281 Miske 1908, Taf. XXXVI. 45.
282 Miske 1908, Taf. XXXVI. 58.
283 Miske 1908, Taf. XXXVI. 60.
284 Foltiny 1958, 10, 65, Taf. IV. 6.
285 Ilon 2002b, 160–161, Abb. 9–11; Költő – Varga – Maclean 2002, 405–408.
286 Miske 1928, 81–94.

European Urnfield culture and that it reached Velem through trade, gift exchange, marriage or alliance, or that it was part of plundered booty.

However, the question of how the objects of the treasure were actually made should be examined, regardless of where it was produced. Following the repeated examination of the artefacts,[287] this issue will be addressed by drawing from the more recent comprehensive studies by Hermann Born[288] and Barbara Armbruster,[289] and my consultations with Géza Szabó.

The following manufacturing procedure seems most likely in the case of the diadem: the bronze backplate[290] was embedded in pitch[291] (*Treib-/Ziselierkitt*; *Fig. 36*) and the pre-drawn motifs were created using positive (*Patrizen*) and negative (*Matrizen*) patterned punches bearing concentric circle, zigzag and cable motifs.[292] The gold foil[293] was then placed and stretched over the decorated bronze backplate (the pull marks can be identified as parallel lines; *Fig. 16. 1*) and the pattern was "copied" to the foil by pressing it against the bronze plate with a flat piece of wood or by rolling a wooden cylinder over it. The edges

---

[287] This was performed in cooperation with master goldsmith András Radics, who was generous with his knowledge during the consultations before and after the photographing of the artefacts.

[288] BORN 2003a-b.

[289] ARMBRUSTER 2000, 111–118, Abb. 40, 42, 44.3, 59. 1, 60, 67; 2012, 379: description of the period's manufacturing techniques, with an overview of the earlier literature.

[290] The thickness of the backplate of the neck ornament (*Goldblechkragen*) of the treasure in the Museum für Vor- und Frühgeschichte in Berlin is 0.5 mm. BORN 2003b, 95–96, Abb. 17–18.

[291] BORN 2003b, 91. A lump of pitch measuring 1.8 x 1.5 x 0.8 cm was found in Pit 167 of the Middle Bronze Age settlement at Szombathely–Zanat-Pap-földek. Péter Skriba's excavation in 2008; the finds are still unpublished; I am grateful to him for calling my attention to this find. HNM temporary inv. no. 48.67829.167.77. Pitch was used to coat vessels found in the cemetery at Zanat dated to the end of the Urnfield period, cf. ILON – SÜMEGI – TÓTH *et al.* 2011, 179, 182–185. There are many large lumps of pitch (still unpublished) in the bronze founder's hoard from nearby Ikervár dating to the Early Iron Age. Cf. NAGY – SÜMEGI – PERSAITS – GULYÁS –TÖRŐCSIK 2012, 36. I am greatly indebted to Marcella Nagy for her kind permission to publish the goldsmith's pitch fragments from Ikervár.

[292] BORN 2003b, 93.

[293] Impressions with a diameter of 3 to 4 mm on the X-ray images of the gold foil were made with a goldsmith's planishing hammer (*Planierhammer*) used for stretching the plate. BORN 2003b, 89, Abb. 5, 14. The marks left by an embossing hammer (*Treibhammer*) have been identified on the X-ray images of the gold artefact from Ezelsdorf. KOCH 2003, 101, Abb. 6–7.

of the foil were folded over and the metal composite was bent into the desired size. Finally, it was attached to an organic base of leather[294] or textile. If made otherwise, it would be difficult to interpret the fragments of the bronze backplate that preserved the patterns of the foils.

The following manufacturing procedure can be assumed in the case of the domed roundels: the soft gold foil was pressed onto the bronze backplate decorated with the desired patterns and set on the goldsmith's pitch applied to a wooden or bronze bar/tool[295]/anvil with a rounded terminal. Its edges were folded over and the gold spiral wound around a bronze wire was fixed to the edge produced in this manner.

Several techniques could be employed for manufacturing the gold wire for the domed roundels of Velem and the pectorals:[296] a very simple procedure described by Hermann Born[297] involved pressing strips of gold into a notch carved into a piece of hardwood and then smoothing the wire's surface. The cross-section of this wire with a flash running along its edge would be a triangle with rounded corners (or rather, a flattened triangle) conforming to the shape of the notch. Such flashes are visible on the digital macrophotos of the specimens that I could examine (Várvölgy: 1926, 2005, *Fig. 37. 3* and Velem: 1929, *Fig. 21. 3–4*). A similar procedure would be hammering on an anvil with a similar notch, called swages,[298] producing a wire with a similar cross-section. Wire could also be made by rolling or drawing between two slabs of stone or hardwood to produce a wire of round cross-section,[299] or by using a wire draw-plate of stone,[300] hardwood[301] or metal. The fragment of a swage block suitable for wire drawing was found in the Cape Gelidonya shipwreck.[302] Wooden tools are only preserved under fortunate circumstances, in wet or extremely arid conditions. Metal draw-plates for producing wire were identified in the Late Bronze Age hoards found at Isleham

[294] This is also confirmed by the bronze mounts of the leather vest of the lady of Blanot. THEVENOT 1991, Figs 42–43; the same has been assumed in the case of the ornamented bronze plate from the Nürnberg–Mögeldorf treasure. BORN 2003b, 94.

[295] ARMBRUSTER 2003, Abb. 10.

[296] FISCHER 1995, 12.

[297] BORN 2003a, 181–182.

[298] Anvils of this type has been published from Keranfinit, Bardouville and Fresné-la-Mère: THEVENOT 1998, Fig. 9. 3–5.

[299] FISCHER 1995, Abb. 4b

[300] OBERFRANK 1986, 26.

[301] THEOPHILUS 1986, Chapter LVI; FISCHER 1995, Abb. 4c-e.

[302] BASS *et al.* 1967. 102, Fig. 112. 136, Fig. 113. 136.

(southern England),[303] Drouwen (northern Netherlands)[304] and Jenišovice[305] (Czech Republic). The perforation through the anvil found in Venarey-les-Laumes (France; *Fig. 31. 8*)[306] and the swages on others (*Fig. 31. 5–7*), may have been used for the same purpose. It is possible that the prismatic fired clay object with seven notches found in Grave 601 at Bologna–S. Vitale had served the same purpose.[307]

Gold wires were wound around thin bronze wires (*Fig. 21. 3*) and the spirals thus produced were used to create the desired pectoral (*Fig. 39. 4–5*); in the case of other adornments, such as the domed roundels, they were mounted onto their edges. In my view, spirals may have been used to trim garments too (*Fig. 41. 2*). Gold bands could be wound around textile or leather ribbons, a more durable variant of ornate pendent adornments. The fragments of such ornaments have luckily survived in the Velem treasure (*Fig. 21. 4*).

The use of pressing moulds came long after the diffusion and widespread use of the techniques of repoussé and combinations of repoussé and chasing (Dunapentele),[308] repoussé and engraving (Dedinka),[309] and repoussé, chasing and engraving (Csabrendek).[310] These popular metalworking techniques were used simultaneously. More archaic techniques (Vácszentlászló[311] and its circle) demonstrably survived into later periods, alongside the improved versions and imitations of archaic techniques.

4.4 The symbolism of the golden artefacts unearthed in Velem

In this section, I shall address this issue but briefly, without any pretension of completeness, because it is not the focus of this work. The colour of gold

---

303 Ha A2–B1 according to the Hungarian chronology. Northover 1995, 15–16, Fig. 1.

304 Fokkens 1997, Fig. 7, centre.

305 Ha B1 period. Kytlicová 1991, Taf. 46. 44–47; Kytlicová 2007, 267, Taf. 102. 35–38.

306 Nicolardot – Verger 1998, Fig. 11. 10.

307 Müller-Karpe 1959, Text 256, Taf. 70. A

308 Bóna 1959, 55–56, Abb. 14.

309 Paulík 1984, 44, 48, Obr. 1; Paulík 1986, Obr. 5, 8; Schmidtová – Baxa – Paulík 2002, 291, Abb. 7. 3.

310 Bóna 1959, 56; Mozsolics 1973, 48, 125, Taf. 1; Mozsolics 1985, 58.

311 Hampel 1886, Taf. XXXVIII. 3a-b; Hampel 1892, 61; Mozsolics 1973, 142, Taf. 24. 2.

has since time immemorial evoked the Sun, light and radiance.[312] As I have already noted,[313] I agree with other scholars that the combination of a boss and concentric circles can be interpreted as a solar symbol.[314] Continuing earlier traditions,[315] the Velem assemblage and the symbolism of its objects reflected the prominence of the Sun cult,[316] as did many other finds from the onset of the 14th–13th centuries BC, i.e. the beginning of the Urnfield period, from Egypt through Central Europe to Scandinavia. The Velem treasure represented the lavish, magnificent costume adornments, or at least part of them,[317] of a person, perhaps a high-ranking woman, at the peak of the social hierarchy, who was in command of celestial, sacral and divine powers, or who was capable of ensuring the benevolence of celestial beings, that had been hidden here thousands of years ago. The eight fields filled with vertical double and triple zigzag motifs arranged in combinations of 3-3-2-3 on the diadem and the concentric zigzag lines on the domed roundels can be interpreted as a serpent symbol,[318] in which case they would refer to the underworld, making the composition denote this world and the otherworld. The striking predominance of solar symbols suggests the worldly powers of the owner of the sumptuous adornments. My contention regarding the portrayal of the duality of the lower world and the upper world – this world and the otherworld – is borne out, for instance, by the stone decorated with a combination of concentric circles, zigzag motifs and bundles of parallel lines found at Illmitz (Burgenland).[319]

---

[312] ELUÈRE 1995, 31; GEBHARD 2003, 152; DAVID 2010, 437; GLEIRSCHER 2014, 142.

[313] ILON 2002b; ILON 2012b.

[314] VLADÁR 1973, 305; MÜLLER-KARPE 1978–79, 23, Abb. 6; HANSEN 1994, 261; KAUL 1998, I: 195–209, II: Cat. nos 136, 157; DAVID 2003, 35; GOLD UND KULT 2003, Kat. Nr. 46, with further literature. MENGHIN 2003, 225–227; SOMMERFELD 2010, 222. Cf. also ARMBRUSTER 2011, 29–30; ARMBRUSTER 2012, 375.

[315] DAVID 2010, 439–486.

[316] BOUZEK 2000, 346; SPRINGER 2003, 20; MÜLLER-KARPE 2003, 147, 151, Abb. 2. 2, 3. 3, 4, 8, 9.

[317] In an ideal case, a complete set of female costume jewellery crafted from durable materials (metal, glass/glass paste, amber) would be made up of adornments for the head, the neck and the chest, the waist, the arms and the legs. One good example is the assemblage recovered from Grave 27, a female burial, of Tumulus 48 at Stična, dated to the Early Iron Age. GABROVEC – KRUH – MURGELJ – TERŽAN 2006, 32–33, Taf. 16–17.

[318] UENZE 1993, 132–136; KAUL 2003, 49.

[319] PITTIONI 1954, 417, Abb. 284.

However, I would also like to point out another possible interpretation. Most archaeoastronomers agree that the central rosette of seven concentric circles on the domed roundels and the corresponding motif on the diadem's peak represent the Seven Sisters of the Pleiades (*Siebengestirn*).[320] The very first portrayal of this constellation dates to 1713 BC;[321] later depictions showing the "path" of the constellation, of which the first five-phased depiction dates to the earlier 16th century BC,[322] include the Nebra sky disc.[323] Homer's description of Achilles' shield seems to echo the elements of the Nebra disc:

> And first Hephaestus makes a great and massive shield,
> blazoning well-wrought emblems all across its surface,
> raising a rim around it, glittering, triple-ply
> with a silver shield-strap run from edge to edge
> and five layers of metal to build the shield itself,
> and across its vast expanse with all his craft and cunning
> the god creates a world of gorgeous immortal work.
> There he made the earth and there the sky and the sea
> and the inexhaustible blazing sun and the moon rounding full
> and there the constellations, all that crown the heavens,
> the *Pleiades* and the Hyades, Orion in all his power too
> and the Great Bear that mankind also calls the Wagon:
> she wheels on her axis always fixed, watching the Hunter,
> and she alone is denied a plunge in the Ocean's baths.
> (Homer, *The Iliad*, Book XVIII: 558–571, tr. Robert Fagles; my italics)

This would explain the design of seven concentric circles appearing twice on the bracelet of the high-ranking woman buried at Blanot, even if in a slightly different composition, probably reflecting a different phase.[324]

At the same time, the Pleiades were one of the crucial constellations aiding orientation in seafaring and overland travel:

---

[320] SCHLOSSER 2010, 919, 921; STEINRÜCKEN 2010, 938–939, 944, Abb. 1. 9; HANSEN 2010, 954.

[321] SCHLOSSER 2010, Abb. 26.

[322] MELLER 2010, Abb. 35.

[323] PÁSZTOR – ROSLUND 2007, 269–274, Figs 2–3.

[324] THEVENOT 1991, Fig. 37a.

> The wind lifting his spirits high, royal Odysseus
> spread sail – gripping the tiller, seated astern –
> and now the master mariner steered his craft,
> sleep never closing his eyes, forever scanning
> the stars, the *Pleiades* and the Plowman late to set
> and the Great Bear that mankind also calls the Wagon:
> she wheels on her axis always fixed, watching the Hunter,
> and she alone is denied a plunge in the Ocean's baths.
> Hers were the stars the lustrous goddess told him
> to keep hard to port as he cut across the sea.
> (Homer, *The Odyssey*, Book V: 295–304, tr. Robert Fagles; my italics)

In peasant societies,[325] this star cluster also marks the beginning and the end of the agricultural year, the so-called Pleiadian year,[326] made up of 221 days, divided into seven synodic lunar months and 14.3 days. The Velem diadem has exactly 219 concentric circles (still visible today!), which is hardly a coincidence and is very close to the astronomical calculation.

> When the Atlas-born *Pleiades* rise, start the
> harvest – the plowing, when they set. They are concealed
> for forty nights and days, but when the year has revolved
> they appear once more, when the iron is being sharpened.
> This is the rule for the plains, and for those who dwell near
> the sea and those far from the swelling sea in the valleys
> and glens, fertile land: sow naked, and plow naked, and
> harvest naked, if you want to bring in all of Demeter's
> works in due season, so that each crop may grow for you in
> its season, lest being in need later you go as a beggar to
> other people's houses and achieve nothing – just as now
> you have come to me. But I shall not give you anything
> extra, nor measure out extra for you. Work, foolish Perses,
> at the works which the gods have marked out for human
> beings, lest someday, sorrowing in your spirit, together
> with your children and your wife you seek a livelihood

[325] LEITSCHUH-WEBER 1994, 93–97.
[326] SCHLOSSER 2010, 922–924.

> among your neighbors, but they pay no attention to you.
> For two times maybe and three times you will succeed; but
> if you bother them again, you will accomplish nothing but
> will speak a lot in vain, and the rangeland of your words will
> be useless. I bid you take notice of how to clear your debts
> and how to ward off famine:
> (Hesiod, *Works And Days*, Book II: 383–404, tr. Glenn W. Most; my italics)

The vertical zigzag lines in the central part of the diadem recall agricultural fields or plots of land, while the wavy lines on the domed roundels can be interpreted as symbols linked to vegetation[327] and fertility.

The edges of the domed roundels of Pair II were originally framed by 27 or 28 concentric circles, each of which can be interpreted as a day (24 hours). We know that 27⅓ sidereal lunar days[328] make up one month.[329] The seven concentric circles in the centre of the domed roundels represent a single lunar phase, i.e. a quarter. In the Nordic Bronze Age, sets of 7 and 28 appear on the Aspeberget rock carvings, one of which portrays a figure holding a sistrum-like object in its right hand, depicted by twenty-eight cup marks arranged in four rows of seven each. In his study devoted to ancient astronomy, Flemming Kaul suggested that it depicted the four lunar phases and the lunar months,[330] a conclusion similar to my own. Viewed from this perspective, the number of the domed roundels found in Velem – four in all – is not a coincidence, and also implies that this part of the costume adornments can be considered complete.

In sum, the symbols[331] appearing on the gold artefacts from Velem representing the Sun and the Moon resemble a series of other objects typical of the European Bronze Age, including the Carpathian Basin,[332] bearing symbols representing

---

327 Teržan 2005, 252–253, Abb. 8.

328 Measured from a fixed point, the period of the orbit of the Moon around the Earth with respect to the fixed stars is defined as a sidereal lunar month (from Lat. *sidus*; its average duration is 27⅓ days. Therefore, one "Moon phase" was assigned to each day of the orbit through a sky divided into 28 parts.

329 Sommerfeld 2010, 230–231, Abb. 12.

330 Kaul 2003, 47, Abb. 17.

331 David 2010, 479.

332 Menghin 2003, 230–234, Abb. 11–13; Pásztor 2012: 192–200, Fig. 9, 2–3. The slab of clay with a diameter of 1 m found at Ság-hegy, which, owing to its fractured surface,

time (calendar)[333] that continued a "conservative" tradition looking back on thousands of years[334] that can be associated with, and portrays, agriculture and fertility, in other words, the cyclicity of nature. The cyclic movement of the Sun and the Moon symbolises, and can be associated with, the cycles of life, as has been argued by Déchelette.[335] The Pleiadian lunar year appears on the diadem; the lunar month and lunar quarter on Pair II of the domed roundels; the lunar quarter on Pair I of the domed roundels. They are, at the same time, illustrations of good and evil, of this world and the otherworld, possibly inspired by the deity[336] that influences the skies and the weather, perhaps a reflection of a dualistic worldview.

---

can never be used for the purpose of accurate calculation, can be regarded as a type of calendar as well. Ilon – Sümegi – Bodor 2006, Fig. 9.

[333] May – Zumpe 2003, 253–265.

[334] Jockenhövel 2003, 112. The new one would be embodied by the symbolism of the bird (*Vogel*) and, in my view, the transition between the two is evidenced by depictions of the sun barque (*Vogel-Sonnenbarke*). Ilon 2012b, esp. 174 and Abb. 1.

[335] Déchelette 1909, 94.

[336] Kaul 2003, 50.

5 Diadem types, how they were worn, and social gender in prehistory

A diadem is a headpiece that signals social rank, regardless of whether made of copper, bronze and/or gold, while the differences in its ornament obviously denote the owner's social status. Over half a century ago, István Bóna noted that the prototypes of the early diadems typical of the Carpathian Basin in the Copper and Bronze Age should be sought in the Southeastern Balkanic-Anatolian culture province.[337] More recently, János Makkay demonstrated the close relationship between the diadems typical in the Aegean, the Balkans, the Carpathian Basin and the Abashevo culture of the Volga-Ural region[338] (for the later pieces, see Type B/2b, below). A list of the fifty Early Bronze Age headbands (diadems) known from Central Europe has been compiled by Rüdiger Krause.[339] First, I shall offer a classification, although without any pretence of perfection, of the copper, bronze and gold artefacts identified as diadems found in the Carpathian Basin and in the neighbouring territories. My main criterion is the relation between the edges of the plate (band/ribbon) and its length. In my view, the two main groups (A and B) also reflect a chrono-typological sequence in view of the general tendency.

A: Plates with parallel edges,
B: Plates with non-parallel edges,
  B/1: Plates with tapering edges,
  B/2: Plates, whose upper edge widens in the centre from the lower one,
    B/2a: Plates with rising central part,
    B/2b: Plates with peaked central part.

Let us see a few examples illustrating the above categorisation.

A: Plates (bands, sheets) with parallel edges, identified as diadems

1. This type comes from burials dating to the Copper Age and the Early Bronze Age in Slovakia.[340] Among the latter, a copper piece decorated with repoussé was recently found in Grave 554 at Ludanice. Length: 32 cm, width: 4 cm.[341] Bronze

---

337 Bóna 1959, 55.
338 Makkay 2000, 54–56, Fig. 12. 3–5.3.
339 Krause 2003, 172–174, 286–287, Abb. 144.
340 Novotná 1984, 67.
341 Bátora Schulzt 2012, 43, Abb. 3.1.

hoard I from Nemecká–Hradiso,[342] interpreted as a votive offering, comprised a single bronze headband. Its decorated ends were fastened with wires. Length: 61.4 cm, width: 4.2 cm, diameter: 18.5 cm, weight: 91.842 g. It was interpreted as representing the second phase of the traditional act of deposition performed by a family. Dating: Ha B1, Lausitz culture.

2. Vörs–Majorság (Somogy County): a unique, repoussé-decorated copper piece with the two terminals twisted together on the forehead, from Grave 2, a female burial,[343] assigned to the Baden culture. This band encircled the entire head.

3. Franzhausen (Lower Austria): the women buried in Graves 110, 334, 747 and 785 of Cemetery I, assigned to the Unterwölbling culture,[344] wore bronze headbands and, in some cases, other unusual frontlets (*Fig. 40. 1*). However, these adornments do not always suggest that their wearers enjoyed a higher social status than the middle social stratum.

4. Melk–Spielberg (Lower Austria): a headband with rolled terminals made of repoussé-decorated bronze plate was found in a female burial[345] assigned to the Unterwölbling culture, dated to the Bz A1–2 period.

5. Arbedo–Castione (Tessin Canton, Switzerland): in addition to other jewellery, the hoard (Bz A1) contained a bronze headband of this type.[346] The edge of the band is decorated with repoussé and there are three perforations on both its terminals. Width: 2.58 cm, diameter: 14.2–13.2 cm. It was probably attached to a backing of organic material.

6. Lovasberény–Jánoshegy (Fejér County): a stray find of a bronze headband dated to the Vatya III period.[347] The terminals of the decorated band are rolled back. Length: 54 cm, width: 5 cm.

---

[342] Ožďáni 2009, 54–55, Obr. 5, Tab. I.

[343] Banner 1956, 111, Taf. LXXXVII; Visy 2003, 123, colour photograph on the title page of the chapter on the Copper Age. From his examination of the skull in 2005, anthropologist Balázs Gusztáv Mende (Institute of Archaeology of the Hungarian Academy of Sciences, Budapest) concluded that the buried individual had female traits. Quoted by Horváth 2006, 109.

[344] Neugebauer 1994, Abb. 40. 5, Abb. 41; Neugebauer – Neugebauer 1997, Teil 1:116, 252, 430, 444, Teil 2:Taf. 450/5, 498/3, 563/6, 571/7.

[345] Leeb 1994, 117, Abb. 10. 11, Abb. 11 (the captions are erroneous in both cases). The dimensions of the headband were not published.

[346] Primas 1997, 292, Abb. 2.1.

[347] Bóna 1959, 56, Abb. 17; Bóna 1975, 71, Taf. 52.3.

7. Ócsa–6 Klapka St. (Pest County): the diadem of a hoard brought to light while digging a well.[348] Length: 54 cm, width: 2.6–3.1 cm, diameter: 18.7 cm. There are twenty-three double perforations along its lower edge, some of which most likely served for the attachment of pendants. Dating: Mozsolics BIIIb, late Koszider period of the Vatya culture, although an earlier date (Bz A2b-c) has also been suggested.[349] Gisela Schumacher-Matthäus proposed a reconstruction with the four disc pendants, whose decoration is identical to the ones from Velem, as having hung in pairs on the back.[350]

8. Nyíregyháza–12–16 Petőfi St. (Szabolcs-Szatmár-Bereg County): the gold hoard placed in a vessel contained a gold headband.[351] Diameter: 18.5 cm, width of the plate: 3.3 cm, weight: 104.25 g. It has a simple decoration (beadrow, herringbone motif, semi-circles, repoussé boss). The rolled-back terminals are connected by a gold pin. Dating: Mozsolics B IVb, Bz D1, Ópályi horizon.

9. Kemecse (Szabolcs-Szatmár-Bereg County): Hoard I contained a bronze diadem with repoussé ornamentation.[352] Length: 58 cm, width: 6 cm; its ends are rounded. Dating: Mozsolics BVb, Kurd horizon.

10 Kék (Szabolcs-Szatmár-Bereg County): the hoard contained a repoussé-decorated bronze diadem,[353] whose main motifs were identical with those of the preceding diadem (perhaps both were manufactured in the same workshop of the Gáva culture). Length: 52 cm;[354] there are two perforations on both terminals. Dating: Mozsolics BVb, Kurd horizon.

11. Márok (Baranya County): diadem fragments decorated with a combination of repoussé concentric circles and bead-like semi-spherical bosses;[355] the other decorated plates[356] most likely adorned a belt. The decoration of the diadem fragments is nearly identical with the ornamentation of the plate from Bingula–Divoš (Serbia)[357] and that of a diadem from Pamuk (perhaps made in the same workshop). Dating: Mozsolics BVb, Kurd horizon.

---

[348] Topál 1973, 3, 8, Abb. 1.

[349] David 2010, 470.

[350] Schumacher-Matthäus 1985, Taf. 44. 1.

[351] Mozsolics 1966, 14, 33, Abb. 1. 6, Abb. 2–3; Mozsolics 1973, 49, 201–202; Kemenczei 1999, 73, Kat. Nr. 39.

[352] Mozsolics 1985, 58–59, 132, Taf. 190. 4a-b.

[353] Mozsolics 1985, 58–59, 131–132, Taf. 192. 1.

[354] According to Kemenczei 1984, 175, it measured 64.4 cm.

[355] Mozsolics 1985, 146–149, Taf. 92. 28, 32–35.

[356] Mozsolics 1985, Taf. 92. 12–17, 36.

[357] Kilian Dierlmeier 1975, Taf. 49. 470.

12. Pamuk (Somogy County): an artefact defined as a bronze diadem broken into three pieces, decorated with concentric circles, was part of a hoard hidden in a vessel.[358] Dating: Mozsolics B Vb, Kurd horizon.

13. Budinščina (Croatia): bronze plate decorated with repoussé cross motifs from the hoard.[359] Dating: Vinski-Gasparini Urnfield period II (Ha A1).

14.) Nadap hoard (Fejér County): bronze plate decorated with repoussé cross motifs.[360] Width: 3 cm. Dating: Ha A1 or A2.

15. Štramberk (Moravia): bronze plate decorated with bundles of repoussé lines, the two ends fastened with two wires, from Hoard 4 (diameter: 16.5 cm, width: 3 cm). Dating: Ha B1.[361]

16. Szombathely hoard (Vas County):[362] a bronze headband decorated with a sun barque motif. Length of the surviving three fragments: 33 cm, width: 6.1 cm. In contrast to my earlier reconstruction, they may come from a belt. The metal analysis indicated that it could have been produced in the workshop of the Velem hillfort. Dating: Ha B1/2, 10th–9th centuries BC, late Urnfield culture.

17. The foil with straight edges of the Fleissig Collection[363] was most likely found in Transdanubia. Owing to its fragmented condition, the function of the plate, whether it came from a diadem or a belt decorated with closely spaced concentric circles resembling the design of the gold foils from Ság-hegy, Hoard II, cannot be determined. Dating: contemporaneous with Ság-hegy, Hoard II, Mozsolics B VIb, Románd horizon, Ha B2.

B/1: Plates (bands, sheets) with tapering edges, identified as diadems

1. Gold foil diadem assigned to the Bell Beaker culture, possibly from Bratislava (Pozsony, Slovakia) in the Lafrakoni Collection of the Hungarian National Museum.[364]

2. Binningen (Baselland Canton, Switzerland): a diadem (or perhaps a breast ornament),[365] presumably worn by a woman, whose stamped ornamentation of

---

358 Mozsolics 1985, 169, Taf. 106. 20.

359 Vinski-Gasparini 1973, I: 212, II: Taf. 79. 20; Mozsolics 1985, 58.

360 Makkay 2006, 41, Pl. XXII. 201.

361 Salaš 2005, I: 458, 461, Obr. 24, II: Tab. 439. 14.

362 Ilon 2002b, 149–169.

363 Mozsolics 1950, 15, Taf. IV. 3.

364 Bátora – Vladár 2002, 201, Abb. 2.1.

365 Mozsolics 1950, 18, Taf. XVI. 2; Bándi 1983, Abb. 6.1; Primas 1998, 344, 374, Abb. 198.

concentric circles connected by S-spirals continues earlier traditions.[366] It was crafted in the earlier Urnfield culture (Bz D2).[367] Its zigzag and cable patterns are remarkable in relation to the ornamentation of the Velem diadem.

3. Ippensheim–Bullenheimer Berg hoard (Bavaria): two gold plates mounted onto bronze backplates.[368] Their decoration is similar, but not identical. In view of their weight (4.08 and 5.55 g) and size (length: 19.5 and 19.9 cm),[369] these plates do not appear to have been diadems because they taper toward their ends and their length is insufficient as well.[370] I believe that they were adornments mounted onto leather or textile worn on the arm or in the hair (braid, chignon). Wolfgang David contends that they were used as costume, neck or breast ornament, or as part of a belt.[371] Some of the artefacts in the hoard were perhaps the ornaments of a ceremonial costume.[372] Dating: Ha A–B, 12th–9th centuries BC;[373] 10th–9th centuries BC, according to other scholars.[374]

4. Paseky (Písek area, Czech Republic): gold plate; length: *ca.* 24 cm. Dating: Bz D.[375] Similarly to the gold plates from Bullenheimer Berg, and for the same reason, I do not consider it to have been a diadem, but to have been worn in a manner similar to the above plates.

5. Drslavice (Moravia): bronze fragment from Hoard 1, almost identical with the bronze bands from Dedinka (Slovakia) and Németbánya (see below). Length: 8.3 cm, greatest width: 4.1 cm. Its ends are rolled back and it is decorated with herringbone and semi-circle motifs in repoussé along its edge. Dating: Bz D2–Ha A1 (Drslavice–Ořechov horizon).[376]

---

366 DAVID 2001, esp. Abb. 1–3, 6, 8, Abb. 6. 1.

367 DELLA CASA – FISCHER 1997, 205, 228, Abb 4. T85; RYCHNER 1998, 254, 374, Abb. 119. 2, Abb. 198.

368 DAVID 2007, 422.

369 DAS PRÄHISTORISCHE GOLD 1997, II: 304, Taf. 63; GOLD UND KULT 2003, Kat. Nr. 40.

370 Its classification as a diadem is treated with reservation by some scholars. Cf. GEBHARD 2003, 150.

371 DAVID 2007, 422–423.

372 DAS PRÄHISTORISCHE GOLD 1997, I: 197.

373 GEBHARD 2003, Abb. 2, Kat. Nr. 40.

374 HÄNSEL 2003, 166, Abb. 12; KEMENCZEI 1999, 76.

375 MOZSOLICS 1950, 17–18; DAS PRÄHISTORISCHE GOLD 1997, I: 180–181, Abb. 6. 17.9, II:268, Taf. 6.

376 SALAŠ 2005, I: 326, 332, II: Tab. 131. 428.

6. Drslavice (Moravia): a bronze fragment virtually identical to the above piece, from Hoard 2. Dating: Bz D2–Ha A1 (Drslavice–Ořechov horizon).[377]

7. Mušov (Moravia): fragments of repoussé decorated and engraved bronze plates (perhaps arm or leg ornaments) from Hoard 2,[378] resembling the pieces from Dedinka and Németbánya, suggesting that they had been worn in a similar manner. Length: 3.7 cm, greatest width: 1.9 cm. Dating: early phase of the Central Transdanubian Urnfield culture, Ha A1.

8. Dedinka (Dunasáp, Slovakia): bronze band decorated with dotted circles and repoussé and incised grooving from a female cremation burial (Grave II/74), dating to the Late Bronze Age.[379] Length of the three fragments: 4.1 cm, 5.1 cm and 2.2 cm, greatest width: 3.5 cm. Its reconstructed length, *ca.* 28 cm, is too short for a diadem, and thus, if mounted on leather or textile, it was probably worn on the arm or in the hair as a type of chignon or braid jewellery. Owing to the rolled-back ends, it could only have been worn as a diadem (tiara, frontlet) if a metal pin or a textile or leather cord was threaded through its ends enabling its placement around the forehead or if it was attached to a cap-like organic backing. Dating: Čaka culture, Bz D/Ha A1.

9. Németbánya–Felsőerdei dűlő (Veszprém County): fragment of a bronze plate described as a diadem, decorated similarly as the piece from Dedinka, from a cremation burial of Tumulus II/3,[380] dated to the late Tumulus–early Urnfield culture. Length: 3.6 cm. It was probably worn in the same manner as the one from Dedinka. Dating: Bz D/Ha A1.

10. Celldömölk–Izsákfa-Guta dűlő (Vas County): the yet unpublished hoard contained a bronze plate resembling the one from Dedinka.[381] A fragment of the slightly tapering, rolled-back terminal, decorated with repoussé herringbone motifs. Length: 5.8 cm, width: 2.8–26 cm, width of plate: 0.6 mm, weight: 13 g. Inv. no. SM Ö.85.1.12. Dating: Ha A1.

---

377 Salaš 2005, I: 337, II: Tab. 164. 268.

378 Kovárník 1998, 513–514, Taf. 8. 12, 17; Salaš 2005, I: 364, 370, II: Tab. 216. 181, 206.

379 Paulík 1984, 44. 48, Obr. 1; Paulík 1986, Obr. 5, 8; Schmidtová – Baxa – Paulík 2002, 291, Abb. 7. 3.

380 Ilon 1986, 83, 87, 93, Taf. I. 1.

381 I managed to acquire this hoard for the museum. Later, Mária Fekete conducted a control excavation, during which many bronze artefacts and the lower part of the vessel partly destroyed by ploughing were found *in situ*.

11. Medvedevcy (Zakarpattia Oblast, Ukraine): Hoard I contained a bronze plate head ornament, decorated with repoussé and engraved spiral hooks (*Spiralhaken*), concentric circles and semi-herringbone motifs along its edges.[382] Dating: Lazy Phase I, Ha A1.

12. Hinova (Iron Gates, Oltenia, Romania): a diadem-shaped gold band with a length of 59 cm and a width of 2.9 cm, from the hoard containing 5 kg of gold jewellery.[383] Its decoration is identical to that of the significantly earlier domed roundels found in Tafalău (Cófalva, Romania). Dating: Ha A.

B/2a: Plates (bands, sheets) with rising central part, identified as diadems

1. Csabrendek (Veszprém County): a decorated bronze diadem from a female burial dating to the early Tumulus culture (Koszider period). There are four perforations at each of its ends for the wire clasp. Length: 55 cm, greatest width: 4.8 cm, diameter: 16.5 cm.[384]

B/2b: Plates (bands, sheets) with peaked central part, identified as diadems

1. Varna (Bulgaria): miniature diadems with tongue-like projections in the centre from Graves 2 and 3 dating to the Copper Age. There is a single perforation on each terminal for the clasp.[385]

2. Tirynthe (Argolid, Greece): a diadem depicted on the head (perhaps placed on the hair) of a terracotta figurine portraying a woman, dated to the end of the Bronze Age (Late Helladic IIIC, 12th century).[386]

3. Bernstorf (Bavaria): a crown-shaped diadem (length: 43 cm, weight: 49.9 g) found by amateur archaeologists after deforestation on a Middle Bronze Age settlement,[387] assigned to the Tumulus culture (Bz C2, dated to 1400–1100 BC by radiocarbon measurements and to around 1370 BC by dendrochronology).[388] Five vertical plates with rounded triangular terminals rise from the band ornamented with concentric circles and hatched triangles, the same motifs adorning another plate.[389] While the forerunner of the diadem can be traced to the Aegean, its

---

[382] Kobaľ 2000, 87, Taf. 60. 6, Taf. 61. 10.

[383] David 2007, 431–432, Abb. 9.

[384] Bóna 1959, 56; Mozsolics 1973, 48, 125, Taf. 1; Mozsolics 1985, 58.

[385] Macht, Herrschaft 1988, 186–188, Abb. 1, 26–27, 40, 219.

[386] L' Europe au temps d'Ulysse 1999, 255, Cat. no. 155.

[387] David 2001, 71, Abb. 8.2; David 2007, 434; Gold und Kult 2003, Kat. Nr. 39.

[388] Gebhard 2003, 149, Abb. 1.

[389] David 2001, Abb. 9. 6.

decoration of simple concentric circles (*Kreisaugen*) and hatched triangles suggests a local manufacture.[390]

4. Cegléd–Öregszőlők (Pest County): a bronze diadem with triangular peak (length: 15 cm, height: 4.5–5 cm) from either a settlement or an inhumation burial,[391] found in 1925. There are two perforations on each terminal, probably for fastening or the clasp. Dating: Middle Bronze Age, late Vatya culture.

5. Pákozd–Várhegy settlement (Fejér County): object with a triangular peak in its centre, interpreted as a woman's bronze diadem (length: 14 cm, height: 5.4 cm), from the settlement dated to the Vatya-Koszider period,[392] found in a condition similar to the Velem diadem. It is decorated with concentric circles, and there are two perforations on each terminal for fastening or a clasp.

In my view, the pieces from Cegléd and Pákozd were more likely wrist- or hand-guards mounted onto organic materials of the type published by Hermann Müller-Karpe from Würtingen, rather than diadems.[393]

6. Istenmezeje (Heves County): diadem,[394] the almost identical counterpart of the one from Vácszentlászló (see below). According to Arnold Ipolyi's report,[395] there were two jewellery items of this type, one of which – specifically the one which came into his possession and which he later donated to the lyceum in Eger, where it disappeared during World War 1[396] – was found on the head of the deceased in an inhumation burial.[397] (However, the people of the Piliny culture cremated their dead.) The other piece is in the collection of the Hungarian National Museum. Diameter on top: 23.2 cm, at the bottom: 20.5 cm. Dating: Mozsolics BIVb, Bz D1, Ópályi horizon, a relic of the Piliny culture.

7. Vácszentlászló (Pest County): bronze diadem[398] with rounded triangular peak in front, terminating in an upward-curving spiral disc at the back. The plate is decorated with repoussé. Height: 9.4 cm, diameter on top: 22 x 23 cm, in the

---

[390] ZEITLER 2000, 93, Abb. 21.

[391] DINNYÉS 1982, 50–52, Abb. 2. 6; DAVID 2002a, 468, Abb. 8. 3. 2.

[392] KOVÁCS 1977, 95, Abb. 38; DAVID 2002, I:465, Abb. 8. 3. 1; HORVÁTH 2004, 35–36.

[393] MÜLLER-KARPE 1980, Taf. 356. E11.

[394] HAMPEL 1886, Taf. XXXVIII. 3a-b; HAMPEL 1892, 61; MOZSOLICS 1973, 142, Taf. 24.2.

[395] IPOLYI 1884, 469–511, esp. 480–481.

[396] PATAY 1967, Abb. 5, caption.

[397] This claim was accepted by Flóris Rómer with some reservation, but was rejected by Pál Patay (1967, note 9).

[398] HAMPEL 1886, Taf. XXXVIII, 2; HAMPEL 1892, 168; MOZSOLICS 1973, 187, Taf. 24.1; KOVÁCS 1977, 96–97, Abb. 56.

centre: 16.7 cm, at the bottom: 21.7 cm. Two disc-headed pins lay next to the diadem. Dating: Mozsolics BIVb, Ópályi horizon, a relic of the Piliny culture.

The reconstructions proposed by Gisela Schumacher-Matthäus must be mentioned here:[399] her drawing has the diadem's spirals curling downward in front for the piece from Nagybátony (Grave 873) or at the back (Rimavská Sobota/Rimaszombat, Slovakia) after being placed on the head. I would reject the latter because of the discomfort it would have caused as well as in view of the *in situ* position of a Vörs diadem, even though it is chronologically earlier. I therefore agree with the reconstruction showing the spirals curving upward in front[400] or at the back.[401]

8. Rimavská Sobota (Rimaszombat, Slovakia): fragment of a diadem's spiral terminal resembling the pieces from Vácszentlászló and Istenmezeje, from a hoard.[402]

9. Nagybátony (Nógrád County): two miniature bronze diadems, one from Grave 873, the other a stray find from the area of the cemetery;[403] they are regarded as smaller versions of the above diadems typical of the Piliny culture (Istenmezeje, Vácszentlászló, Rimavská Sobota). Patay dated this type to the Bz D–Ha A1 and considered them to be the relics of the Piliny culture.[404] Václav Furmánek agreed with the cultural classification, but dated the miniature variants earlier, to the Bz B1–C1.[405]

10. Balatonboglár–Borkombinát (Somogy County): an object with a peaked centre and two perforations on each terminal, resembling a cast bronze diadem, from the Urnfield settlement.[406] Its diameter is *ca.* 8 cm;[407] its other measurements have not been published. The excavators suggested that it was a chignon band rather than a diadem, which seems quite plausible to me.

---

[399] Schumacher-Matthäus 1985, Taf. 45. 2, Taf. 46. 1.

[400] Mozsolics 1973, Taf. 24. 2.

[401] Kovács 1977, Abb. 56.

[402] Hampel 1886, Taf. XXXVIII. 4.

[403] Patay 1967, 53, and Fig. 3. 1 and Fig. 4. 1.

[404] Patay 1967, 56–57.

[405] Furmánek 1977, 292.

[406] Published without data on size: Honti – Belényesy – Fábián *et. al.* 2004, 8, Taf. II, 3.

[407] It was displayed as part of a temporary exhibition in Kaposvár, where I culd personally view it in February 2007.

11. Celldömölk–Ság-hegy (Vas County): Hoard II[408] contained fragments of two gold foils with curved ends ("semi-oval" according to Amália Mozsolics, and "semi-elliptic" according to Jenő Lázár). Mozsolics and Tibor Kemenczei interpreted them as the ends of a diadem. The central, peaked part of the foil interpreted as part of a diadem was missing, and the end fragments disappeared during World War 2. However, a photo of the object's original condition (*Fig. 39. 2*)[409] survived in an album compiled by Jenő Lázár,[410] the collection's owner. One of the photos shows a frontal view of one fragment, the other a reverse view of another fragment, which reveals that the edge of the gold foil was folded over backward in the same way as the foil of the Velem diadem, and similar perforations were made along its edge. However, the position of the perforations on the more intact piece suggest attachment rather than a clasp mechanism. Therefore, I believe that Frigyes Kőszegi's contention that this artefact could have adorned the ear-guard of a bronze helmet[411] should not be rejected out of hand, even though it could only be confirmed by the straight portion of the plates. However, the photograph of the artefact's unrestored condition does not confirm that one of the foil's edges had a prominent peak, as suggested by a schematic reconstruction drawing made by Mozsolics,[412] and therefore an interpretation as a diadem must be treated with caution. It was mounted onto a bronze backplate as noted by Jenő Lázár in his description.[413] Dating: Mozsolics: BVIb, Románd horizon, Ha B2; Kemenczei: IVb treasure horizon, Ha B2; Turk:[414] Late Bronze Age III, Ha B1(2).

Other head ornaments

1. Szigetszentmiklós–Üdülősor (Pest County): the silver headband from Grave 863 of the cemetery[415] assigned to the Csepel Group of the Beaker culture cannot be reconstructed with certainty and thus it cannot be assigned to a particular type.

---

408 Mozsolics 1950, Taf. IV. 1a-b; Mozsolics 1981, 302; Mozsolics 2000, 38, Taf. 18; Kemenczei 1996b, 84, 87, Abb. 37; Kemenczei 1999, 74–75, Abb. 43.

409 Mozsolics 1950, Taf. IV. 1.

410 SM Archaeological Archives, inv. no. 2378-08; it is a large album. Treasure II was unearthed on December 20, 1932. The treasure was published by Jenő Lázár in 1941, in which he described the restored gold sheets. Lázár 1941, Fig. 1.

411 Kőszegi 1988, 130; Bouzek 1981, Abb. 4. 1.

412 Mozsolics 2002, Taf. 18. 2.

413 Lázár 1941, 371.

414 Turk 2012a, 219, 223, Abb. 6.

415 Endrődi 2012, 16, Fig. 1. 3, Fig. 6. 2, Fig. 7. 1.

2. Ordacsehi (Somogy County): the cylindrical bronze pendants found in the head region in Grave 400, the burial of a middle-aged woman, in the cemetery of the Kisapostag culture[416] have been interpreted as the pendent adornments of a cap (*Fig. 40. 2*), probably worn in daily life.

3. Franzhausen (Lower Austria): the reconstruction of the unusual head ornament of the woman buried in Grave 110 of Cemetery I, assigned to the Unterwölbling culture,[417] is confirmed by the fragment of an Early Bronze Age figurine discovered in Budapest (*Fig. 40. 3*).[418]

4. Medvedze (Medvedzie, Slovakia): the bronze diadem is a combination of Types A and B/2b.[419] Dating: Mozsolics: BVc Gyermely horizon, Ha A2. Wire jewellery conceived in a similar spirit (*Drahtkunst*) is also known from Hoard I of Velem and thus the two can be regarded as contemporaneous.[420]

Since the interpretation of these objects as a diadem or a belt is often controversial, it is instructive to examine the diameter and length of the debated objects as well as the basic measurements of an average human body in order to find an acceptable answer and to bolster the claims made here regarding the function of the plates. The waistline of an average, slim female aged around 25 and 175 cm tall is 75 cm, while the circumference of her head is 17–22 cm. (The measurements of a male of the same age and height are obviously greater.) Regarding females, this means that bands shorter than 75 cm could not have been worn as belts because they would not have reached around the waist, unless worn by a child or if the plates were used to decorate the belt's front part only. The waistline of a small girl of average stature aged three is 47 cm. At the same time, there are several figurines dating to the Bronze Age of the Carpathian Basin, although from an earlier period than the Urnfield culture, on which the decorative plate mounted onto organic, textile or leather material, embellished the wearer's costume in front, but not on the back, where it was fastened (Cîrna, Figurine 3: Grave 26; Figurine 5: Grave 66).[421] Taking the average female as an example, the minimal length of a plate-decorated belt of this type could not be less than 40–45 cm because only in this case could it be securely positioned above the pelvis. A similar mode of wearing can be assumed in the case of diadems too, as

[416] SOMOGYI 2004, 363–365, Abb. 16A-C; ZOFFMANN 2004, 384–385.

[417] NEUGEBAUER 1994, Abb. 40. 4, Abb. 41. 1–2.

[418] ZSIDI 2005, 84; REMÉNYI 2005.

[419] HAMPEL 1886, Taf. XXXVIII. 1a-b; MOZSOLICS 1985, 59.

[420] MOZSOLICS 1985, 59, Taf. 231A. 23, Taf. 231B. 4.

[421] SCHUMACHER-MATTHÄUS 1985, Taf. 8. 2b, Taf. 12. 2b.

already noted for the plate found in Dedinka, which indicates that the two ends of the plate did not reach around the head and that the plate was mounted onto a some organic material. The diadem from in Grave 27 of Tumulus 48 at Stična,[422] which is later than the Velem diadem, was worn in a similar manner. The diameter of this diadem was 18.1 cm and was probably worn like a hairband whose ends did not reach around the back of the head.

In sum, headbands were widely used, popular head adornments from the Copper Age to the end of the Urnfield culture in Central Europe, whose use extended into the Hallstatt culture as shown by the "mask" from Kleinklein–Kröllkogel.[423] Plates with a peaked centre, although not the most widespread type, were known in the Copper Age and in the ensuing Bronze Age. They were fastened with wire or a clasp mechanism on the back (Csabrendek, Pákozd, Štramberk), although they may have been flexible like hairbands. It seems likely that diadems were mounted onto organic backings, although this yet remains to be proven.

In the light of the above, the Velem diadem can be assigned to Type B/2b. Its mode of wearing will be discussed in Chapter 8. While gold foil covered objects such as coronet-shaped cones (*Kegel*), or caps (*Hut*) and necklaces (*Halskragen*/*cape*) were all the rage in Western Europe,[424] gold foil covered bands appear to have been the dominant fashion in Central and Eastern Europe. Irrespective of their shapes, diadems were worn by young and old females alike, although they might also have been part of the male costume as insignia of rank and prestige.

---

[422] GABROVEC – KRUH – MURGELJ – TERŽAN 2006, 33, Taf. 17/1.
[423] EGG – KRAMER 2005, Abb. 14.
[424] GERLOFF 1995, Abb. 8.

6 Analogies of the gold domed roundels of the Velem type[425]

The bronze[426] and gold variants of this artefact type are similarly domed roundels (*Buckeln*) and not flat discs (*Scheiben*). This has been conclusively proven during the new conservation work in the case of the pieces from Velem or it is obvious from the published photos in the case of other finds.[427] Decorated gold foil was mounted onto a copper or bronze backplate and was framed with spiral decoration of gold wire. A list of this ornament type was published over two decades ago by Lothar Sperber,[428] who noted that it was worn by females. His list is here complemented with the new finds and a few observations on manufacturing techniques.

1. Óbuda (?): pair of gold domed roundels[429] in the Museum of Natural History in Vienna. Their ornamental motifs and the framing with spirals are identical to that of the Velem pieces. Weight: 2.4 and 2.9 g. Dating: Nordic Bronze Age IV (Ha A).

2. Celldömölk–Ság-hegy (Vas County):[430] Hoard II contained a single round gold plate decorated with touching concentric circles in repoussé. The perforations along its edge indicate attachment by spiral wires (now missing) and that it was mounted on a bronze backplate, as described by Jenő Lázár.[431] A photograph of its condition before conservation can be found in the album of the Lázár Collection. It shows the bronze backplate (*Fig. 39. 2*) and the shadow effect reveals that the foil is domed. In 1950, Amália Mozsolics published a photo of the artefact after conservation.[432] Dating: Mozsolics: Hajdúböszörmény horizon

---

425 SPERBER 1992, note 4.

426 HÄNSEL 1997, Abb. 1. 2; TOMEDI 1998, 42, Abb. 3. 2.

427 In many cases, the photographs reveal that the "discсs" actually have a domed shape (e.g. DAVID 2003, Abb. 2), as shown by the roundel from Bullenheimer Berg. GOLD UND KULT 2003, Abb. 2, Kat. Nr. 40. The flattened ones were cracked radially or were broken, as the pices from Velem amd Várvölgy.

428 SPERBER 1992, note 4.

429 MOZSOLICS 1950, Abb. 7; MOZSOLICS 1981, 302–303; BARTH 1988/1989, 158, 160–161, Taf. I. 12–13; DAVID 2003, Abb. 2. 7–8.

430 MOZSOLICS 1950, 13–14, Taf. IV. 2; MOZSOLICS 1981, 302, 306; MOZSOLICS 2000, 38, Taf. 18/1; KEMENCZEI 1999, 75, Abb. 43.

431 LÁZÁR 1941, 371.

432 MOZSOLICS 1950, Taf. IV. 2.

(BVIa: Ha B1),[433] later modified to Románd horizon (BVIb: Ha B2);[434] Turk: Late Bronze Age III, Ha B1(2).[435]

3. Várvölgy–Felsőzsid (Zala County):[436] six[437] (or seven[438]) pieces, found in 1926 in a fragmented condition on Nagy-Lázhegy, in an area known as "Kis Lénia" (today called "Arany lénia", a deforested area) in the southwestern part of the hillfort,[439] part of a gold treasure hidden in a ceramic vessel. They had been mounted onto bronze backplates,[440] similarly to the Velem pieces,[441] but they were not framed with spiral gold wire. One of them bears concentric circle motifs[442] in an arrangement that is virtually identical to that of the domed roundels of Pair II from Velem. Dating: Mozsolics BVc, Ha A2, Gyermely horizon.

4. Rothengrub (Lower Austria): the hoard interpreted as containing female costume ornaments[443] included a domed roundel of gold,[444] a close counterpart of the pieces in Pair I from Velem. In his reconstruction, Richard Pittioni envisioned them as adorning a belt end. However, the decoration of the triple discs is made up of densely spaced concentric circles in repoussé resembling the plates of the Ság-hegy treasure. Pittioni dated the treasure to the Ha A2 horizon,[445] while Amália Mozsolics considered it to be contemporaneous with the golden treasure discovered in Velem[446] and assigned it to the Gyermely horizon (Ha A2). Tibor

---

433 Mozsolics 1981, 306; Sperber 1992, note 4.

434 Mozsolics 2000, 38.

435 Turk 2012a, 219, 223, Abb. 6.

436 Tompa 1928, 204–207, Abb. 95. 15–20; Mozsolics 1950, 14–15; Mozsolics 1981, Taf. 13. 7–12.

437 Tompa 1928, Abb. 95; Mozsolics 1981, Taf. 13; Kemenczei 1999, Abb. 44.

438 According to chief conservator Csaba E. Kiss, with whom I examined the finds on January 28, 2008, the fragments of domed roundels (inv. no. Ő. 735; Mozsolics 1983, Taf. 13a-b) listed in the inventory of gold artefacts of the Hungarian National Museum do not come from the same object.

439 Müller 2006b, note 1; Müller 2007, 5–26, esp. 16.

440 Mozsolics 1981, 300.

441 Mozsolics 1981, 301, Taf. 13. 7, 9–10.

442 Kemenczei 1999,74, Abb. 44, upper left corner.

443 Male according to Amália Mozsolics. Cf. Mozsolics 1981, 302.

444 Pittioni 1952, 90, 96, 98, Taf. II. 4a-b; David 2003, Abb. 2. 5, Abb. 3. 2; Lauermann – Rammer 2013, 84, Abb. 21.

445 Pittioni 1952, 96.

446 Mozsolics 1981, 306.

Kemenczei dated it to the 12th century BC. More recently, it has been dated to the Ha B2–3 period.[447]

5. Innsbruck–Mühlau cemetery (Tyrol, Austria): the piece from Grave 1, an inurned burial,[448] has been interpreted as a button, rather than a domed roundel by Lothar Sperber.[449] However, a bronze plate perhaps functioning as a backplate to a domed roundel was recovered from Grave 46. Dating of the "button": v. Merhart: Bz D–Ha A transition, the Kurd horizon;[450] Kemenczei: 12th century BC.[451] Lothar Sperber dated Grave 46 to the Ha A2.[452]

6. Innsbruck–Wilten (Tyrol, Austria): Graves 86, 98 and 110, all cremation burials,[453] yielded fragments of domed roundels as well as of the bronze backplates. Dating: Bz D (Grave 110) and Ha A1.

7. Sistrans (Tyrol, Austria): one piece from one of the excavated graves.[454]

8. Volders (Tyrol, Austria): Lothar Sperber mentions Graves 340 (Ha A1), 337 (Ha A2) and 374 (Bz D2–Ha A2) in connection with this jewellery type.[455]

9. Aislingen (Bavaria): fragments of a pair of gold plates decorated with concentric circles[456] found together with a pectoral (*Fig. 39. 6*) and other jewellery dated to the late Tumulus /earlier Urnfield period, probably from a cremation burial.

10. Deggendorf–Fischerdorf (Bavaria): fragments of two gold plates decorated with stamped concentric circles found on the pelvis in Grave 3, an inhumation burial, of Tumulus 2.[457] The burial has been assigned to the Tumulus culture and is dated to the later phase of the Bz C period.

11. Dietzenbach (Hessen, Germany): a piece recovered from a grave.[458]

---

447 Kemenczei 1999, 76; Gleirscher 2014, 141, quoting Anton Kern's new date.
448 Mozsolics 1950, 16; David 2003, Abb. 2. 6.
449 Sperber 1992, note 41.
450 Mozsolics 1981, 305–306.
451 Kemenczei 1999, 76.
452 Sperber 1992, note 4.
453 Sperber 1992, 67–68, notes 4 and 41, Abb. 6. 5.
454 Sperber 1992, note 4; David 2007, note 13.
455 Sperber 1992, 73, note 4.
456 Wels-Weyraucht 1995, 117, 119, Abb. 1. 2, 4.
457 Schmotz 1985, 319, 321, Abb. 9.
458 Wels-Weyraucht 1995, 127.

12. Goldbach (Bavaria): a gold piece from Grave 3.[459] While the decorative motifs were identical to the ones on the domed roundels from Velem, their arrangement differed. Dating: Ha A1.

13. Glüsing bei Hennstedt (Schleswig-Holstein, Germany): a gold piece from the tumulus burial,[460] decorated with stamped concentric circles as the domed roundels from Velem, although their arrangement differed slightly. Dating: Nordic Bronze Age, Period II, 14th century BC.

14. Ippensheim–Bullenheimer Berg (Bavaria): the hoard contained six domed roundels of gold (the diameter and ornamentation of 2 + 4 pieces were identical).[461] According to Wolfgang David, they may have adorned the tip of a cap.[462] They are variously dated to the Urnfield culture, Bz D,[463] and the Ha A–B (12th–9th centuries[464] and 10th–9th centuries[465] BC).

15. Landau–Wollmesheim (Rheinland-Pfalz, Germany): six gold plate pendants were found in a double female burial (Grave 2).[466] Each of the artefacts was decorated with a stamped concentric circle and had a suspension loop. Dating: Ha A1.

16. Three unprovenanced gold foils (two larger) in the Archäologische Staatssammlung München.[467] They are decorated with concentric circles and seven of these are placed in the centres. Perforations that demonstrate the fastening of spirals can be distinguished on their edges.

17. Petterweil (Hessen, Germany).[468]

18. Waldalgesheim (Rheinland-Pfalz, Germany).[469]

19. Wollmesheim (Rheinland-Pfalz, Germany):[470] five pieces with suspension loops, from Grave 2.

---

459 Das prähistorische Gold 1997, I: 196, II: 305, Taf. 62.

460 Gold und Kult 2003, 285, Kat. Nr. 13.

461 David 2003, Abb. 2. 10; Gebhard 2003, Abb. 2; Hänsel 2003, 166, 173, Abb. 12, Abb. 17.

462 David 2007, 423.

463 Das prähistorische Gold 1997, II: 304, Taf. 63.

464 Gold und Kult 2003, Kat. Nr. 40.

465 David 2007, 422; Hänsel 2003, 166, Abb. 12; Kemenczei 1999, 76.

466 Sperber 1999, 614, Abb. 5. 2.

467 David 2007, Abb. 5.

468 Wels-Weyrauch 1995, 127.

469 Wels-Weyrauch 1995, 127.

470 Müller-Karpe 1959, Taf. 208. B/2; Wels-Weyrauch 1995, 127.

20. Worms (Rheinland-Pfalz, Germany):[471] two gold domed roundels found at an unknown site ("in den Weinbergen nördlich der Liebfrauenkirche"). Dating: Bz C–Ha B, 14th–11th centuries.

21. Han-sur-Lesse (Belgium): a piece found in the cave.[472]

It is quite obvious that the distribution of domed roundels is significantly wider than suggested by Ulrike Wels-Weyraucht[473] and that they were fashionable from the classical Tumulus period to the end of the Urnfield period. The chain of archaeological sites forming clusters extends from northern, southwestern and southern Germany through Tyrol to western Hungary. The similarities in their ornamentation (Bullenheimer Berg, Worms)[474] and the identical decoration of the pieces from Lower Austria and western Hungary (Rothengrub, Várvölgy, Velem) and of a vessel base found in Biia (Erdőbénye, Transylvania, Romania) seem to reflect – despite the chronological difference of approximately one to one and a half centuries – connections between these regions, perhaps established through the copper and salt trade controlled by local elites, a possibility that needs to be explored by future studies.

It must here be noted that the origins of the decoration on the domed roundels, although in differing in arrangement and produced using different techniques[475] can be found in the hoards of the Apa-Hajdúsámson horizon in the eastern Carpathian Basin and in the ornamentation of the weapons and pottery of the Bronze Age tell cultures preceding the Urnfield period. The similar design of concentric circles connected with S-spirals on plates found at Tafalău (Cófalva) and other sites[476] and on the piece from Binningen, already noted by Gábor Bándi,[477] reflect the style of a workshop active in the east[478] or drawing from eastern traditions. The long-standing debate on the motifs themselves – whether they reflect cultural impacts from Mycenae[479] or the Near East[480] in the Carpathian Basin – yet

[471] Mozsolics 1950, 16–17; Menghin – Schauer 1983, 142, Abb. 65. Nr. 26a-b; David 2003, Abb. 2. 11–12; Gold und Kult 2003, 286, Kat. Nr. 14.

[472] Wels-Weyraucht 1995, 127.

[473] Wels-Weyraucht 1995, 130, Abb. 9.

[474] David 2003, 38.

[475] Das prähistorische Gold 1997, I: 183; David 2001; David 2003, 44.

[476] Mozsolics 1950, Taf. VIII. 8–9, 11–12; for further analogies up to the Bz A2b–Bz C period, cf. David 2007, 432–433, Abb. 6.

[477] Bándi 1983, 86, Abb. 6.

[478] Montag 2000, 95.

[479] Bouzek 1985; Bouzek 1996; Lichardus – Vladár 1996; David 2007, 435–436.

[480] Penner 1998; Dietrich – Dietrich 2011.

remains to be resolved in my view. At the same time, two distinct provinces can be distinguished regarding the ornamentation of the gold foils appearing on costume jewellery: one to east of the boundary marked by the Danube in the Carpathian Basin, and the other one to its west.[481] Designs of spiralling motifs and meanders made with pointed punches were more popular in the eastern province, while concentric circles created by stamps/patterned punches were typical of the western one. Obviously, there was contact between the two regions, as shown by the plate from Binningen in the west and, for instance, the gold foil of the vessel from Biia in the east.

The role of domed roundels in costume will be discussed below, in Chapter 8. What is quite clear is that there is nothing to suggest that the Velem foils had adorned plate brooches (*Plattenfibel*).[482]

---

[481] David 2007, 434.
[482] Barth 1988/1989, 160–161, Taf. II. 3.

7 Analogies of the gold spiral tangle: the assumed breast ornament (pectoral)[483]

1–2. Várvölgy–Felsőzsid: the two hoards both contained a tangle of gold wires. The tangle of Hoard I (1926) was made up of spirals and plain gold threads.[484] Bronze corrosion was noted both on the exterior and in the interior of the spirals, alongside a few millimetres of the bronze wire (*Fig. 33. 3*), similarly to the ones from Velem (*Fig. 21. 3*). The diameter of the wire from which the spirals were wound is 0.66 mm. The cross-section of the gold thread of the spirals is triangular with a flash running along the edges. The threads' thickness varies between 0.11–0.65 mm. The weight of the tangle is 8.17 g. Hoard II, weighing 110 g, recovered from a settlement (Feature 422) on the Nagy-Lázhegy in 2005,[485] contained a similar tangle (13.1g),[486] although no domed roundels. There were a few regularly twisted spirals among the gold threads. The spirals had a diameter of 19 mm, suggesting a leather or textile band with a thickness of 17–18 mm. (The Velem spirals were probably attached to similar bands.) The gold threads have a flattened triangular cross-section and a flash running along the edges. Width of threads: 0.68 mm, thickness: 0.13 mm. Dating: the two hoards can be assigned to the Gyermely horizon, based on Amália Mozsolics' dating of the golden treasure from Velem.[487]

3. Rothengrub (Lower Austria): the treasure contained a nearly undamaged specimen.[488] According to Richard Pittioni, who published the assemblage, it may have been mounted onto a textile ribbon, which hung down the chest of the woman who wore it.[489] Dating: IIa A.

---

483 Mozsolics 1981, 302, Taf. 1.

484 Tompa 1928, 205, Abb. 95. 21; Mozsolics 1981, Taf. 13. 5. Inventoried under inv. no Ő. 730 in the inventory of gold artefacts of the Hungarian National Museum.

485 Müller 2006a, 334–335; Müller 2006b, 235, Fig. 5; Müller 2013.

486 Chief restorer Csaba E. Kiss and I recorded the weight and size data on February 19, 2008, at the Balaton Museum in Keszthely. I am grateful to archaeologist Róbert Müller for his kind permission to study the artefacts of the treasure. The treasure, including weight data, has since been published: Müller 2013, 85.

487 Mozsolics 1981, 306; Kemenczei 1999, 76; Müller 2013, 99, dated it somewhat differently, to the Ha A2–B1 period.

488 Pittioni 1952, 90, Taf. 1a-b; Lauermann – Rammer 2013, Abb. 21.

489 Pittioni 1952, 95.

4. Koppental (Styria, Austria): in addition to gold bracelets, the hoard dated to the early Urnfield period (1200–1000 BC) contained gold wires, which may have been part of a pectoral. The hoard has been variously interpreted as a goldsmith's or trader's hoard, or a votive hoard deposited as part of a ritual event.[490]

5. Bled (Slovenia): in addition to fifty-six bronze and two other gold artefacts, Hoard 2 also contained the nearly undamaged gold foil from the centre of what was probably a pectoral. The basic motifs of the plate's ornamental design and its manufacturing technique as well as the employed tools resemble those on the one from Velem. Dating: Ha A1.[491]

Pectorals also had bronze components, structural elements made of bronze wires. In some cases, only their framed "inner" element (perhaps an amulet), often made of boar's tusk plaque, survived.

6. Aislingen (Bavaria): a pectoral, probably from a cremation burial (dated to the late Tumulus/earlier Urnfield period),[492] of which its centre, a fragmented bronze plate survives, decorated with leaf- and swallow tail-shaped bronze pendants. Width: 12 cm, height with the pendants: 13.7 cm (*Fig. 39. 6*). The other grave goods included the fragments of two gold domed roundels, which lay beside the pectoral.

7. Grünwald (Bavaria): the fragment from Grave 1 had a row of rings along its lower part.[493]

8. Straubing (Bavaria): fragments from Grave 31, a child burial, dated to the early Urnfield period.[494]

9. Gammertingen (Baden-Württemberg): The specimen from a double burial dated to the Ha A2 had a similar structure as the pieces from Twann (Switzerland) and Rixheim (France).[495]

10. Karlsruhe–Neureut (Baden-Württemberg): the votive hoard recovered from the former channel of the Rhine contained a pectoral made up of a boar's

490 GRUBER 2008, 72–77, Abb. 89, Katalog 177, 4. 2. 9.

491 TURK 2012b, 305, Fig. 3.

492 WELS-WEYRAUCHT 1991, 85–86, Taf. 29, note 734, and 4, Taf. 48. B3; WELS-WEYRAUCHT 1995, 117, 119, Abb. 1. 2–4.

493 WELS-WEYRAUCHT 1995, 127, Abb. 8F.

494 KUBACH-RICHTER 1978–79, 134, 149, Abb. 5. 13–16; WELS-WEYRAUCHT 1995, 122, Abb. 6A.

495 WELS-WEYRAUCHT 1995, 126, note 130, and 47, Abb. 8C.

tusk plate, two pairs of three bronze spirals on top and swallow-tailed bronze pendants at the bottom.[496]

11. Taumering (Oberpfalz): the lower part of the fragment from an adult female's burial (Grave 51) has a row of pendent rings.[497]

12–13. Barbey, Cent Arpents (France): two pieces, from Graves 4 and 26.[498]

14–15. Barbuise-Courtavant (France): one of the two pieces recovered from the burials is fragmented, but a part of the boar's tusk plate survived.[499]

16. Beaujeu (France): fragments (spiral and pendant) from a hoard.[500]

17. Beaumont, Crot aux Moines (France):[501] incomplete piece.

18. Blanot (France):[502] a hoard dated to the Ha B1 contained a piece believed to have been owned by a high-ranking woman, whose possessions included a cauldron from the Upper Tisza region. A slightly oval bronze plate decorated with five concentric circles (width: 9.44 cm, weight: 8 g) attached to a (possibly leather) backing by tiny loops turned backward. The hoard also contained combinations of leather and bronze and leather and gold beads, interpreted as parts of necklaces. In my view, one (or all) of the latter may have been used for framing a pectoral. In view of its size, the decorated bronze plate could be fitted within a frame of ribbed gold beads. Stéphane Verger interpreted the assemblage of three necklaces and three pairs of leg adornments as the ornaments worn by the woman during three major phases of her life cycle.[503]

19. Champlay-la-Columbine (France):[504] Grave 101 yielded ten pendants of a pectoral made from concentrically twisted threads framing a boar's tusk plate (*Fig. 39. 5*).

20. Durrenentzen–Haut-Rhin (France): a piece recovered from a burial.[505]

21–23. La Saulsotte (France): three burials (Graves 38, 43, 52) yielded pectorals,[506] found *in situ* directly above the pelvis in the abdominal region. The

---

496 WELS-WEYRAUCHT 1995, 122, 130, Abb. 6C; BEHRENDS 1999, 85, Cat. no. 107.

497 WELS-WEYRAUCHT 1995, 127, 130, Abb. 8E.

498 PIETTE 1998, 130, Fig. 1. 5.

499 WELS-WEYRAUCHT 1995, 123, Abb. 7B-C; PIETTE 1998, 129–130, Fig. 1. 3–4.

500 WELS-WEYRAUCHT 1995, 126, Abb. 6E.

501 PIETTE 1998, 129, Fig. 1. 2.

502 THEVENOT 1991, 52, 57–58, 106, 152, Figs 54–56, 60–65; VERGER 1998, Fig. 3, centre.

503 VERGER 1998, Fig. 3.

504 PIETTE 1998, 129, Fig. 1. 1.

505 WELS-WEYRAUCHT 1995, 123, 126, Abb. 6D; PIETTE 1998, 138.

506 PIETTE 1998, 130, 135, Figs 2–4.

one from Grave 38 has seven rings, six of which were found in their original position.

24. Rixheim (France): the fragment of a pectoral from Grave 2 had a structure resembling the ones from Twann and Gammertingen.[507]

25. Bienne (Switzerland):[508] no details are known.

26. Binningen (Switzerland): a piece recovered from a female burial.[509]

27. Twann–Petersinsel (Switzerland): the lower part of a pectoral, a stray find, decorated with a row of rings.[510]

28. Vallamand–Les Ferrages (Switzerland):[511] no details are known.

Jacques Piette assigned the breast ornaments, traditionally considered to have been female jewellery, discovered in France, Germany and Switzerland dating to the beginning of the Late Bronze Age, into four main types.[512] In view of the concentric circle motifs on the gold foils from Velem, I believe that the tangle of gold spirals can be added to Piette's Type 1 – obviously, only if its pieces reinforced by a bronze wire (!) had been part of a pectoral prior to its unravelling, as I assumed, because the other pieces, if twisted with thread, may have been used for trimming the neckline, the sleeves and/or the hemline[513] or ever as a hair ornament.[514] Pectorals were worn in the lower chest region, near the pelvis. However, it is also possible that the spirals of the pectoral had framed a pair of gold domed roundels (*Fig. 42. 6*). This reconstruction is borne out by the specimen from Aislingen and, even more, by the position of the Deggendorf gold plates on the pelvis. This piece of jewellery suggests that it had been worn by a woman, perhaps a priestess, and that it had signalled status and rank.[515] Its owner's social status was indicated by its materials (e.g. gold, bronze, ivory). Evidence for the later fashion of pectorals comes from male warrior burials.[516]

---

507 Wels-Weyraucht 1995, 126, Abb. 8D.

508 Piette 1998, 138.

509 Beck 1980, 103–104, 128, Taf. 20. A/6; Piette 1998, 138; Wels-Weyraucht 1995, 122, Abb. 6B; Rychner 1998, 254, 374.

510 Primas 1971, Abb. 8. 2; Wels-Weyraucht 1995, 126, 130, Abb. 8B.

511 Rychner-Faraggi 1993, 59, Fig. 62.

512 Piette 1998, 136, 138.

513 Assumed on the basis of the gold threads found in many cremation burials unearthed at Vösendorf (Lower Austria). Grömer 2006, 42, 59, Abb. 11.

514 Born 2003a, 182, Abb. 4.

515 Wels-Weyraucht 1995, 130.

516 "Rechteckige Panzerplatten mit rein geometrischem Dekor stammen sowohl aus dem jungen Rom wie auch aus dem südlichen Etrurien der zweiten Hälfte des 8. Jhs. v.

A glance at their distribution (*Fig. 38*) reveals that while most of the twenty-five pectorals of the western Urnfield culture were recovered from burials (only three come from hoards), the pieces from Austria (Koppental, Rothengrub), Slovenia (Bled) and western Hungary (Várvölgy, Velem) were parts of hoards.

Chr., wurden also sowohl von Etruskern als auch von Latinern getragen. Mit sehr großer Wahrscheinlichkeit kann man diese Platten mit einer Notiz des Livius (Liv. 1, 20) in Verbindung bringen, der »eherne Brustplatten *(aeneum pectori tegumentum)*« als Teil der Tracht der zwölf Palatinischen Salier – einem Krieger-Priester-Kollegium – beschreibt. Damit kann der hohe Status der Träger solcher Herzpanzer als erwiesen gelten. Gleiches lässt sich nach dem Schema der Quantitätsverhältnisse aus der relativen Seltenheit gegenüber anderen Kriegergräbern erschließen. Das besonders reich ausgestattete sog. Kriegergrab von Tarquinia enthielt neben einer Panzerplatte der Übergangsform zudem ein weiteres Stück aus Gold, das zwar in der Dekorsyntax den älteren Stücken gleicht, jedoch bereits Ziermotive aus dem frühorientalisierenden Fundus trägt." TOMEDI 2005, 519.

8 Reconstructions of how the jewellery of the golden treasure was worn

Version 1

In this version, each piece of jewellery was worn on the head (*Fig. 41. 2. 4, 6*). It is possible that both men and women wore them, even if not exclusively on the forehead (terracotta figurines: Gazi, Crete,[517] Budapest–Kőérberek[518]), but also mounted onto a cap-like headwear made of organic material such as leather or textile (resembling the ones of the bronze figurines from Nurag), or in the hair twisted into a chignon/topknot. In cases when domed roundels were found beside diadems, I believe Jiří Hrala's explanation is acceptable, namely that the domed roundels were attached to a leather or textile backing (a cap or other headwear),[519] or to the hair, or to a band holding the hair down (see the reconstruction of Grave 23 unearthed at Grundfeld).[520] This ornament may have been complemented with spirals attached to a wide band resembling a hairband, perhaps trimming the edges, as suggested by Voβ for the bronze spirals from Grave 2 unearthed at Grundfeld.[521] The latter could even be defined as a diadem.

Version 1a

The domed roundels attached to a wider leather or textile band trimmed with gold spirals (*Fig. 21. 4*) suspended from the perforations (two or four) on the diadem (*Fig. 41. 6*).[522]

Version 1b

The domed roundels were attached directly to the diadem by means of its perforations (*Fig. 41. 4*).

Version 1c

The domed roundels were attached to textile or leather ribbons/bands braided into the hair. Evidence for attachment by means of a loop made of spirals was

---

[517] L' Europe au temps d'Ulysse 1999, 10, 255, Cat. no. 154.

[518] Zsidi 2005, 84.

[519] Das prähistorische Gold 1997, I: 183.

[520] Voss 1986, 50–53, Abb. 2, 4.

[521] Voss 1986, 49–50, Abb. 1; Das prähistorische Gold 1997, I:196.

[522] This version and version 4 was also suggested by Amália Mozsolics (1950, 7).

identified on the domed roundels during conservation (except for domed roundel 1 that was very fragmentary).

The second version is evidenced by one of the gold jewellery items from Grave 4 of Grave Circle A of Mycenae:[523] three sheet pendants suspended by means of gold spirals from the perforations along the diadem's lower edge. My reconstruction is illustrated also by Homer's description of the costume of Andromache, the wife of Hector:

> She flung to the winds her *glittering headdress*,
> *the cap* and *the coronet*, braided band and veil,
> all the regalia golden Aphrodite gave her once,
> the day that Hector, helmet aflash in sunlight,
> led her home to Troy from her father's house
> with countless wedding gifts to win her heart.
> (Homer, *The Iliad*, Book XXII: 550–555, tr. Robert Fagles; my italics)

The diadems of the Abashevo culture of the Volga-Ural region, reconstructed similarly, are also noteworthy in this respect.[524]

Version 2

In this version, the diadem was worn on the head, while the domed roundels were attached to a finely spun, perhaps veil-like fabric fastened to the headwear used as a backing. This version is illustrated by the following Homeric passage:

> Circe dressed me quickly in sea-cloak and shirt
> while the queen slipped on a loose, glittering robe,
> filmy, a joy to the eye, and round her waist
> she ran a brocaded golden belt
> and over her head a *veil* to shield her brow.
> (Homer, *The Odyssey*, Book X: 597–601, tr. Robert Fagles; my italics)

Version 3

In this version, the diadem is worn on the head.

---

[523] MÜLLER-KARPE 1980, Taf. 224. 34.

[524] MAKKAY 2000, Fig. 12. 3–5.

Version 3a1

The other adornments are worn around the neck (*Fig. 41. 5*, *Fig. 42. 2–4*), on the chest (*Fig. 42. 5*), or even suspended as low as the pelvis (*Fig. 42. 6*). This reconstruction has a combination of gold threads, gold spirals and gold domed roundels mounted onto a leather or textile backing whose design and appearance resembles that from Grave 101 unearthed at La Colombine (Yonne, France) and Grave I/8 uncovered at Augsburg–Haunstetten[525] as well as the costume of a bronze figurine from Sardinia.[526] The technique with which the domed roundels were framed with spirals is illustrated by the Rothengrub pectoral[527] and the Aislingen pectoral.[528]

Version 3a1a: The domed roundels were attached to a pectoral/necklace (*Fig. 42. 4*)

Version 3a1b: The domed roundels were (partly) suspending from a pectoral/necklace.

The pieces from hoards and cremation burials are of little help in reconstructing how domed roundels were worn. We can only turn to Bronze Age figurines or distant, but more or less contemporaneous inhumation burials in this respect. The symbols (tiny punctates around a circular impression, see *Fig. 40. 4*) on the clay figurine of the Kyjatice culture from Ludas[529] can be interpreted as the stylised depiction of pendent domed roundels that were combined with a string of beads. The fragment of a gold plate of this type was found on the pelvis of the deceased in Grave 3, an inhumation burial, of Tumulus 2 at Deggendorf–Fischerdorf (Bavaria, Tumulus culture, later Bz C).[530] One disc lay on the pelvis and four on the legs in Grave Γ at Vergina–Feld Malamas (Macedonia, Greece; Macedonian Iron Age I, 11th–9th centuries BC).[531] If the tangle of gold spirals (perhaps a pectoral) and the domed roundels are combined, the pendants are framed with spiral beads, as, for example, in the reconstruction based on the *in situ* position of the ornaments on the chest in Tumulus 98 at Plzeň–Nová

---

[525] L' EUROPE AU TEMPS D'ULYSSE 1999, 80, Cat. no. 108; WIRTH 1999, 581, Abb. 12.

[526] SPERBER 2003, 208, Abb. 8.

[527] PITTIONI 1952, Taf. I. Lothar Sperber derives the mode of how disc pairs were worn from Middle Bronze Age costume. Cf. SPERBER 1999, 620.

[528] WELS-WEYRAUCHT 1995, 117, 119, Abb. 1. 2, 4.

[529] DOMBORÓCZKI 2012, 164–166, Fig. 196.

[530] SCHMOTZ 1985, 319, 321, Abb. 9.

[531] PABST 2011, 213, 217, Abb. 10.

Hospoda[532] and on their *in situ* position in Graves 38, 43 and 52 uncovered at La Saulsotte (France),[533] suggesting that this combination was worn above the pelvis in the abdominal region. The pectoral from Aislingen, repeatedly quoted in the above, is also noteworthy in this respect.[534]

Version 3a2

In this version, the other adornments hang on the back (*Fig. 41. 2*). Although a chronologically distant analogy, four cast discs – two pairs, each made up of identical discs (just like in the Velem assemblage!) – ornamented the costume's back according to Gisella Schumacher-Matthäus' reconstruction based on the Ócsa hoard.[535] This arrangement with four discs – alongside a significant number of other variants[536] – is not uncommon in the Bronze Age material of the Carpathian Basin. A most delightful depiction is the figurine from Kličevac (Serbia).[537] Cast pieces were also arranged in this manner as shown by Set A from Gálya (Gaj, Serbia),[538] the four pendent bands of the jewellery from Magyargoroszló (Guruslău, Romania)[539] and the two pairs of opernwork discs from Rimaszombat.[540] Although ornamented in a different manner and cast, the four elements of the pendent part on the back has been documented in the Urnfield period too (Jedenspeigen, a child's cremation burial, Ha A).[541] The back side of the figurines depicting three pendants known from Szurdokpüspök (Nógrád County)[542] and Bárca (Barca, Slovakia) must be mentioned in this respect.[543] In this version, the domed roundels from Velem were attached to a backing of organic material by the suspension loop of the beading-like spiral border (the suspension loop could be noted on the domed roundels with the exception of no. 1, the heavily fragmented piece).

---

[532] Wels-Weyrauch 2011, 262, Abb. 7–8.
[533] Piette 1998, 130, 135, Figs 2–4.
[534] Wels-Weyrauch 1991, 81–82, 85, Taf. 27. 671–682, Taf. 28. 698, Taf. 29. 734, Taf. 48. B/3.
[535] Schumacher-Matthäus 1985, Taf. 44. 1.
[536] Schumacher-Matthäus 1985, 80.
[537] Schumacher-Matthäus 1985, Taf. 5. 3b.
[538] Schumacher-Matthäus 1985, Taf. 47. 1a.
[539] Schumacher-Matthäus 1985, Taf. 50. 4.
[540] Schumacher-Matthäus 1985, Taf. 51.
[541] Schumacher-Matthäus 1985, 80, 129, Taf. 48. 1.
[542] Schumacher-Matthäus 1985, 25–26, Taf. 16. 1b.
[543] Schumacher-Matthäus 1985, 25, Taf. 16. 2b.

Version 3a3

The other ornaments are worn in combination around the neck and on the back.

Versions 3b1

The domed roundels were worn as part of an ornate belt around the waist, mounted onto a leather or textile backing similarly to belt mounts (*Fig. 41. 1*).[544] In this case, the four domed roundels were worn frontally, although it seems to me that four pieces would have been insufficient for adorning a belt, even though this arrangement would have been quite spectacular. I can envision some of the gold spirals mounted onto textile to embellish the chest, to ensure that this body part would also be accentuated.

Version 3b2

The domed roundels adorned an ornate belt around the waist, but were suspended from it (*Fig. 42. 1*). The belt described by Homer was not unlike the costume accessory from Velem, but it was embellished with infinitely more pendants:

> Kneading her skin with this to a soft glow and combing her hair,
> she twisted her braids with expert hands, and sleek, luxurious,
> shining down from her deathless head they fell, cascading.
> Then round her shoulders she swirled the wondrous robes
> that Athena wove her, brushed out to a high gloss
> and worked into the weft an elegant rose brocade.
> She pinned them across her breasts with a golden brooch
> then sashed her waist with *a waistband*
> *floating a hundred tassels*, and into her earlobes,
> neatly pierced, she quickly looped her earrings,
> ripe mulberry-clusters dangling in triple drops
> and the silver glints they cast could catch the heart.
> Then back over her brow she draped her headdress,
> fine fresh veils for Hera the queen of gods,
> their pale, glimmering sheen like a rising sun,

[544] PITTIONI 1952, Abb. 1. Gábor Bándi followed this reconstruction when he displayed the domed roundels from Velem as part of the permanent exhibition of the Savaria Museum opened, in 1984.

and under her smooth feet she fastened supple sandals.
(Homer, *The Iliad*, Book XIV: 214–229, tr. Robert Fagles; my italics)

If the domed roundels embellished an ornamental belt, the neck and the chest would have remained unaccentuated and therefore the gold spirals were probably used for trimming the costume. It is also possible that only a part of the ceremonial costume was hidden.

Version 4

A part or the entire assemblage can be conceptualised as having decorated an ornate belt, at least theoretically.[545] In this version, the "diadem" is the centrepiece of the belt around the waist. In this case, however, its peak would prevent its wearer from bending forward and if worn in this manner, the foil would bear use-wear traces such as horizontal creasing as a result – but no such traces were observed on it, only an oblique one (*Fig. 16. 1*). Moreover, as a result of the conservation work, the gold foil "reverted" to its original size, from which it is obvious that it could not have been used as a belt plaque owing to its diameter.

Regarding the manner in which it was worn, yet one other doubt must be voiced. How exactly should we interpret the "undersized" pieces (whose length is less than 50 cm or have a diameter below 15 cm) described as diadems in the archaeological literature? Were they symbolic objects used, for example, for ceremonial purposes? Or were they parts of cult paraphernalia, perhaps the adornments of figurines or statuettes? In my view, these objects were (a) either attached to headdresses of the type worn in the Middle Ages by ribbons and worn on the forehead (e.g. Bullenheimer Berg, Dedinka, Németbánya, etc.), in which case they can be defined as diadems or frontlets; or (b) they were set into chignons/topknots or braids (e.g. Balatonboglár, Bullenheimer Berg), and were braid ornaments, braid ribbon adornments, in which case they can hardly be identified as diadems.

In the light of above, I can only confidently conclude that the peaked gold foil from Velem, first mounted onto a bronze backplate and then attached to some organic material, was used as a diadem that signalled social status (Type B/2b). The treasure's other jewellery items remain open to interpretation and

---

[545] This was first suggested by Amália Mozsolics in 1941 when she inventoried the treasure. Cf. *Fig. 11,* the line under the photograph in the inventory book. Ferenc Tompa was the first to publish it: TOMPA 1934–35, 105.

we can at most only offer a variety of possible reconstructions until a stroke of archaeological luck will present us with the key to this particular enigma.

The value of the assemblage of costume ornaments to the community can be determined if the following aspects are considered:

1. Whether its raw material is rare or more quotidian:
- gold plate or foil, perhaps only cut-out pieces (such as spangles),[546] mounted onto a copper or bronze backplate, or a textile or leather backing;[547]
- copper or bronze plate, perhaps only cut-out pieces (such as spangles), mounted onto a textile or leather backing.

2. The craftsmanship of the piece, i.e. the amount and quality of work[548] invested by the goldsmith/blacksmith[549] is hardly negligible. Viewed from this perspective, we can only speak of products made from durable (i.e. not organic) raw materials, whose craftsmanship is of an increasingly high standard, making them more valuable:
- plain, undecorated plate;
- sparsely decorated plate;
- profusely decorated plate (50 to 70% of its surface is decorated);
- the entire surface of the plate is decorated.

The diadem and the domed roundels from Velem are gold foils, which had originally been mounted onto bronze backplates, which were then mounted onto organic backings. The entire surface of the gold foils is decorated; in other words, they had been crafted from the rarest (most valuable[550] and sacral) raw material, embellished with an exceptionally fine design and produced with the greatest work investment. The colour yellow, the colour of gold, was the perhaps most pronounced element of the costume. In Homer's epics, gold is the attribute of women (golden Aphrodite, Artemis of the golden distaff, and Hera, goddess of the golden throne) and gold is the most distinct trait of their costume:

---

546 The use of spangles for adorning headdresses of organic material was first suggested by BÓNA 1959, 56. A new reconstructions has been recently proposed by SCHUMACHER-MATTHÄUS 1985, Taf. 20. 4a, Taf. 30. 2b.

547 The vest of the Lady of Blenot is a good example: THEVENOT 1991, 45–58, Figs 39–45.

548 KUIJPERS 2008, 32–33.

549 FONTIJN 2002, 27–28, Table 3.

550 The high prestige of gold is indisputable. CLAUSING 1998, 310.

They armed for a raid, hoping to break the siege –
loving wives and innocent children standing guard
on the ramparts, flanked by elders bent with age
as men marched out to war. Ares and Pallas led them,
both burnished gold, *gold the attire they donned*, and great, magnificent
in their armor – gods for all the world,
looming up in their brilliance, towering over troops.
(Homer, *The Iliad*, Book XVIII: 598–604, tr. Robert Fagles; my italics)

9 The dating of the golden treasure in the light of radiocarbon data from northwestern Transdanubia

In her monograph,[551] Amália Mozsolics assigned the golden treasure discovered in Velem, and Hoard I from Velem (the "great" treasure of 1896, parts Ia and Ib, or perhaps two separate hoards),[552] the since lost gold plates of Hoard II found at Ság-hegy, the Várvölgy (Felsőzsid) hoard and the Rothengrub hoard to the same period (Ha B). Later, she dated the treasures from Rothengrub, Velem and Felsőzsid to the Gyermely horizon (Mozsolics BVc, Ha A2),[553] and Hoard II with its gold plates from Ság-hegy to the Hajdúböszörmény and, later still, to the Románd hoard horizon (Mozsolics BVIa-b, Ha B1–2).[554] In my view, she was correct to revise her initial dating after realising that the gold foils from Ság-hegy were later than the ones from Velem. In line with Mozsolics's revised dating, Tibor Kemenczei assigned the Velem treasures and the Várvölgy hoard as well as Hoard I from Velem to the middle Urnfield period by regarding them as assemblages of the Ha A2 period (hoard horizon III in his periodisation). At the same time, he dated the gold finds from Mühlau, Rothengrub and Worms to the earlier Urnfield period (Ha A1).[555] In my view, he was correct in separating the plates from Mühlau and Rothengrub and assigning them to an earlier period. In contrast, Gábor Bándi dated the Velem treasure to a broader and earlier time interval (Bz D–Ha A1) within the Urnfield period.[556] For my part, I would assign the golden treasure towards the end of the period proposed by Bándi.

According to Alix Hänsel, the diadem and treasure from Velem as well as Hoard II with its gold artefacts from Ság-hegy and the neck adornments recently purchased by the Museum für Vor- und Frühgeschichte in Berlin[557] can be assigned to the late phase of the Urnfield culture, to the Ha B period (10th–9th centuries BC). I believe this date is too early for the Velem treasure and hence unacceptable. In his comprehensive overview of the gold objects of the Bronze Age, Károly Kacsó also assigns the assemblages from Velem and Ság-hegy to the

---

551 Mozsolics 1950, 24–25, 41.
552 Czajlik 1993, 326.
553 Mozsolics 1979, 95–96.
554 Mozsolics 1981, 305–306; Mozsolics 1984, Taf. 1; Mozsolics 2000, 38.
555 Kemenczei 1996b, 77, Abb. 37; Kemenczei 1996a, 105; Kemenczei 1999, 76.
556 Bándi 1983, 92.
557 Hänsel 2003, 171–173.

later Urnfield period.[558] As noted in the above, this date is only acceptable for the gold artefacts from Ság-hegy. Peter Turk[559] dated all five hoards found at Velem, including the treasure containing the gold foils, to the Ha B1(2) period. This date is untenable, not only in my opinion, but according to other scholars too.

As regards the cross-dating of the treasures, the following need to be noted: if Hoard I of Velem was actually two hoards (Ia and Ib),[560] they must be dated separately, unless they were deposited at the same time. Amália Mozsolics linked Hoard Ia (containing jewellery, tools and weapons)[561] to Hoard Ib (containing only jewellery)[562] on account of the bronze twisted lockrings with passmanterie-like hook and clasp terminals, and then associated both hoards with the gold treasure from Várvölgy.[563] To which we may add that the Velem treasure can now also be linked to second gold hoard from Várvölgy containing two lockrings of this type.[564] According to Mozsolics's chronology, these treasures were buried in period BVc, corresponding to the Gyermely horizon (Ha A2).[565] Gold bracelets of an identical design came to light as part of a gold treasure found in Arikogel (Salzkammergut, Upper Austria) in 2005, which has been dated to the early Urnfield period (Ha A). [566]

When studying the Velem treasure and its "circle", the hoard from Rothengrub can be considered one of the Archimedean points. It was initially dated to the Ha A period, but has more recently been assigned to the Ha B2–3 period.[567] The other oft-quoted assemblage is the more distant hoard from Bullenheimer Berg, which had been dated to a broader time interval (Ha A–B).[568] These two examples, and

[558] KACSÓ 2006, 86.

[559] TURK 2012a, 219. 223, Abb. 6.

[560] MOZSOLICS 1985, 211–213; MISKE 1925, 47. Hoard Ia was found at the end of May 1896. 400 pieces were collected from the villagers by Kelemen Kárpáti (today in the collection of the Savaria Museum), but Miske also acquired a few pieces, some of which he donated to the Hungarian National Museum. A few days later, Kárpáti unearthed Hoard Ib at a distance of 4.5 m from the alleged findspot of Hoard Ia. Cf. CZAJLIK 1993, 326–327, for a detailed discussion.

[561] HAMPEL 1896, Taf. CCXXXVIII. 23; MOZSOLICS 1985, 211–213, 231. A/23.

[562] HAMPEL 1896, Taf. CCXLI. 4; MOZSOLICS 1985, 213, Taf. 231. B/4.

[563] MOZSOLICS 1981.

[564] MÜLLER 2007, 16, and the colour photograph of the artefact on the cover of the book; MÜLLER 2006b, 235, Fig. 5; MÜLLER 2013, Fig. 1, 8–9; Fig. 5. 1.

[565] MOZSOLICS 1985, 213.

[566] GRUBER 2008, 75–76, Abb. 84, 86, Katalog 172, Nr. 4. 1. 7–8.

[567] PITTIONI 1952; GLEIRSCHER 2014, 141, quoting Anton Kern's new dating.

[568] GEBHARD 2003, 150–151, Abb. 2, Kat. Nr. 40/c; DAVID 2007, 422.

the wide range of dates proposed for the Velem treasure serve as an eloquent illustration of the chronological uncertainties.

In sum, a wide range of dates has been proposed for the gold foils from Velem, ranging from Bz D2 to Ha B 1–3, i.e. roughly between the 14th/13th and the 9th/8th centuries BC, although the assemblage is most often assigned to the Ha A–early Ha B1 period, i.e. the 12th–10th centuries BC (corresponding to the Gyermely and Hajdúböszörmény horizons as defined by Mozsolics). Accordingly, the jewellery items of the Velem treasure were made and buried within this time interval. In my view, however, its precise date within the latter half-millennium is still open to debate. In this respect, the broad time interval reflecting the many uncertainties in dating seems the most appropriate position, as in the catalogue to the *Gold und Kult der Bronzezeit* exhibition, listing some of the closest analogies to the Velem treasure. Even so, it is my belief that a more accurate dating is possible, as we shall see below.

A series of radiocarbon dates, even if not too many, for the Koszider period in western Hungary can be enlisted for the absolute dating of the Velem treasure (*Fig. 43*).

1. Ménfőcsanak–Széles földek (Győr-Moson-Sopron County). The results of the AMS dating of Pit 7765, dating to the Koszider period (Bz B1), performed in Debrecen;[569] animal bones (DeA-1753): 3269±27 BP, 1618–1475 cal BC (2 σ); child bone (DeA-1854): 3293±26 BP, 1629–1503 cal BC (2 σ).

2. Nagydém–Középrépáspuszta (Veszprém County). Human bones from Grave 1.A,[570] Koszider period of the early Tumulus culture: 3450±60 BP, 1498 cal BC (Deb-1999); 3470±60 BP, 1518 cal BC (Deb-2021).

3. Németbánya Felsőerdei dűlő (Veszprém County). Dates for animal bone samples from the settlement dated to the late Tumulus-early Urnfield period:[571]

- Trench C, 48 cm (Deb-3434): 2992±55 BP, 1384 (1211) 1024 cal BC (2 σ).
- Trench A, 220-245 cm (Deb-3435): 3082±41 BP, 1423 (1362, 1350) 1216 cal BC (2 σ).
- Trench D, Pit b (Deb-3437): 3051±44 BP, 1408 (1292) 1129 cal BC (2 σ).
- Trench B, from the floor of the earliest house (Deb-3760): 3039±48 BP, 1408 (1279) 1108 cal BC (2 σ).

---

569 Ilon 2014a, Abb. 5.

570 Two measurement from samples of a human phalanx. Cf. Ilon 1999, 266.

571 Ilon 1996c, 153–154, 208; Ilon 2005, 135–145; Ilon 2014b, 128.

Most dates falls within the first half of the Urnfield period (14th–12th centuries BC, Bz C2/D–Ha A1), indicating that this small settlement was occupied for approximately 150 years.

4. Bezi–Nagy-Sarok (Győr-Moson-Sopron County). Sample taken from the wood remains of the settlement's well lined with a wickerwork of oak twigs.[572] dated to the Urnfield period (PRI-10-13-434): 3260–3080 cal BP, 1310–1130 cal BC (2 σ).

5. Börcs–Paphomlok dűlő (Győr-Moson-Sopron County). Samples taken from a settlement of the Urnfield culture dated to the Bz D–Ha A1 period:[573] 3053±40 BP, 1294 cal BC (Deb-3141); 2997±56 BP, 1216 cal BC (Deb-3001); 2982±54 BP, 1191 cal BC (Deb-3200); 2919±54 BP, 1075 cal BC (Deb-3060).

6. Ménfőcsanak–Széles földek (Győr-Moson-Sopron County). Samples of charred wood from two graves of the cemetery containing twelve burials, dated to Urnfield period, submitted for AMS dating: 1σ: 1113–1096 cal BC, 1092–1009 cal BC; 2σ: 1191–1176 cal BC, 960–935 cal BC (DeA-1745); 1σ: 1114–1012 cal BC; 2σ: 1192–1171 cal BC, 959–937 cal BC (DeA-1747).

7. Gór–Kápolnadomb. Samples taken from animal bones gave the following dates:[574]

Sample code	Feature	BP	cal BC (1 σ)
Deb-1512	Trench H-6, Pit d/2	2690±40	892–872
Deb-2588	Trench E-15, Pit b/1	2800±40	987 (924) 894
Deb-1506	Trench K-6, Pit a	2830±40	1032–928
Deb-2589	Trench K-6, Pit c	2830±40	1017 (947) 914
Deb-1683	Trench I-6, Pit d/2	2880±40	1138–992

The settlement's occupation falls into the late phase of the later Urnfield period, i.e. the 10th–9th centuries BC, corresponding to the Ha B1–2 period in Müller-Karpe's periodisation.[575]

8. On my request, Pál Sümegi and his team performed palaeoenvironmental corings, down to the bedrock lying at a depth of 180 cm, in a small alder bog

---

572 EGRY 2010, 11, Fig. 3–4; Kathryn Puseman: *Identification and AMS dating of wood from M85 Enese elkerülő 5., Bezi–Nagy-Sarok archaeological site (9-0142) and Kony-Proletar dűlő II., Enese elk. 2. archaeological site (9-0142), Hungary*. PaleoResearch Institute Technical Report 10–13, Golden, Colorado. February 2010, in the archives of the Service for Cultural Heritage, Hungarian National Museum, Budapest.

573 FIGLER 1996, 12.

574 ILON 1992; ILON 1996a; ILON 1996b; ILON 1998; ILON 2001a; ILON 2003.

575 MÜLLER-KARPE 1959, 228. és Abb. 64.

lying at the foot of the St. Vid Hill of Velem (*Fig. 1*).[576] The unstratified greyish-brown clayey marl between 180–140 cm contained charcoal fragments, often a centimetre large, embedded into the deposit. The first pollens were identified between 164–160 cm. The pollen remains indicated a species-rich gallery wood of arboreal and non-arboreal species. The most typical local arboreal species were oak (*Quercus*), maple (*Acer*) and willow (*Salix*), while the significant proportion of fir (*Abies*), Scots pine (*Pinus*) and spruce (*Picea*) pollens were wind-bone from the Alpine region. The presence of walnut (*Juglans*) and cereals as well as weeds such as dock (*Rumex*) and dandelion (*Taraxacum*) indicating trampling attest to ploughlands and meadows, and reflect intensive arable farming activity in the surrounding area. The pollen record indicates that walnut appeared in the Carpathian Basin from the Middle Bronze Age onward,[577] and its presence thus indicated that this sequence could be dated to a period after the Middle Bronze Age. The radiocarbon measurements of samples taken from a depth of 175–176 cm confirm this: 2915±35 BP, 1121±66 (GDa-632), indicating a date in the middle/late period of the Urnfield culture.

Therefore, within the Urnfield period, the sample from Velem suggests a later date than the end of the Németbánya settlement (not later than Ha A1) and is contemporaneous with or a little earlier than the beginning of the settlement in Gór (Ha B1?).[578] This harmonizes with my dating based on conventional archaeological chronology. The dates cited here can be fitted into a coherent sequence, which complements the currently accepted absolute chronology for western Hungary.[579]

In the light of the above, I would date the prestigious gold costume ornaments (ceremonial dress),[580] or rather, what has survived of it, because jewellery such as bracelets and armlets as well as a belt are probably missing,[581] to the Bz D–Ha B2/3 = Mozsolics B IVb–B VIb = roughly the $14^{th}/13^{th}$–9th centuries BC, although the assumed changes in the manufacturing technique of the diadem (foil

576 Palaeoenvironmental sampling was performed on approximately a dozen archaeological sites in Vas County, Hungary. The findings have been partly published in Jakab – Juhász – Sümegi – Ilon 2007.

577 Sümegi – Bodor 2000, 87.

578 The assessment of the finds from the settlement is still in progress, and thus the date for the beginning of the settlement's occupation is not final.

579 Hänsel 1982, 2–4, Abb. 1, and note 2; Della Casa – Fischer 1997, 196, 221–227; Kemenczei 1984, 96.

580 Falkenstein 2011, 95.

581 Verger – Dumont – Moyat – Mille 2007, 147–160.

and wire[582]) and the transitional traits of the domed roundels and the assumed pectoral (ornamented plates framed with wire), would allow a closer dating to the Ha A 1/2 transition (close of 12th century BC), roughly corresponding to the transition between the Kurd and Gyermely horizons in Amália Mozsolics's periodisation. The treasure was no doubt owned by a member,[583] probably a woman,[584] of one of the "ancestral" and traditional families (perhaps of the ruling family) of the "urban"[585] elite, which controlled the surrounding land within a range of approximately 30–50 km[586] from its stronghold on the St. Vid Hill of Velem during the Urnfield period. It is possible that she also fulfilled the role[587] of a sacral or high priestess.[588] Gold jewellery items simultaneously expressed social status and power, and were a means of social display and transmitted a coded message[589] through their chosen raw materials, ornamentation and the very fact that they had been buried. At the same time, we cannot reject Rupert Gebhard and Wolfgang David's contention that assemblages made up of costume accessories were possibly connected with cult statues.[590] Comparable assemblages of costume jewellery are represented by the hoard from Bernstorf, assigned to the Tumulus culture and dated earlier than the Velem treasure, and the hoard from Bullenheimer Berg, dated to the later Urnfield period.[591]

Thus, as we have seen, the high-ranking members of the elite in Bronze Age Europe were proud owners of gold foil-covered costume adornments and symbols of status and power[592] as well as of golden vessels, objects of social display (*Fig. 32*), decorated with an identical set of symbols.[593] The St. Vid Hill of Velem lies on the easternmost fringes of the spatial distribution of the assemblages embodying what was presumably an identical and coherent spiritual background.[594]

---

582 Mozsolics 1985, 59.
583 Janssen 1985, 52.
584 Sperber 1999, 614, 627.
585 Hänsel 2003, esp. 208–209.
586 Müller-Karpe 1975, 12–14; Ilon 2007a; Ilon 2007b.
587 Kemenczei 1999, 77; Metzner-Nebelsick 2009, 13–26.
588 Gerloff 1995, 168–169.
589 Armbruster 2013, 461.
590 Gebhard 2003, 153; David 2007, 423, 434.
591 Gebhard 2003, 149–152, Abb. 1–2.
592 Gerloff 2003, 191–203.
593 Kemenczei 1999, 77.
594 Hansen 1994, 261, note 117.

10 The deposition of the golden treasure

Today, we know much more about the treasure's findspot and find circumstances than did Amália Mozsolics when she penned her laconic description of the find spot that became internationally known: "Baron Kálmán von Miske fand im Jahre 1929 bei einer Probegrabung in Velem auf der obersten Terasse am *südlichen* Abhang unter der Szent Vid (Sankt Veit) Kapelle *unter zwei kleineren Felsen* den hier zu besprechenden Goldfund [my italics]."[595] This description, however, stands in stark contrast to what she wrote in the museum inventory book in 1941: "It was allegedly discovered by a tree in 1929." This might even be true given the hill's tree cover, but she made no mention of stones, stone slabs or rocks at the time. Kálmán Miske's already cited letter dated to 1929[596] clearly stated that the findspot was not located on the hill's southern slope or on its upper terrace, but on the uppermost terrace of the three terraces cut by his trial trench. Amália Mozsolics tried to coax more accurate information out of Ferenc Tompa, who flatly refused her request. His reaction was no doubt fuelled by some jealousy over the publication of the treasure because Kálmán Miske had conferred the right to do so on Ferenc Tompa.

Miske's letter records that the gold objects lay underneath a pointed slab of stone, and Szilveszter Katona mentioned that his grandfather, János Katona, always told him that the treasure had been found at a shallow depth, not long after the leaves were swept away. Later, Amália Mozsolics interpreted the unconfirmed presence of one or more stones overlying the assemblage as a marker;[597] more recently, however, stone slabs have come to be regarded as commemorating the location of votive offerings.[598] Tudor Soroceanu's studies on the customs association with hoard deposition suggest that the Velem treasure had been buried on the slope near a spring.[599] The household (the "palace") of the treasure's owner was most likely located on the plateau, suggesting that the assemblage of costume jewellery had been hidden somewhat farther, on a lower terrace, near a spring

[595] MOZSOLICS 1950, 7.

[596] KVM Local History Archives, inv. no. 1426/XXXIX.43 and 1942/XXXIX.109.

[597] MOZSOLICS 1987, 96.

[598] FALKENSTEIN 2011, 87.

[599] SOROCEANU 1995, Abb. 3b, Abhang VI; SOROCEANU 2005, 394, Abb. 4.

or some other source of water. It is possible that the location itself lay within eyesight of the settlement, and forged a link between different social spheres.[600]

The general condition of the gold objects at the time of their discovery – the diadem was folded several times,[601] the domed roundels were flattened into discs, the tangle of gold threads (perhaps the remnants of a pectoral and/or a fabric woven with gold threads), indicating that every single object was damaged/ altered compared to its original condition – leaves room for speculation about the general arrangement of the treasure.[602] A previously unknown manuscript of Kálmán Miske contains important information about another element of how the treasure had been deposited:

> "the gold assemblage [...] is made up of a folded band of pure gold with a width of ca. 6 cm, whose length, give or take a little, is 80 to 100 cm, and *an adornment of hopelessly tangled twisted gold wires* to which *round gold discs had been attached* to form a necklace. [my italics]"

In my interpretation, the gold threads (of the damaged pectoral) were used to bind the folded diadem and the four flattened domed roundels, or they were wrapped up in a piece of textile woven with gold threads. The condition of the artefacts (crumpling, flattening, folding, rolling into a ball, fragmentation, etc.) conforms to the general deposition rites of the Bronze Age as described by Louis D. Nebelsick.[603]

The custom of burying valuables underneath a stone slab is illustrated by a bronze hoard dated to the Early Iron Age discovered on January 10, 1910, in nearby Németkeresztes-[604] or Magyarkeresztes[605] (today known as Vaskeresztes, after the two villages were merged): "It was a mild Saturday morning, so the

[600] FONTINJ 2002, 211, 264–266, Fig. 10. 1, Fig. 14. 3; BALLMER 2010, 124–126, 129, Abb. 3–4.

[601] The hoard dated to the Vatya-Koszider period from Pákozd–Várhegy had been deposited in the same manner (see above, Chapter 5).

[602] SOROCEANU 1995, 35, Abb.11.

[603] NEBELSICK 1997, 35–41.

[604] The newspapers of Vas County reported on the find circumstances. Quotation taken from *Vasmegyei Független Hírlap* [Vas County Independent Journal], vol. 7, no. 7 (January 11, 1910), p. 1, from the article entitled "Őskori lelet Németkeresztesen" [A Prehistoric Artefact at Németkeresztes].

[605] MOZSOLICS 1942.

village judge of Keresztes ordered his farm-hands to turn over the soil in the vineyard. While working, one of them struck his shovel against a large stone. The men wanted to move the stone, but they soon realised that they would first have to dig around it because it covered almost a square meter of land. After lifting the regularly carved slab of stone, they were surprised to find a sizeable bronze bucket filled with small bronze objects." In this case, the bronze objects had quite clearly been placed in a bronze bucket, which correlates well with Soroceanu's classification of deposition practices.[606] We know of two other, likewise reliably documented depositions of the Urnfield period in Vas County. The bronze objects discovered at Izsákfa, located at the foot of Mt. Ság-hegy, had been placed into a clay vessel on the terrace of the Kodó Stream;[607] the upper part of the vessel was destroyed by ploughing. The hoard buried on the terrace of the Perint Stream in Szombathely was similarly hidden in a clay vessel, which was broken by the finders, and only the few sherds that reached the museum attest to the one-time find circumstances.[608]

The deposition of the Velem treasure can be associated with a rite of passage or votive offering (*Weihe- oder Opfergabe*):[609] given that its pieces had been crafted from gold, the most prestigious raw material, it can be categorised as an assemblage presented to the highest supernatural being[610] by a high-ranking member of the community's social elite.[611] It was, at the same time, deposited in a fragmented/folded state (*Brucherzfund*), conforming to the traditions in Transdanubia in the western part of the Carpathian Basin during the Bronze Age.[612] Its deposition in a high place, specifically on the St. Vid Hill, in a frequently-visited location in the proximity of the Szentkút Spring, where one (Hoard I) or two hoards (Hoards Ia and Ib) had been discovered in 1896, suggest the existence of a sacred precinct (a by no means unique phenomenon in that period) that was

---

606 SOROCEANU 1995, 35, Abb. 11k.

607 I acquired the pieces from the finder who had discovered the hoard and the vessel damaged by ploughing, and donated them to the Savaria Museum. The control excavation, in which I also participated, was conducted by Mária Fekete in 1982. The assemblage is still unpublished, except for the sword fragments. KEMENCZEI 1988, 62, Taf. 37. 334A; KEMENCZEI 1991a, 79, Taf. 65, 323A-B.

608 ILON 2002b.

609 SOROCEANU 1995, 56; KACSÓ 2006, 88–89.

610 It can also be associated with cyclicity and the constant rebirth of nature. NEBELSICK 2000, 171.

611 CLAUSING 2005, 87; KACSÓ 2006, 90.

612 HANSEN 2006, 64–65.

used by the community's wealthy families.[613] In view of the treasure's dating proposed here, of the currently known treasures and hoards from Velem,[614] the golden treasure – the most valuable among them all – was buried first, slightly preceding Hoard I, an act that may also have symbolised "taking possession" of the sacred area. The act of deposition, the sacrifice of the ceremonial costume (*Goldornat*), or of a portion of it, once worn by the community's leading family but now stripped of its wearer[615] may reflect the intention of creating an Ancestor, a local hero.

---

[613] NEBELSICK 2000, 160, Fig. 11.2; HRALA 1997, 179–180; HANSEN 2013, 379.

[614] MOZSOLICS 1985, 211–213; MOZSOLICS 2000, 89–90; KEMENCZEI 1996b, 77, 84, Abb. 35.

[615] HÄNSEL – HÄNSEL 1997, 66–68.

11 Conclusion

In the light of the arguments presented in the foregoing, we may reasonably assume that the diadem and the domed roundels (*Fig. 24*) were manufactured with the same tools and probably in the same workshop. Whether this was a local workshop or one active farther west yet remains to be established – what we do know is that the necessary tools and skills were available locally, on the St. Vid Hill and in the broader area. The diadem's original diameter is larger than previously assumed from its condition while it was mounted onto the copper plate. The difference in the colour of the gold foils, noted during earlier examinations, turned out to be irrelevant and cannot serve as a springboard for any hypothetical conjectures (such as some being later replacements) because the difference in colour disappeared during cleaning in the first phase of the conservation work, and their identicalness has been confirmed by the metal analyses. Additionally, the iconography of the design adorning the pairs of domed roundels only makes sense if they are viewed simultaneously as a set.

The material of the foils (gold) and the colour (glittering yellow) of the artefacts as well as their symbols (concentric circles) are all reflections of a Sun (solar) cult. The metal analyses unambiguously confirmed the connection between the domed roundels. Moreover, the number of domed roundels (four) that depict the four lunar phases and the lunar month is hardly coincidental because this is how they conveyed a meaningful concept (synodic lunar month) through an iconographical scheme, which in turn again serves to confirm that this part of the costume jewellery can be regarded as being contemporaneous and complete. The set of symbols on the gold artefacts from Velem fits into the conservative tradition of the symbols embodying time (the calendar) appearing on objects of the European Bronze Age, a tradition that had been associated with arable farming and fertility, and had essentially recorded the cyclicity of nature since long millennia. The Pleiadian lunar month is symbolised on the diadem, while the lunar month and the lunar quarter appear on Pair II of the domed roundels and the lunar quarter alone on Pair I of the domed roundels. Their symbolic design perhaps also served to illustrate good and evil, this world and the otherworld, and possibly the deity that ruled the sky and the weather, suggesting a dualistic perception of the world. The direct forerunner of this pattern (with an emphasis on sets of seven such as seven concentric circles) can be traced to the Tumulus culture as evidenced by the gold disc from Zelene (Bz B2/C).

The magnificent gold adornments of a ceremonial costume (or, better said, a portion of them) were buried under an upright slab of stone as an act of sacrifice near a spring known as Szentkút Spring today. The remnants of the pectoral were wound around the folded diadem and the flattened domed roundels. Certain jewellery items such as bracelets, anklets and the belt are lacking from the assemblage, perhaps following some logic.[616] The Velem treasure was buried at the beginning of the second major wave of hoard depositions on settlements in the Bronze Age.[617] The treasure was no doubt owned by a member, probably a woman, of one of the "ancestral" and traditional families (perhaps of the ruling family) of the "urban" elite, which controlled the surrounding land within a range of approximately 30–50 km from its stronghold on the St. Vid Hill of Velem during the Urnfield period. It is possible that she also fulfilled the role of a sacral or high priestess. Neither can we reject the possibility that assemblages made up of costume accessories were possibly connected with cult statues. It seems to me that the jewellery pieces could be worn in several combinations: (a) as headwear: a diadem with two or four suspended domed roundels hanging down on the side(s), or the domed roundels as pendent ornaments of textile/leather ribbons woven into braids or placed on the top of the head; (b) the domed roundels worn as adornments of the upper part of the chest, with two to four domed roundels attached to textiles, and/or worn on the lower part of the chest,[618] with two to four domed roundels perhaps combined to form a pectoral; (c) the domed roundels worn suspended from the diadem on the back, or mounted onto textile; (d) the domed roundels mounted onto a leather/textile belt clasped around the waist or suspended from the latter (*Figs 41–42*). Similar assemblages of costume adornments are represented by the Bernstorf treasure assigned to the Tumulus culture, predating the Velem treasure, and the Bullenheimer Berg treasure dated to the second half of the Urnfield period.

In dating the Velem treasure (*Fig. 24*), I prefer the approach used in German research as exemplified by the catalogue to the *Gold und Kult der Bronzezeit* exhibition held in Nuremberg, according to which the treasure can be assigned to broad time interval spanning the entire Urnfield period (Bz D–Ha B2/3, Mozsolics B IVb–B VIb, *ca.* 14th/13th–10th/9th centuries BC). However, if certain details of the manufacturing techniques are considered, this date can be narrowed.

[616] These jewellery types all occur in the Blanot hoard. THEVENOT 1991, Pl. I–III.

[617] TURK 2012a, 222.

[618] See above for the position of the gold plate fragment from Deggendorf and of many breast ornmanets from France found near the pelvis.

The treasure reflects the transition from the fashion of plate jewellery (*Gold-Diademstyls*) to wire jewellery (*Drahtkunst*) since it incorporates both plate and wire elements. The domed roundels and the assumed pectoral(s) confirm this because the decorated foils are framed with wire spirals. At the same time, the adornments lack the incised and linear repoussé patterns typical of the preceding Urnfield period (e.g. the necklace of bronze plates from Blanot, and the plate jewellery from Dedinka, Drslavice, Izsákfa, Mušov, Németbánya and Paseky) as well as patterns made up of linked concentric circles (e.g. Binningen).

Thus, a date to the Ha A1/2 transition (Mozsolics BVb/c: Kurd and Gyermely horizons), i.e. the end of the 12th century BC, would seem acceptable at first sight for the treasure's manufacture. One caveat in this respect in the fragmented necklace with incised, linear motifs in repoussé from the Blanot hoard dated to the Ha B1 period.[619] This jewellery could have been part of a family heirloom, a piece inherited from a previous generation, reflecting an earlier fashion and manufacturing technique. This would be in line with Stéphane Verger's interpretation that the assemblage represents the jewellery worn during the three major phases of the life cycle and reflects changes in social status,[620] even though I do not wholly agree with this reasoning.

The elites of Bronze Age Europe monopolised the trade of luxury and prestige commodities such as copper, gold, silver, amber and salt that symbolised power and wealth. They used a uniform weight and value standard,[621] they wore costumes displaying their rank, had golden vessels for social display (*Fig. 32*), and wielded golden insignia of rank,[622] all bearing the same set of symbols.[623] The St. Vid Hill of Velem represents one of the easternmost sites[624] of the distribution of assemblages of gold costume jewellery embodying a more or less identical tradition in the Urnfield period (*Fig. 38*). At the same time, we cannot reject the possibility of a local Transdanubian, or perhaps more likely, eastern Alpine[625]

---

619 Thevenot 1991, Fig. 56. 12; Verger 1998, Fig. 3. 7.

620 Verger 1998, 37–38, Fig. 3.

621 David 2007, 437; Pare 2013, 519–520.

622 Gerloff 2003.

623 Kemenczei 1999. 77. To the best of my knowledge, the single pieces found farther to the east are repreented by the foil-covered plate jewellery dated slightly earlier from Nyíregyháza and the more or less contemporaneous specimens from Óbuda and Hinova (Iron Gates, Oltenia, Romania).

624 Hansen 1994, note 261, 117.

625 One of the main sources of the copper used in Transdanubia for long centuries. Kiss 2009, 207.

goldsmithing tradition and development (*Fig. 32* and *Fig. 38*),[626] which was closely connected to the period's flourishing metal provinces north of the Alps and in the Upper Tisza region.

In sum, the assemblage of golden jewellery yet again confirms Margarita Primas' earlier contention[627] for another smaller region, namely the eastern Alpine foreland, that traditions and knowledge as well as the customs and symbols grounded in them, and weight and value standards were uniform, even while part of the larger provinces/regions of the extensive Urnfield distribution with more sweeping cultural trajectories and cultural contacts.[628]

---

626 KEMENCZEI 1999, 77.

627 PRIMAS 1997, 295.

628 The cultural irradiation is confirmed by the gold plate and its symbols from Rocavecchia (the eastern coastline of Apulia, Italy), which in my view is more or less contemporaenous with, or perhaps slightly later, than the Velem treasure. Cf. JUNG 2007, 222, 226, note 42, Abb. 3.

12 Epilogue

The freshly restored treasure and the reconstruction drawings of the costume as well as the bronze treasures from Velem were displayed in the Castle Museum of Kőszeg as part of an exhibition opened on May 31, 2008. The exhibition was organised by the present author in cooperation with archaeologist Marcella Nagy and historian József Révész. We published a modest catalogue[629] containing information such as the weight of the treasure as well as several drawings and reconstructions that were published for the very first time. This exhibition was visited by prominent Hungarian archaeologists specialising in prehistory as well as our foreign colleagues, among them Mireille David-Elbiali, Wolfgang David, Attila László and Peter Romsauer on the occasion of the 6th National Conference on Prehistory held on March 19–21, 2009. Together with Marcella Nagy, we published another report on the treasure in 2009,[630] and I completed two smaller studies on the results of the metal analyses of the domed roundels.

One task of archaeological research, hopefully in a not too distant future more receptive to cultural heritage protection, is to conduct a series of control excavations over a 200–500 m² large area, during which the exact findspots of the treasures and hoards found in the 19th and 20th centuries could be identified, and perhaps additional artefacts that were deemed worthless at the time could be collected.[631]

Future studies and instrumental analyses should definitely cover the identification of the trace elements of the gold used for the treasure's adornments for provenancing,[632] A complex analysis of this type was performed for the Copper Age gold treasure from Hencida,[633] which indicated that the different pieces of the treasure had been crafted from many different types of raw materials at different times. The lack of tin (Sn) indicated that the gold used was not alluvial (washed) gold, and that it did not appear to have been imported from the

---

629 NAGY – ILON – RÉVÉSZ 2008.

630 ILON – NAGY 2009, 52–53.

631 Unless, of course, illegal local metal detectorists have not already looted the entire area and stripped the site of its metal finds. Metal detectoring spread like fire after the 1989 transition.

632 In Transylvania, Sb (antimony), Te (tellurium), Pb (lead) trace elements indicate mined gold, while Sn (tin) suggests alluvial washed gold. Cf. CONSTANTINESCU – CRISTEA-STAN – VASILESCU – SIMON – CECCATO 2012, 20.

633 CSEDREKI – DANI 2011.

so-called "gold province" in the vicinity of Verespatak (Romania). A similarly complex examination taking advantage of the many available instrumental analytical techniques (identification of mined *vs.* washed gold, provenancing) could contribute to determining the provenance of the treasure's raw material. It is my conviction that CT[634] and 3D scanning could contribute to identifying the bronze backplates to the gold foil of the diadem and the domed roundels from the imprints of the ornamentation. An international research project in the not too distant future would be able to identify the goldsmithing tools used in the manufacture of the adornments through the computer-aided processing of the images of tools, tool-marks and decorative patterns, which would in turn contribute to the identification of workshops and/or craftsmen (itinerant, hired or perhaps even kidnapped or part of an exchange). As a result, we would be afforded a glimpse into yet another dimension of the network of connections among the elites of the Bronze Age. It would be instructive to examine the mines whence the craftsmen of Velem are assumed to have procured their copper (Stadtschlaining–Antimon-Bergwerk),[635] which could be complemented with a complex analysis of the bronze artefacts from the site and of the bronze granule, as well as a new examination of the bronze backplates.

---

[634] As in the case of two treasures lifted *in situ* in 2011: a bronze hoard dating to the Early Iron Age found at Ikervár and a gold treasure dated to the later 14th century BC found at Gessel (Germany). NAGY – SÜMEGI *et al.* 2011; HASSMANN – HEINTGES – RASINK – INGHART – WULF 2012.

[635] CZAJLIK 2013.

13 Acknowledgements

My first debt of gratitude goes to Dr. Sándor Horváth, director of the county museums, and Dénes Ádám, chief finance director, for their support, because without their assistance, I would not have been able apply for various research grants. The conservation and restoration of the gold foils, and the production of their replicas was funded by an amount of HUF 1.1 million granted in response to Applications 2311/0920 (2003–04) and 2311/1302 (2005), announced by the Museological Professional College of the National Cultural Program. The funds for the metal analyses were secured through a grant from the archaeological projects of the Savaria Museum operating under the Directorate of the Museums of Vas County.

I would also like to thank Dr. Zoltán Nagy, director of the county museums, and Andrea Csapláros, director of the Savaria Museum, for permitting research on the treasure following my retirement from the museum as of June 1, 2008,.

I can never be grateful enough to chief conservator Katalin T. Bruder, sadly no longer among us, for her meticulous work, her attention the tiniest details and her inspiring comments and ideas. I thank physicist Attila L. Tóth (Institute of Technical Physics and Materials Science of the Hungarian Academy of Sciences, Budapest) for the instrumental measurements, and chemist Márta Járó (Department of Conservation and Restoration of the Hungarian National Museum, Budapest) for generously sharing with me their findings.

Special thanks are due to chief restorer Csaba E. Kiss (Savaria Museum, Szombathely) for his accurate drawings of the artefacts (the gold foils) and for his invaluable insights on the gold treasure from Várvölgy–Felsőzsid. I would like to thank archaeological technician Tamás Tárczy (Szombathely) and Gábor Papp (Söpte) for their excellent photographs, and Magdolna Mátyus (Regional Office II of the National Heritage Protection Center of the Hungarian National Museum, Szombathely) for her drawings of artefacts and her spectacular reconstructions. I am most grateful to goldsmith and archaeological technician András Radics (Regional Office II of the National Heritage Protection Center of the Hungarian National Museum, Szombathely) for sharing with me his knowledge on the finer details of ancient goldsmithing techniques, and archaeological technician Tibor Takács (Regional Office II of the National Heritage Protection Center of the Hungarian National Museum, Szombathely) for his macrophotographs made during the new examination of the treasure.

I am most grateful to the Expert College of Literature and Knowledge Dissemination of the National Cultural Fund for providing a grant of HUF 500,000 (coded: 3802/04630 (2013–2014)) enabling the final touches to the manuscript of this short monograph.

Special thanks go to my reviewers, Viktória Kiss (PhD) and Géza Szabó (PhD) for their useful and insightful comments. Any errors that remain are entirely of my own making.

I would also like to thank Zoltán Törőcsik for translating the text into English and Stephen Pow for revising the English text.

My greatest debt of gratitude goes to my spouse, Marcella Nagy, not only for her professional advice, but also for being a constant source of support and inspiration, for her faith in my work, and for her constant encouragement. She has been a loyal companion during the years, whom I can never thank enough.

Abbreviations

KVM = Municipal Musuem, Kőszeg

HNM = Hungarian National Museum, Budapest

SM = Savaria Museum, Szombathely

References

ALBERTI 1998

Alberti, Maria Emanuela: A stone or a weight? *Annali* (Roma), 45 (1998) 9–22.

ALBERTI 2003

Alberti, Maria Emanuela: Weighing and dying between East and West. Weighing materials from LBA Aegean funerary contexts. In: Foster, P. K. – Laffineur, R. (eds) *Metron. Measuring the Aegean Bronze Age*. Aegaeum, 24 (2003) 277–284.

ARMBRUSTER 2000

Armbruster, Barbara Regina: *Goldschmiedekunst und Bronzetechnik. Studien zum Metallhandwerk der Atlantischen Bronzezeit auf der Iberischen Halbinsel*. Monographies Instrumentum 15, Montagnac, Monique Mergoil, 2000.

ARMBRUSTER 2003

Armbruster, Barbara Regine: Edelmetallgefäβe der Bronzezeit – eine technologische Betrachtung. In: Grebe, A. – Springer, T. et al. (Red.) *Gold und Kult der Bronzezeit.* Ausstellungskatalog. Nürnberg, Verlag des Germanischen Nationalmuseums, 2003, 64–86.

ARMBRUSTER 2011

Armbruster, Barbara Regina: Gold der Bronzezeit – Technologie, Ästhetik und Funktion. In: Dietz, U. E. – Jockenhövel, A. (Hrsg.) *Bronzen im Spannungsfeld zwischen Nutzung und symbolischer Bedeutung. Beiträge zum internationalen Kolloquium am 9. und 10. Oktober 2008 in Münster.* Prähistorische Bronzefunde XX, 13. Stuttgart, Franz Steiner Verlag, 2011, 19–38.

ARMBRUSTER 2012

Armbruster, Barbara: Goldgefäße der Nordischen Bronzezeit – eine Studie zur Metalltechnik. *Praehistorische Zeitschrift* 87 (2012) 370–432.

ARMBRUSTER 2013

Armbruster, Barbara: Gold and goldworking of the Bronze Age. In: Fokkens, H. – Harding, A. (eds) *The Oxford Handbook of the European Bronze Age*. Oxford University Press, 2013, 454–468.

BÁCSKAY 1985

Bácskay, Erzsébet: Prehistoric mining and utilization of some mineral raw materials in the Carpathian Basin and in the adjacent areas. In: *Neogene mineral resources in the Carpathian Basin. Historical studies on their utilization.* VIIIth RCMNS Congress – Hungary. Budapest, Hungarian Geological Survey, 1985, 559–576.

BADER 1978

Bader, Tiberiu: *Epoca bronzului nord-vestul Transilvanei.* Bucureşti, Editura ştiinţifică şi enciclopedică, 1978.

BÄHR – KRAUSE – GEBHARD – LÜHR – HERBIG 2012

Bähr, Vanessa – Krause, Rüdiger – Gebhard, Rupert – Lühr, Christoph – Herbig, Christoph: Neue Forschungen zu den Befestigungen auf dem Bernstorfer Berg bei Kranzberg im Landkreis Freising (Oberbayern). *Bayerische Vorgeschichtsblätter* 77 (2012) 5–41.

BALLMER 2010

Ballmer, Ariane: Zur Topologie des bronzezeitlichen Deponierens. Von den Handlungstheorie zur Raumanalyse. *Prähistorische Zeitschrift* 85 (2010) 120–131.

BALOGH – VÉGH 1982

Balogh Lajos – Végh József (szerk.) *Vas megye földrajzi nevei.* Szombathely, Vas Megyei Múzeumok Igazgatósága, 1982.

BÁNDI 1983

Bándi, Gábor: Das Golddiadem von Velem. *Savaria, A Vas Megyei Múzeumok Értesítője* 16 (1983) 81–93.

BANNER 1956

Banner, János: *Die Péceler Kultur*. Budapest, Akadémiai kiadó, 1956.

BARTELHEIM 2009

Bartelheim, Martin: Die Nutzung mineralischer Ressourcen in der Bronzezeit Mittel- und Südeuropas. In: Bartelheim, M. – Stäuble, H. (Hrsg.) *Die wirtschaftlichen Grundlagen der Bronzezeit Europas.* Forschungen zur Archäometrie und Altertumswissenschaft 4. Rahden (Westf.), Verlag Marie Leidorf, 2009, 177–188.

BARTH 1988/1989

Barth, Fritz Eckart: Zum Goldscheibenfund von Óbuda. *Mitteilungen der Antropologischen Gesellschaft in Wien* 118/119 (1988/1989) 155–162.

BARTÍK 2009

Bartík, Juraj: Bronzezeitliche Gegenstände aus einer Privatsammlung II. Zborník Slovenského Národného Múzea CIII – *Archeológia* 19 (2009) 37–52.

BASS et al. 1967

Bass, George F. et al.: Cape Gelidonya: a Bronze Age shipwreck. American Philosophical Society New Ser. Vol. 57. Part 8. Philadelphia, 1967.

BÁTORA – SCHULZT 2012

Bátora, Jozef – Schulzt, Michael: Ein beachtenswertes frühbronzezeitliches Grab aus Ludanice, Ortsteil Mýtna Nová ves (SW Slowakei). In: Kujovský, R., Mitáš, V. (Hrsg.) *Václáv Furmánek a doba bronzová. Zborník k 70. narodeninám.* Nitra, Archeologický ústav SAV Nitra, 2012, 43–50.

BÁTORA – VLADÁR 2002

Bátora, Jozef – Vladár, Jozef: Die Besiedlungsproblematik der Glockenbecherkultur in der Südwestslowakei. Beitrag zu den Anfängen der Bronzezeit. *Budapest Régiségei* 36 (2002) 199–209.

BECK 1980

Beck, Adelheid: *Beiträge zur frühen und älteren Urnenfelderkultur im nordwestlichen Alpenvorland.* Prähistorische Bronzefunde XX, 2. München, C. H. Beck`sche Verlagsbuckhhandlung, 1980.

BEHRENDS 1999

Behrends, Rolf-Heiner: La défense de sanglier sertie de bronze de Karlsruhe–Neureut. In: *L' Europe au temps d' Ulysse. Dieux et Héros de l' âge du bronze.* Copenhague – Bonn – Paris – Athènes, Musée national du Danemark, Copenhague, Kunst und Ausstellungshalle der BRD, Bonn, Réunion des musées nationaux, Paris, ministère de la Culture, Athènes, 1999.

BÓNA 1959

Bóna István: Bronzkori övkapcsok és diadémák. Adatok a Közép-Duna-medence bronzkori viseletéhez. Bronze Age girdle-clasps and diadems. Data to the costumes of the Bronze Age in the Middle Danube Basin. *Archaeologiai Értesítő* 86 (1959) 49–59.

BÓNA 1975

Bóna, István: *Die Mittlere Bronzezeit Ungarns und ihre südöstlichen Beziehungen.* Budapest, Akadémiai kiadó, 1975.

BORN 2003a

Born, Hermann: Herstellungstechnische Voruntersuchungen an dem spätbronzezeitlichen Goldschmuck der Neuerwerbung. *Acta Praehistorica et Archaeologica* 35 (2003) 177–184.

BORN 2003b

Born, Hermann: Herstellungstechnische Voruntersuchungen am Berliner Goldhut. In: Grebe, A. – Springer, T. et al. (Red.) *Gold und Kult der Bronzezeit.* Ausstellungskatalog. Nürnberg, Verlag des Germanischen Nationalmuseums, 2003, 87–98.

BOUZEK 1981

Bouzek, Jan: Die Anfänge der Blechernen Schutzwaffen im Östlichen Mitteleuropa. In: Lorenz, H. (Hrsg.) *Studien zur Bronzezeit. Festschrift für Wilhelm Albert v. Brunn.* Mainz/Rhein, Verlag Philipp von Zabern, 1981, 21–38.

BOUZEK 1985

Bouzek, Jan: *The Aegean, Anatolia and Europe: Cultural Interrelations in the Second Millennium B.C.* Göteborg–Prague, Paul Aströms Förlag – Academia, Publishing House of the Czechoslovak Academy of Sciences, 1985.

BOUZEK 1996

Bouzek, Jan: Greece and the Aegean area and its relationship with continental Europe. *Acta Archaeologica* (København) 67 (1996) 175–181.

BOUZEK 2000

Bouzek, Jan: Versuch einer Rekonstruktion des Pantheons der Urnenfelderzeit. In: Gediga, B. – Piotrovska, D. (Hrsg.) *Die symbolische Kultur des Urnenfelderkreises in der Bronze- und Frühen Eisenzeit Mitteleuropas.* Warszawa – Wrocław – Biskupin, State Archaeological Museum in Warsaw, 2000, 345–354.

BUCHHOLZ 1959

Buchholz, Hans-Günter: Keftiubarren und Erzhandel im zweiten vorchristlichen Jahrtausend. *Praehistorische Zeitschrift* 37 (1959) 1–40.

ČERČE – ŠINKOVEC 1995

Čerče, Peter – Šinkovec, Irena: Catalogue of Hoards of the Urnfield Culture. In: Teržan, B. (ed.) *Hoards and Individual Metal Finds from the Eneolithic and Bronze Ages in Slovenia. I.* Catalogi et Monographiae 29. Ljubjana, Narodni muzej, 1995, 129–232.

CHERNEL 1877

Chernel Kálmán: *Kőszeg szab. kir. Város jelene és múltja.* Első rész. Jelenkor. Szombathely, Seiler Henrik kiadása, 1877.

CLAUSING 1998

Clausing, Christof: Zur Bedeutung der Bronze als Anzeiger urnenfelderzeitlicher Sozialstrukturen. In: Mordant, C. – Pernot, M. – Rychner, V. (eds) *L' Atelier du bronzier en Europe du XXe au VIIIe siècle avant notre ère. Actes du colloque international „Bronze 96" Neuchâtel et Dijon Tom. III. Production, circulation et consommation du bronze.* Paris, Comité des travaux historiques et scientifiques, 1998, 309–322.

CLAUSING 2001

Clausing, Christof: Spätbonze- und eisenzeitliche Helme mit einteiliger Kalotte. *Jahrbuch des Römisch-Germanischen Zentralmuseums* 48 (2001) 199–225.

CLAUSING 2003

Clausing, Christof: Ein urnenfelderzeitlicher Hortfund von Slavonski Brod, Kroatien. *Jahrbuch des Römisch-Germanischen Zentralmuseums* 50 (2003) 47–205.

CLAUSING 2005

Clausing, Christof: *Untersuchungen zu den urnenfelderzeitlichen Gräbern mit Waffenbeigaben vom Alpenkamm bis zur Südzone des Nordischen Kreises. Eine Analyse ihrer Grabinventare und Grabformen.* British Archaeological Reports international series, 1375. Oxford, 2005.

CONSTANTINESCU – CRISTEA-STAN – VASILESCU – SIMON – CECCATO 2012

Constantinescu, Bogdan – Cristea-Stan, Daniela – Vasilescu, Angela – Simon, Rolf – Ceccato, Daniele: Archaeometallurgical characterization of ancient gold artifacts from Romanian museums using XRF, micro-PIXE and micro-

SR-XRF methods. Proceedings of the Romanian Academy, Series A, Vol. 13, 2012:1, 19–26.

CZAJLIK 1993

Czajlik, Zoltán: Exploration geoarcheologique du mont Szent Vid. *Acta Archaeologica Academiae Scientiarum Hungaricae* 45 (1993) 317–347.

CZAJLIK 2012

Czajlik Zoltán: *A Kárpát-medence fémnyersanyag-forgalma a későbronzkorban és a vaskorban.* Budapest, ELTE Bölcsészettudományi Kar, 2012.

CZAJLIK 2013

Czajlik, Zoltán: Lokaler, regionaler oder Fernhandel? Probleme der spätbronzezeitlichen Metallversorgung am Velem–St. Veit Berg (Westungarn). In: Rezi B. – Németh R. – Berecki S. (eds): *Bronze Age Crafts and Craftsmen in the Carpathian Basin.* Proceedings of the International Colloquium from Târgu Mureş, 5–7 October 2012. Bibliotheca Mvsei Marisiensis Ser. Archaeologica VI. Târgu Mureş, Edutera MEGA, 2013, 167–180.

CSEDREKI – DANI 2011

Csedreki János – Dani János: A hencidai rézkori aranykincsen végzett PIXE vizsgálatok tanulságai. Experiences of the PIXE analyses performed on the Copper Age Gold treasure of Hencida. *Archeometriai Műhely* X:4 (2011) 285–291.

DAS PRÄHISTORISCHE GOLD 1997

Das prähistorische Gold in Bayern, Böhmen und Mähren. Band I. Textband. Band II. Herkunft – Technologie – Funde. Lehrberger, G. – Fridrich, J. – Gebhard, R. – Hrala, J. (eds) *Památky Archeologické* Supplementum 7. Prague, Institute of Archaeology, 1997.

DAVID 2001

David, Wolfgang: Zu den Beziehungen zwischen Donau–Karpatenraum, osteuropäischen Steppengebieten und ägäisch-anatolischem Raum zur Zeit der mykenischen Schachtgräber unter Berücksichtigung neuerer Funde aus Südbayern. In: *Anodos: studies of ancient world 1.* Trnava, Fakulta humanistiky Trnavskej university v Trnave, 2001, 51–80.

DAVID 2002a

Dawid, Wolfgang: *Studien zu Ornamentik und Datierung der bronzezeitlichen Depotfundgruppe Hajdúsámson-Apa-Ighiel-Zajta. I–II.* Alba Iulia, Verlag ALTIP S.A., 2002.

DAVID 2002b

David, Wolfgang: Die ältesten verzierten Bronzegürtelhaken der donauländischen Bronzezeit. In: *Anodos: studies of ancient world 2. In honour of Mária Novotná.* Trnava, Fakulta humanistiky Trnavskej university v Trnave, 2002. 67–90.

DAVID 2003

David, Wolfgang: Zum Ornament der Goldblechkegel von dem Hintergrund bronzezeitlicher Goldfunde Mittel- und Südosteuropas. *Anzeiger des Germanischen Nationalmuseums,* 2003, 35–53.

DAVID 2007

David, Wolfgang: Bronzezeitliche Goldornate aus Süddeutschland und ihre donauländisch-balkanischen Beziehungen. In: Todorova, H. – Stefanovich, M. – Ivanov, G. (eds) *The Struma/Strymon River Valley in Prehistory. In the Steps of James Harvey Gaul* 2. Sofia, Gerda Henkel Stiftung, 2007, 421–441.

DAVID 2010

David, Wolfgang: Die Zeichen auf der Scheibe von Nebra und das altbronzezeitliche Symbolgut des Mitteldonau–Karpatenraumes. In: Meller, H. – Bertemes, F. (Hrsg.) *Der Griff nach den Sternen. Internationales Symposium in Halle (Saale) 16.–21. Februar 2005.* Halle, Landesamt für Denkmalpflege und Archäologie Sachsen-Anhalt – Landesmuseum für Vorgeschichte Halle (Saale), 2010, 439–486.

DÉCHELETTE 1909

Déchelette, Joseph: Le culte du soleil aux temps préhistoriques. *Revue Archéologique* (juillet-décembre 1909) 94–123.

DELLA CASA – FISCHER 1997

Della Casa, Philippe – Fischer, Calista: Neftenbach (CH), Velika Gruda (YU), Kastanas (GR) und Trindhøj (DK) – Argumente für einen Beginn der Spätbronzezeit (Reinecke Bz D) im 14. Jahrhundert v. Chr. *Praehistorische Zeitsrift* 72 (1997) 195–233.

DIETRICH – DIETRICH 2011

Dietrich, Laura – Dietrich, Oliver: Wietenberg ohne Mykene? Gedanken zu Herkunft und Bedeutung der Keramikverzierung der Wietenberg-Kultur. *Praehistorische Zeitschrift* 86 (2011) 67–84.

DINNYÉS 1982

Dinnyés István: A táj a honfoglalás koráig. *Studia Comitatensia* 11 (1982) 45–64.

DOMBORÓCZKI 2012

Domboróczki, László: Recherches archéologiques à Ludas–Varjú-dűlő. In: Szabó, M. (Dir.): *La nécropole celtique à Ludas–Varjú-dűlő.* Budapest, L' Harmattan, 2012, 155–169.

DOMBÓVÁRI 2012

Dombóvári Judit: In memoriam T. Brúder Katalin. *Archeometriai Műhely* IX:4 (2012) 293.

EGG – KRAMER 2005

Egg, Markus – Kramer, Diether: *Krieger – Feste – Totenopfer. Der letzte Hallstattfürst von Kleinklein in der Steiermark. Mosaiksteine.* Forschungen am Römisch-Germanisches Zentralmuseum, Band 1. Mainz, Verlag des Römisch-Germanisches Zentralmuseums, 2005.

EGRY 2010

Egry Ildikó: Bezi, Nagy-sarok. Előzetes beszámoló a bronzkori falu feltárásáról (2008–2009). Bezi, Nagy-sarok. Preliminary report on the excavation of the Bronze Age village (2008–2009). In: Kisfaludi J. (ed.) *Régészeti kutatások Magyarországon 2009 – Archaeological Investigations in Hungary 2009.* Budapest, Kulturális Örökségvédelmi Hivatal – Magyar Nemzeti Múzeum, 2010, 5–18.

EIWANGER 1989

Eiwanger, Josef: Talanton. Ein bronzezeitlicher Goldstandard zwischen Ägäis und Mitteleuropa. *Germania* 67 (1989) 443–462.

ELIADE 2004

Eliade, Mircea: *Kovácsok és alkimisták.* Budapest, Cartaphilus Könyvkiadó, 2004.

ELUÈRE 1995

Eluère, Christiane: Gold and society in prehistoric Europa. In: Morteani, G. – Northover J. P. (eds): *Prehistoric Gold in Europe. Mines, Metallurgy and Manufacture.* NATO ASI Ser. E: Applied Sciences 280. Dordrecht – Boston – London, Kluwer Academic Publishers, 1995, 29–31.

ENDRŐDI 2012

Endrődi, Anna: Early Bronze Age headdress. Markers of the social status in the Bell Beaker-Csepel Group. *Archaeologiai Értesítő* 137 (2012) 7–26.

FALKENSTEIN 2011

Falkenstein, Frank: Zu Struktur und Deutung älturnenfelderzeitlicher Hortfunde im nordalpinen Raum. In: Dietz, U. E. – Jockenhövel, A. (Hrsg.) *Bronzen im Spannungsfeld zwischen Nutzung und symbolischer Bedeutung. Beiträge zum internationalen Kolloquium am 9. und 10. Oktober 2008 in Münster.* Prähistorische Bronzefunde XX, 13. Stuttgart, Franz Steiner Verlag, 2011, 71–105.

FEKETE 1986

Fekete, Mária: Früheisenzeitliche Forschungen im Komitat Vas. In: Jerem, E. (Red.) Hallstatt Kolloquium Veszprém 1984. *Antaeus. Mitteilungen des Archäologischen Instituts der Ungarischen Akademie der Wissenschaften*: Beiheft 3. Budapest, 1986, 57–67.

FEKETE 2007

Fekete Mária: *Események és szemelvények.* Egyetemi segédkönyv. Pécs, Pécsi Tudományegyetem BTK Ókortörténeti és Régészeti Tanszék, 2007.

FEKETE 2008

Fekete Mária: A kincs, a lelőhely, a védett terület és a cross-pálya. *Vasi Szemle* LXII:5 (2008) 525–540.

FEKETE 2010

Fekete, Mária: Sankt Veit. Angaben zu den prähistorischen Feiern und Götter (Namen) sowie dem Schmuck der Zeremonienbekleidung aus Pannonien. In: Bolohan, N. – Măţău, F. – Adrian, F. (eds): *Signa Praehistorica. Studia in honorem magistri Attila László septuagesimo anno.* Iaşi, Editura Univ. „Alexandru Ioan Cuza", 2010, 381–411.

FELCMAN 1910–12

Felcman, Jan: Hromadný nález v katastru Nová Ves u Velími. *Památky Archaeologické* 24 (1910–12) [1913] 375–382.

FIGLER 1995

Figler András: Adatok Győr környékének bronzkorához. Angaben zur Bronzezeit in der Umgebung von Győr. *Acta Musei Papensis* 6 (1996) 7–29.

FISCHER 1995

Fischer, Calista: Klein, aber Fein – Beobachtungen Goldverbindungs- und Drahtherstellungsverfahren an einem spätbronzezeitlichen Fund aus Neftenbach (ZH). In: Schmid-Sikimić, B. – Della Casa, Ph. (Hrsg.) *Trans Europam. Beiträge zur Bronze- und Eisenzeit zwischen Atlantik und Altai.*

Festschrift für Margarita Primas. Bonn, Dr. Rudolf Habelt GmbH, 1995, 7–14.

FOKKENS 1997
Fokkens, Harry: The genesis of urnfields. *Antiquity* 71 (1997) 360–373.

FOLTINY 1958
Foltiny, Stephan: *Velemszentvid, ein urzeitliches Kulturzentrum in Mitteleuropa.* Wien, Österreichische Arbeitsgemeinschaft für Ur- und Frühgeschichte – Urgeschitliches Institut der Univ. Wien, 1958.

FONTINJ 2002
Fontinj, R. David: Sacrifical Landscapes. Cultural Biographies of Persons, Objects and 'natural' Places in the Bronze Age of the Southern Netherlands, C. 2300-600 BC. *Analecta Praehistorica Leidensia* 33/34 (2002).

FONTINJ 2012
Fontijn, David: Landscapes without boundaries? Some thoughts on Bronze Age deposition areas in north-west Europe. In: Hansen, S. – Neumann, D. – Vachta, T. (Hrsg.) *Hort und Raum. Aktuelle Forschungen zu bronzezeitlichen Deponierungen in Mitteleuropa.* Berlin – Boston, De Gruyter, 2012, 49–68.

FURMÁNEK 1977
Furmánek, Václav: Pilinyer Kultur. *Slovenská Archeológia* XXV:2 (1977) 251–370.

GABROVEC – KRUH – MURGELJ – TERŽAN 2006
Gabrovec, Stane – Kruh, Ane – Murgelj, Ide – Teržan, Biba: *Stična II/1. Grabhügel aus der Älteren Eisenzeit.* Katalog. Catalogi et Monographiae 37. Ljubljana, Narodni muzej, 2006.

GEBHARD 2003
Gebhard, Rupert: Zwei Goldornate der Bronzezeit. In: Grebe, A. – Springer, T. et al. (Red.) *Gold und Kult der Bronzezeit.* Ausstellungskatalog. Nürnberg, Verlag des Germanischen Nationalmuseums, 2003, 148–153.

GEDL 2001
Gedl, Marek: *Die Bronzegefäße in Polen.* Prähistorische Bronzefunde II, 15. Stuttgart, Franz Steiner Verlag, 2001.

GERLOFF 1995
Gerloff, Sabine: Bronzezeitliche Goldblechkronen aus Westeuropa. In: Jockenhövel, A. (Hrsg.) *Festschrift für Hermann Müller-Karpe zum 70. Geburtstag.* Bonn, Dr. Rudolf Habelt GMBH, 1995, 153–194.

GERLOFF 2003
Gerloff, Sabine: Goldkegel, Kappe und Axt: Insignien bronzezeitlichen Kultes und Macht. In: Grebe, A. – Springer, T. et al. (Red.) *Gold und Kult der Bronzezeit.* Ausstellungskatalog. Nürnberg, Verlag des Germanischen Nationalmuseums, 2003, 191–203.

GLEIRSCHER 2014
Gleirscher, Paul: Frühes Gold aus Kärnten. In: Tecco Hvala, S. (ed.) *Studia Praehistorica in Honorem Janez Dular. Opera Instituti Archaeologici Sloveniae* 30 (2014) 137–147.

GOGÂLTAN 2005
Gogâltan, Florian: Zur Bronzeverarbeitung im Karpatenbecken. Die Tüllenhämmer und Tüllenambosse aus Rumänien. In: Soroceanu, T. (Hrsg.) *Bronzefunde aus Rumänien II.* Biblioteca Muzeului Bistriţa 11. Bistriţa – Cluj-Napoca, Complexul Muzeal Bistriţa-Năsăud, 2005, 343–386.

GOLD UND KULT 2003
Gold und Kult der Bronzezeit. Grebe, A. – Springer, T. et al. (Red.) Ausstellungskatalog. Nürnberg, Verlag des Germanischen Nationalmuseums, 2003.

GRIMMER-DEHN 1991
Grimmer-Dehn, Beata: Die Urnenfelderkultur im südöstlichen Oberrheingraben. *Materialhefte zur Vor- und Frühgeschichte in Baden-Württemberg* 15. Stuttgart, Kommissionsverlag – Konrad Theiss Verlag, 1991.

GRÖMER 2006
Grömer, Karina: Textilien der Bronzezeit in Mitteleuropa. *Archaeologia Austriaca* 90 (2006) 31–72.

GRUBER 2008
Gruber, Heinz: Schätze aus Gold die urnenfelderzeitlichen Depotfunde vom Arikogel und aus dem Koppental. In: *Schätze, Gräber, Opferplätze. Traunkirchen 08. Archäologie im Salzkammergut.* Katalog zur Ausstellung im ehemaligen Kloster Traunkirchen 29. April bis 2. November 2008. *Fundberichte aus Österreich Materialhefte A*, Sonderheft 6, Wien, 2008, 72–77.

HAGBERG 1998

Hagberg, Ulf Erik: Die westschwedischen Bronzeschilde von Fröslunda – eine große Gabe an die Götter. In: Hänsel, B. (Hrsg.) *Mensch und Umwelt in der Bronzezeit Europas.* Kiel, Oetker-Voges Verlag, 1998, 507–508.

HAMPEL 1864

Hampel József: Marosmegyei aranylelet. *Archaeologiai Értesítő* 14 (1864) 29–32.

HAMPEL 1886

Hampel József: *A bronzkor emlékei Magyarhonban I.* Budapest, Az Orsz. Régészeti és Embertani Társulat kiadványa, 1886.

HAMPEL 1892

Hampel József: *A bronzkor emlékei Magyarhonban II.* Budapest, Az Orsz. Régészeti és Embertani Társulat kiadványa, 1892.

HAMPEL 1896

Hampel József: *A bronzkor emlékei Magyarhonban III.* Budapest, Az Orsz. Régészeti és Embertani Társulat kiadványa, 1896.

HÄNSEL 1997

Hänsel, Alix: Museum und Universität – ein Konflikt ohne Ende? Eine Fallstudie anhand der Auseinandersetzungen um das bronzezeitliche Depot von Vorland. In: Becker, C. – Dunkelmann, M-L. – Metzner-Nebelsick, C. et al. (Hrsg.) *Χρόνος. Beiträge zur prähistorischen Archäologie zwischen Nord- und Südosteuropa. Festschrift für Bernhard Hänsel.* Studia honoraria 1. Espelkamp, Verlag Marie Leidorf GmbH, 1997, 409–414.

HÄNSEL 2003

Hänsel, Alix: Goldschmuck der Spätbronzezeit – Zu einer Neuerwerbung des Berliner Museums für Vor- und Frühgesichte. *Acta Praehistorica et Archaeologica* 35 (2003) 157–175.

HÄNSEL 1982

Hänsel, Bernhard: Südosteuropa zwischen 1600 und 1000 v.Chr. In: *Südosteuropa zwischen 1600 und 1000 v.Chr.* Prähistorische Archäologie in Südosteuropa, Band 1. Berlin, Moreland Editions – Bad Bramstedt, 1982, 1–38.

HÄNSEL 2003

Hänsel, Bernhard: Bronzezeitliche Stadtkultur im Karpatenbecken? In: Kacsó, C. (Hrsg.) *Bronzezeitliche Kulturerscheinungen im Karpatischen*

Raum. Die Beziehungen zu den benachbarten Gebieten. Ehrensymposium für Alexandru Vulpe zum 70. Geburtstag. Baia Mare 10.–13. Oktober 2001. Bibliotheca Marmatia 2 (2003) 207–216.

HÄNSEL 2009

Hänsel, Bernhard: Frühformen des Geldes im bronzezeitlichen Europa. *Godišnjak* (Sarajevo) 36 (2009) 23–35.

HÄNSEL – HÄNSEL 1997

Hänsel, Alix – Hänsel, Bernhard: Herrscherinsignien der älteren Urnenfelderzeit. Ein Gefäßdepot aus dem Saalegebiet Mitteldeutschlands. *Acta Praehistorica et Archaeologica* 29 (1997) 66–68.

HANSEN 2010

Hansen, Rahlf: Sonne oder Mond? Verewigtes Wissen aus der Ferne. In: Meller, H. – Bertemes, F. (Hrsg.) *Der Griff nach den Sternen.* Internationales Symposium in Halle (Saale) 16.–21. Februar 2005. Halle, Landesamt für Denkmalpflege und Archäologie Sachsen-Anhalt – Landesmuseum für Vorgeschichte Halle (Saale), 2010, 953–962.

HANSEN 1994

Hansen, Svend: *Studien zu den Metalldeponierungen während der älteren Urnenfelderzeit zwischen Rhônetal und Karpatenbecken.* Universitätsforschungen zur Prähistorischen Archäologie 121. Bonn, Verlag Dr. Rudolf Habelt GmbH, 1994.

HANSEN 1997

Hansen, Svend: Sacrificia ad flamina – Gewässerfunde im bronzezeitlichen Europa. In: Hänsel, A. – Hänsel, B. (Hrsg.) *Gaben an die Götter. Schätze der Bronzezeit Europas.* Berlin, Seminar für Ur- und Frühgeschichte der Freien Univ. – Museum für Vor- und Frühgeschichte, 1997, 29–34.

HANSEN 2006

Hansen, Svend: Elemente einer Geschichte der Hortung. In: Kobal', J. (Hrsg.) *Bronzezeitliche Depotfunde – Problem der Interpretation.* Užgorod, IBA, 2006, 55–75.

HANSEN 2013

Hansen, Svend: Bronzezeitliche Deponierungen in Europa nördlich der Alpen. Weihgaben ohne Tempel. In: Gerlach, I. – Raue, D. (Hrsg.) *Sanktuar und Ritual. Heilige Plätze im archäologischen Befund.* Rahden (Westf.), Verlag Marie Leidorf, 2013, 371–387.

HARTMANN 1968

Hartmann, Axel: Über die spektralanalytische Untersuchung einiger bronzezeitlicher Goldfunde aus dem Donauraum. *Bericht der Römisch-Germanischen Kommission* 46–47 (1968) 63–73.

HARTMANN 1970

Hartmann, Axel: *Prähistorische Goldfunde aus Europa.* Berlin, Gebr. Mann Verlag, 1970.

HARTMANN 1982

Hartmann, Axel: *Prähistorische Goldfunde aus Europa II.* Studien zu den Anfängen der Metallurgie. Band 5. Berlin, Gebr. Mann Verlag, 1982.

HASE 1995

Hase, Friedrich-Wilhelm von: The ceremonial jewellery from the Regolini-Galassi tomb in Cerveteri. Some ideas concerning the workshop. In: Morteani, G. – Northover J. P. (eds): *Prehistoric Gold in Europe. Mines, Metallurgy and Manufacture.* NATO ASI Ser. E: Applied Sciences 280. Dordrecht – Boston – London, Kluwer Academic Publishers, 1995, 533–559.

HASSMANN – HEINTGES – RASINK – WINGHART – WULF 2012

Haßmann, Henning – Heintges, Tina – Rasink, Bernd – Winghart, Stefan – Wulf, Friedrich-Wilhelm: Der bronzezeitliche Hortfund von Gessel, Stadt Syke, Landkreis Diepholz. *Berichte zur Denkmalpflege in Niedersachsen. Niedersächsisches Landesamt für Denkmalpflege* 32 (2012) 23–28.

HIDDE 1997

Hidde, Birgit: Eberswalde, Kr. Oberbarnim, Prov. Brandenburg. In: Hänsel, A. – Hänsel, B. (Red.) *Gaben an die Götter.* Berlin, Seminar für Ur- und Frühgeschichte der Freien Univ. – Museum für Vor- und Frühgeschichte, 1997, 128–130.

HONTI – BELÉNYESY – FÁBIÁN et. al. 2004

Honti Szilvia – Belényesy Károly – Fábián Szilvia et. al.: A tervezett M7-es autópálya Somogy megyei szakaszának megelőző régészeti feltárásai (2002–2003). Előzetes jelentés III. (Preliminary report III. The preceding archaeological excavations /2002–2003/ of the M7 highway in Somogy county.) Separatum: *Somogyi Múzeumok Közleményei* 16 (2004) 3–70.

HORVÁTH 2004

Horváth Tünde: Néhány megjegyzés a vatyai kultúra fémművességéhez – technológiai megfigyelések a kultúra kőeszközein. Die Metallkunst der

Vatya-kultur. Technologische Beobachtungen an Ihren Steingeräten. *Communicationes Archaeologicae Hungariae* 2004, 12–64.

HORVÁTH 2006
Horváth Tünde: A badeni kultúráról – rendhagyó módon. About Baden Culture – an irregular approach. *A nyíregyházi Jósa András Múzeum Évkönyve* 48 (2006) 89–133.

HRALA 1997
Hrala, Jiří: Die frühurnenfelderzeitlichen goldenen Hortfunde in Ostböhmen. Ein profanes wie auch kultisches Phänomen. In: *Beiträge zur Deutung der bronzezeitlichen Hort- und Grabfunde in Mitteleuropa.* Kraków, Oficyna Cracovia, 1997, 173–181.

ILON 1986
Ilon Gábor: Egy sírépítménytípus a Bakony-vidéki késő bronzkorban. Ein Grabbau-Typ in der Spätbronzezeit der Bakony-Gegend. *Veszprém Megyei Múzeumok Közleményei* 18 (1986) 83–93.

ILON 1992
Ilon, Gábor: Keftiubarren/ingot from Urn-Grave culture settlement at Gór–Kápolnadomb (C. Vas). *Acta Archaeologica Academiae Scientiarum Hungaricae* 44 (1992) 239–259.

ILON 1996a
Ilon, Gábor: Beiträge zum Metallhandwerk der Urnenfelderkultur – Gór (Kom. Vas, Ungarn). In: Jerem, E. – Lippert, A. (Hrsg.) *Die Osthallstattkultur. Akten des Internationalen Symposiums, Sopron, 1994.* Budapest, Achaeolingua, 1996, 171–186.

ILON 1996b
Ilon, Gábor: Beiträge zum Metallhandwerk der Urnenfelderkultur: Gór–Kápolnadomb (Komitat Vas). *Acta Archaeologica Academiae Scientiarum Hungaricae* 48 (1996) 35–47.

ILON 1996c
Ilon Gábor: A késő halomsíros – kora urnamezős kultúra temetője és tell települése Németbánya határában. Das Gräberfeld und Tell der Späthügelgräber–Frühurnenfelderkultur in der Gemarkung Németbánya. *Acta Musei Papensis* 6 (1996) 89–208.

ILON 1998

Ilon, Gábor: Celtic period fortifications and an experiment to reconstruct the rampart – Gór (Vas county). In: Költő, L. – Bartosiewicz, L. (eds): *Archaeometrical Research in Hungary II.* Budapest – Kaposvár – Veszprém, Hungarian National Museum – Dir. of Somogy Museums – Archaeocomp Ass. and the Working Group of Industrial Archaeology and Archaeometry of the Veszprém Reg. Comm. of the HAS, 1998, 227–243.

ILON 1999

Ilon Gábor: A bronzkori halomsíros kultúra temetkezései Nagydém–Középrépáspusztán és a hegykői edénydepot. Die Bestattungen der bronzezeitlichen Hügelgräberkultur in Nagydém–Középrépáspuszta und das Gefässdepot von Hegykő. *Savaria Pars Archaeologica* 24:3 (1999) 239–276.

ILON 2001a

Ilon, Gábor: Siedlungswesen und Bestattungssitten in Gór. Zum Übergang von der Urnenfelder- zur Hallstattzeit. In: Lippert, A. (Hrsg.) *Die Drau-, Mur- und Raab-Region im 1. vorchristlichen Jahrtausend. Akten des internationalen und interdisziplinären Symposiums vom 26. bis 29. April 2000 in Bad Radkersburg.* Universitätsforschungen zur Prähistorischen Archäologie 78, Bonn, Verlag Dr. Rudolf Habelt GmbH, 2001, 243–267.

ILON 2001b

Ilon Gábor: Pénzrendszer a bronzkorban? Währungssystem in der Bronzezeit? In: Dani J. – Hajdú Zs. – Nagy E. Gy. – Selmeczi L. (szerk.): *ΜΏΜΟΣ I.* „Fiatal Őskoros Kutatók" I. Összejövetelének konferenciakötete. Debrecen, Déri Múzeum, 2001, 217–224.

ILON 2002a

Ilon Gábor: Miske Kálmán, br. In: Élesztős L. (szerk.): *Magyar múzeumi arcképcsarnok.* Budapest, Pulszky Társaság – Tarsoly kiadó, 2002, 616–617.

ILON 2002b

Ilon, Gábor: Ein spätbronzezeitlicher Hortfund aus Szombathely (Steinamanger), Kom. Vas (Ungarn). *Das Altertum* 47 (2002) 149–169.

ILON 2002c

Ilon, Gábor: Früheisenzeitliches rituelles Zentrum auf dem Kalapos-kő (Hutstein) in Bozsok bei Velem–Szent Vid? *Specimina Nova. A Janus Pannonius Tudományegyetem Történeti Tanszékeinek Évkönyve* XVI (2002) 19–30.

ILON 2003

Ilon, Gábor: Metallhandwerkstatt der Urnenfelderkultur in Gór. In: Kacsó, C. (Hrsg.) *Bronzezeitliche Kulturerscheinungen im Karpatischen Raum. Die Beziehungen zu den Benachbarten Gebieten. Ehrensymposium für Alexandru Vulpe zum 70. Geburtstag. Baia Mare 10.–13. Oktober 2001.* Bibliotheca Marmatia 2. Baia Mare, Editura Casei Corpului Didactic, 2003, 239–248.

ILON 2004

Ilon Gábor: *Szombathely őskori településtörténetének vázlata. Avagy a római kor előtt is volt élet. Outline of the Pre-historic settlement of Szombathely, or life before the Roman Age.* Szombathely, Vas Megyei Múzeumok Igazgatósága, 2004.

ILON 2005

Ilon, Gábor: Houses of the Late Burial Mound–Early Urnfield Culture. In connection to a house reconstructed in Németbánya. *Ősrégészeti Levelek – Prehistoric Newsletter* 7 (2005) [2007] 135–145.

ILON 2007a

Ilon, Gábor: Settlement patterns in the Velem–Szent Vid area. In: Zatykó, Cs. – Juhász, I. – Sümegi, P. (eds): *Environmental archaeology in Transdanubia.* Varia Archaeologica Hungarica XX. Budapest, Archaeological Institute of the Hungarian Academy of Sciences, 2007, 281–307.

ILON 2007b

Ilon, Gábor: Über die Zusammenhänge zwischen Siedlungsnetz und Metallurgie im Gebiet Nordwesttransdanubiens in der Spätbronzezeit. *Acta Archaeologica Academiae Scientiarum Hungaricae* 58 (2007) 135–144.

ILON 2009

Ilon Gábor: A régészettudomány múltja, jelene és lehetséges jövője. Számvetés a centenárium jegyében. Past, present and possible future of archaeological science. An account on behalf of the centenary. *Savaria* 32:2 (2009) 37–111.

ILON 2010

Ilon Gábor: A bronzkor emlékei a víztározó területén. In: Ilon G. – Kreiter E. (szerk.): *Vízelőtti régészet. A Lukácsházi árvízcsúcs-csökkentő tározó területén végzett régészeti feltárások.* [Pre-Water Archaeology. Archaeological excavations in the area of the Lukácsháza flood-attenuation reservoir.] A K.Ö.SZ. Tudományos-népszerűsítő füzetei 3. Budapest, 2010, 16–17.

ILON 2012a

Ilon Gábor: A velemi Szent Vid aranykincsének gömbszeleteiről (Buckeln). A brief report on the globule segments (Buckeln) of the treasure found on Szent Vid hill in Velem. *Archeometriai Műhely* IX:2 (2012) 123–132.

ILON 2012b

Ilon, Gábor: Das Rad, die Sonne, das Wasservogel und der Vogelbarken auf spätbronzezeitlichen Schwertern... mögliche Ausdrucksformen des Handels oder anderer Beziehungen? In: Marta, L. (Hrsg.) *Die Gáva-Kultur in der Theißebene und Siebenburgen.* Satu Mare Studii şi Comunicări, Ser. Arheologie XXVIII:1, Satu Mare, 2012, 169–209.

ILON 2013a

Ilon Gábor: *Gyűjtő a velemi Szent Vid-hegy lábánál. Vezető Kern István magángyűjteményében. Sammler am Fuße des St. Veit Berges bei Velem. Führer in der Privatsammlung von István Kern.* Kőszeg, Pannon Kulturális Örökség Egyesület, 2013.

ILON 2013b

Ilon, Gábor: Das II. Buckelpaar des Goldschatzes von St. Veit bei Velem. In: Rezi B., – Németh R. – Berecki S. (eds): *Bronze Age Crafts and Craftsmen in the Carpathian Basin.* Proceedings of the International Colloquium from Târgu Mureş 5–7 October 2012. Bibliotheca Mvsei Marisiensis Ser. Archaeologica VI. Târgu Mureş, Editura MEGA, 2013, 181–190.

ILON 2014a

Ilon, Gábor: Opfergrube der Hügelgräberkultur in der Gemarkung von Ménfőcsanak. Spiralornament auf einem Tonfries eines Gebäudes. *Acta Archaeologica Academiae Scientiarum Hungaricae* 65 (2014) 5–42.

ILON 2014b

Ilon, Gábor: Der Anfang der Urnenfelderzeit (Bz D) im Bakonygebirge (Ungarn). Das Gräberfeld und die mehrschichtige Siedlung der Spät-Hügelgräberzeit und der Früh-Urnenfelderzeit in der Gemarkung von Németbánya. In: Dizdar, L. D. – Dizdar, M. (eds): *The Beginning of the Late Bronze Age between the Eastern Alps and the Danube.* Proceedings of the International Conference in Osijek, October 20–22. 2011. Zbornik Instituta za Archaeologiju 1. Zagreb, 2014, 101–177.

ILON – KÖLTŐ 2000

Ilon Gábor – Költő László: Középső bronzkori emlékek a velemi Szent Vidről. Egy tolnanémedi típusú (VII: velemi) kincslelet? Middle Bronze

Age artifacts from Szent Vid of Velem. Another of the Tolnanémedi-type (VII. Velem) artifact sortiment? *Komárom-Esztergom Megyei Múzeumok Közleményei* 7 (2000) 69–95.

ILON – RASZTOVICS 2000

Ilon Gábor – Rasztovics János: Őskori lelőhelyek Vas megyében. Előmunkálatok Vas megye régészeti topográfiájához. Őskor I. Prehistoric sites in Vas County. Preparations for the archaeological topography of County Vas. Prehistory No.1. In: Ilon G. (szerk.): *Pannicvlvs* Ser. B. No. 5. Szombathely, Pannicvlvs, 2000, 145–235.

ILON – SÜMEGI – BODOR 2006

Ilon Gábor – Sümegi Pál – Bodor Elvira: A Ság hegy környékének története a régészeti adatok és a környezetrégészeti vizsgálat tükrében. The history of Ság Hill's immediate vicinity as reflected by archaeological data and the survey of environmental archaeology. *Zalai Múzeum* 15 (2006) 295–314.

ILON – NAGY 2009

Ilon Gábor – Nagy Marcella: Arany diadém. Gold diadem. *Savaria, A Vas Megyei Múzeumok Értesítője* 32:1 (2009) 52–53.

ILON – SÜMEGI – TÓTH et al. 2011

Ilon Gábor – Sümegi Pál – Tóth Gábor et al.: *Szombathely–Zanat késő urnamezős korú temetője és a lelőhely más ős- és középkori emlékei. Természettudományos vizsgálatokkal kiegészített anyagközlés. The Late Urnfield period cemetery from Szombathely–Zanat supplemented by an assessment of Prehistoric and Medieval settlement features and interdisciplinary analyses.* VIA – Kulturális örökségvédelmi kismonográfiák 2/VIA – Monographia minor in cultural heritage 2. Kvassay J. (szerk./ed.) Budapest, Magyar Nemzeti Múzeum – Nemzeti Örökségvédelmi Központ/ Hungarian National Museum – National Cultural Heritage Protection Centre, 2011.

IPOLYI 1884

Ipolyi Arnold: Egy hazai vidék. (Heves és K.-Szolnok megyék) őskori régiségleletei és középkori műemlékei vázlata. In: Ipolyi Arnold. *Magyar műtörténelmi tanulmányai.* Budapest, Ráth Mór, 1884, 469–511.

JACOB 1995

Jacob, Christiana: *Metallgefäße der Bronze- und Hallstattzeit in Nordwest-, West- und Süddeutschland.* Prähistorische Bronzefunde II, 9. Stuttgart, Franz Steiner Verlag, 1995.

JAKAB – JUHÁSZ – SÜMEGI – ILON 2007

Jakab, Gusztáv – Juhász, Imola – Sümegi, Pál – Ilon, Gábor: The Alpine foreland. In: Zatykó, Cs. – Juhász, I. – Sümegi, P. (eds): *Environmental archaeology in Transdanubia.* Varia Archaeologica Hungarica XX. Budapest, Archaeological Institute of the Hungarian Academy of Sciences, 2007, 267–307.

JANSSEN 1985

Janssen, Walter: Hortfunde der jüngeren Bronzezeit aus Nordbayern. Einführung in die Problematik. *Archäologisches Korrespondenzblatt* 15 (1985) 45–54.

JOCKENHÖVEL 1975

Jockenhövel, Albrecht: Zum Beginn der Jungbronzezeitkultur in Westeuropa. *Jahresbericht des Inst. für Vorgeschichte der Univ. Franfurt a.M.* 1975. München, Verlag C. H. Beck, 1975, 134–181.

JOCKENHÖVEL 2003

Jockenhövel, Albrecht: Querverbindungen in Handwerk und Symbolik zwischen Gold- und Bronzetoreutik. In: Grebe, A. – Springer, T. et al. (Red.) *Gold und Kult der Bronzezeit.* Ausstellungskatalog. Nürnberg, Verlag des Germanischen Nationalmuseums, 2003, 106–118.

JUNG 2005

Jung, Reinhard: Aspekte des mykenischen Handels und Produktenaustauschs. In: Horejs, B. – Jung, R. – Kaiser, E. – Teržan, B. (Hrsg.) *Interpretationsraum Bronzezeit. Bernhard Hänsel von seinem Schülern gewidmet.* Universitätsforschungen zur Prähistorischen Archäologie 121. Bonn, Verlag Dr. Rudolf Habelt GmbH, 2005, 45–70.

JUNG 2007

Jung, Reinhard: Goldene Vögel und Sonnen. Ideologische Kontakte zwischen Italien und der postpalatialen Ägäis. In: Alram-Stern, E. – Nightingale, G. (Hrsg.) *Keimelion. Elitenbildung und elitärer Konsum von der mykenischen Palatszeit bis zur homerischen Epoche. Akten des internationalen Kongresses vom 3. bis 5. Februar 2005 in Salzburg,* Österreichische Akademie der Wissenschaften. Philosophisch-Historische Klasse, Sitzungsberichte 350. Veröffentlichungen der Mykenischen Kommission 27. Wien, Verlag der Österreichischen Akademie der Wissenschaften, 2007, 219–255.

KACSÓ 2006

Kacsó, Carol: Bronzefunde mit Goldgegenständen im Karpatenbecken. In: Kobal', J. (Hrsg.) *Depotfunde – Problem der Interpretation.* Užgorod, IBA, 2006, 76–123.

KALLA 2000

Kalla Gábor: Megjegyzések a Kárpát-medencei „Keftiu-tömbök" és az őskori „pénz" kérdéséhez. *Ősrégészeti Levelek – Prehistoric Newsletter* 2 (2000) 83–87.

KÁROLYI 1990

Károlyi Mária: Miske Kálmán (1860–1943). *Vasi Szemle* 44:3 (1990) 389–407.

KÁROLYI 2004

Károlyi Mária: *Napszülöttek. Savaria földjének őskori kultúrái a rómaiak előtt. Ancient cultures of Savaria before the Romans.* Szombathely, Magánkiadás, 2004.

KAUL 1998

Kaul, Fleming: *Ships on Bronzes. A Study in Bronze Age Religion and Iconography I–II.* Copenhagen, Publications from the National Museum, 1998.

KAUL 2003

Kaul, Flemming: Der Mythos von der Reise der Sonne. In: Grebe, A. – Springer, T. et al. (Red.) *Gold und Kult der Bronzezeit.* Ausstellungskatalog. Nürnberg, 2003. Verlag des Germanischen Nationalmuseums, 36–51.

KAUS – KAUS 2012

Kaus, Karl – Kaus, Margarete: Zum Kultgerät von Haschendorf. In: Anreiter, P. – Bánffy, E. – Bartosiewicz, L. – Meid, W. – Metzner-Nebelsick, C. (eds): *Archaeological, Cultural and Linguistic Heritage. Festschrift for Erzsébet Jerem in Honour of her 70th Birthday.* Budapest, Archaeolingua, 2012, 303–319.

KEMENCZEI 1984

Kemenczei, Tibor: *Die Spätbronzezeit Nordostungarns.* Budapest, Akadémiai kiadó, 1984.

KEMENCZEI 1988

Kemenczei, Tibor: *Die Schwerter in Ungarn I.* Prähistorische Bronzefunde IV, 6. München, Verlag C. H. Beck, 1988.

KEMENCZEI 1991a

Kemenczei, Tibor: *Die Schwerter in Ungarn II.* Prähistorische Bronzefunde IV, 9. München, Verlag C. H. Beck, 1991.

KEMENCZEI 1991b

Kemenczei Tibor: A pécskai/Pecica második bronzlelet. Die zweite Depotfund von Pecica/Pécska. *Folia Archeologica* 42 (1991) 28–48.

KEMENCZEI 1996a

Kemenczei, Tibor: Zum Übergang von der Bronze- zur Eisenzeit in NW-Transdanubien. *Folia Archaeologica* 45 (1996) 91–131.

KEMENCZEI 1996b

Kemenczei, Tibor: Angaben zur Frage der endbronzezeitlichen Hortfundstufen im Donau–Theiβgebiet. *Communicationes Archaeologicae Hungariae*, 1996, 53–92.

KEMENCZEI 1999

Kemenczei, Tibor: Spätbronzezeitliche Goldschatzfunde. In: Kovács, T. – Raczky, P. (Hrsg.) *Prähistorische Goldschätze aus dem Ungarischen Nationalmuseum.* Budapest, Ungarisches Nationalmuseum – Institut für Archäologie der Eötvös-Loránd-Universität, 1999, 63–79.

KILIAN-DIRLMEIER 1975

Kilian-Dirlmeier, Imma: *Gürtelhaken, Gürtelbleche und Blechgürtel der Bronzezeit in Mitteleuropa.* Prähistorische Bronzefunde XII, 2. München, C. H. Beck`sche Verlagsbuchhandlung, 1975.

KISS E. 2009

Kiss E. Csaba: A restaurálás története a szombathelyi Savaria Múzeumban. The history of restoration in Szombathely Savaria Múzeum. *Savaria, A Vas Megyei Múzeumok Értesítője* 32:2 (2009) 326–334.

KISS F. 1859

Kiss Ferencz: A karikapénzről. *Archaeologiai Közlemények* 1 (1859) 174–215.

KISS V. 2007

Kiss, Viktória: Contacts along the Danube: a boat model from the Early Bronze Age. In: Galanaki, I. – Tomas, H. – Galanakis, Y. – Laffineur, R. (eds): *Between the Aegean and Baltic Seas. Prehistory across borders.* Aegaeum 27 (2007) 119–129.

KISS V. 2009

Kiss Viktória: A fém nyersanyag-felhasználás kérdései a Dunántúl kora és középső bronzkorában. Questions of the use of metal as raw material in the Early and Middle Bronze Age of Transdanubia. In: Ilon G. (szerk.): *ΜΩΜΟΣ VI. Őskoros kutatók VI. összejövetelének konferenciakötete. Nyersanyagok és kereskedelem.* Kőszeg, 2009. március 19–21. *Proceedings of the 6th meeting for the researchers of prehistory. Raw materials and trade.* Szombathely, Kulturális Örökségvédelmi Szakszolgálat – Vas Megyei Múzeumok Igazgatósága, 2009, 197–212.

KOBAL' 2000

Kobal', V. Josip: *Bronzezeitliche Depotfunde aus Transkarpatien (Ukraine).* Prähistorische Bronzefunde XX, 4. Stuttgart, Franz Steiner Verlag, 2000.

KOCH 2003

Koch, Susanne: Herstellungstechnische Untersuchungen am Goldkegel von Ezelsdorf. In: Grebe, A. – Springer, T. et al. (Red.) *Gold und Kult der Bronzezeit.* Ausstellungskatalog. Nürnberg, Verlag des Germanischen Nationalmuseums, 2003, 98–105.

KOSSACK 1995

Kossack, Georg: Mitteleuropa zwischen dem 13. und 8. Jahrhundert v. Chr. Geb. Geschichte, Stand und Probleme der Urnenfelderforschung. In: *Beiträge zur Urnenfelderzeit Nördlich und Südlich der Alpen.* Römisch-Germanisches Zentralmuseum Monographien 35. Bonn, Dr. Rudolf Habelt GmbH, 1995, 1–64.

KOVÁCS 1977

Kovács Tibor: *A bronzkor Magyarországon.* Budapest, Helikon kiadó, 1977.

KOVÁCS 1991

Kovács, Tibor: Das bronzezeitliche Goldarmband von Dunavecse. *Folia Archaeologica* 42 (1991) 7–25.

KOVÁRNÍK 1998

Kovárník, Jaromír: Neuer Funde eines Bronzedepots in Mušov/Südmähren. (Vorbericht). In: Hänsel, B. (Hrsg.) *Mensch und Umwelt in der Bronzezeit Europas.* Kiel, Oetker-Voges Verlag, 1998, 509–523.

KÖLTŐ – VARGA – MACLEAN 2002

Költő, László – Varga, K. Miklós – Maclean, Paul: Analysis of high antimony concentration finds with various methods XRF analysis of antimony bronzes. In: Jerem, E. – Biró, T. K. (eds): *Archaeometry 98. Proceedings of the 31st*

Symposium Budapest, April 26 – May 3 1998. British Archaeological Reports International Series 1043 (II), Archaeolingua Central European Sr. 1. 2002, 405–408.

KÖNIG 2004
König, Peter: *Spätbronzezeitliche Hortfunden aus Bosnien und der Hercegowina.* Prähistorische Bronzefunde XX, 11. Stuttgart, Franz Steiner Verlag, 2004.

KŐSZEGI – FARKAS 2007
Kőszegi Ádám – Farkas Csilla: Előzetes felszíni kutatások (szisztematikus terepbejárás, geofizikai felmérés) és a megelőző feltárás eredményeinek összevetése a Vát–Bodon-tábla nevű lelőhely kapcsán. Vorherige Untersuchungen (systematische Geländebegehungen, geophysikalische Messungen) und der Vergleich der Freilegungsergebnisse in Verbindung mit dem Fundort Vát–Bodon-tábla. *Savaria, A Vas Megyei Múzeumok Értesítője* 31 (2007) 263–278.

KŐSZEGI 1988
Kőszegi Frigyes: *A Dunántúl története a későbronzkorban. The history of Transdanubia during the Late Bronze Age.* BTM Műhely, 1. Budapest, Budapesti Történeti Múzeum, 1988.

KRAUSE 2003
Krause, Rüdiger: *Studien zur Kupfer- und frühbronzezeitlichen Metallurgie zwischen Karpatenbecken und Ostsee.* Vorgeschichtliche Forschungen 24. Rahden (Westf.), Verlag Marie Leidorf GmbH, 2003.

KUBACH-RICHTER
Kubach-Richter, Isa: Amulettbeigaben in bronzezeitlichen Kindergräbern. *Jahresbericht des Instituts für Vorgeschichte der Universität Frankfurt a. M.* 1978–79. München, Verlag C. H. Beck, 1979, 127–178.

KUIJPERS 2008
Kuijpers, H. G. Maikel: *Bronze Age metallworking in the Netherlands (c. 2000 – 800 BC). A research into the preservation of metallurgy related artefacts and the social position of the smith.* Leiden, Sidestone Press, 2008.

KULCSÁR 1999
Kulcsár Gabriella: Kora bronzkori belsődíszes talpas tálak a Dunántúlon. The Early Bronze Age internally decorated bowls from the Transdanubia. *Savaria Pars Archaeologica* 24:3 (1999) 115–139.

KYTLICOVÁ 1991

Kytlicová, Olga: *Bronzegefäße in Böhmen.* Prähistorische Bronzefunde II, 12. Stuttgart, Franz Steiner Verlag, 1991.

KYTLICOVÁ 2007

Kytlicová, Olga: *Jungbronzezeitliche Hortfunde in Böhmen.* Prähistorische Bronzefunde XX, 12. Stuttgart, Franz Steiner Verlag, 2007.

L' EUROPE AU TEMPS D'ULYSSE 1999

L' Europe au temps d' Ulysse. Dieux et Héros de l' âge du bronze. Copenhague – Bonn – Paris – Athènes, Musée national du Danemark, Copenhague, Kunst und Ausstellungshalle der BRD, Bonn, Réunion des musées nationaux, Paris, ministère de la Culture, Athènes, 1999.

LA NIECE – CARTWRIGHT 2009

La Niece, Susan – Cartwright, Caroline: Bronze Age Gold Lock-rings with Cores of Wax and Wood. In: Kienlien, T. L. – Roberts, B. W. (eds): *Metals and Societies. Studies in honour of Barbara S. Ottaway.* Universitätsforschungen zur Prähistorischen Archäologie 169. Bonn, Verlag Dr. Rudolf Habelt GmbH, 2009, 307–312.

LASSEN 2000

Lassen, Hanne: Introduction to weight systems in the Bronze Age East Mediterranean: the case of Kalavasos-Ayios Dhimitrios. In: Pare, E. F. C. (ed.) *Metals Make the World Go Round. The Supply and Circulation of Metal in Bronze Age Europe.* Oxford, Oxbow Books, 2000, 233–246.

LAUERMANN – AMMER 2013

Lauermann, Ernst – Rammer, Elisabeth: *Die urnenfelderzeitlichen Metallhortfunde Niederösterreichs.* Universitätsforschungen zur Prähistorischen Archäologie, 226. Bonn, Verlag Dr. Rudolf Habelt GmbH, 2013.

LAUX 2005

Laux, Friedrich: *Die Axte und Beile in Niedersachsen II (Lappen- und Tüllenbeile, Tüllenmeisel und -hammer).* Prähistorische Bronzefunde IX, 25. Stuttgart, Franz Steiner Verlag, 2005.

LÁZÁR 1941

Lázár Jenő: A sághegyi I. és II. számú bronzleletek ismertetése. Zwei Schatzfunde vom Ságbereg. *Dunántúli Szemle* 8 (1941) 371–379.

LÁZÁR 1943

Lázár Jenő: A sághegyi őskori telep bronzművessége. Die Bronzeindustrie der urzeitlichen Siedlung am Ságberg. *Dunántúli Szemle* 10:7-8 (1943) 280–287.

LEEB 1994

Leeb, Alexandra: Das frühbonzezeitliche Gräberfeld von Melk/Spielberg – Flur Pielamünd, Niederösterreich. *Zalai Múzeum* 5 (1994) 113–130.

LEHRBERGER 1995

Lehrberger, Gerhard: The gold deposits of Europe: an overview of the possible metal sources for prehistoric gold objects. In: Morteani, G. – Northover J. P. (eds): *Prehistoric Gold in Europe. Mines, Metallurgy and Manufacture.* NATO ASI Ser. E: Applied Sciences 280. Dordrecht – Boston – London, Kluwer Academic Publishers, 1995. 115–144.

LEITSCHUH-WEBER 1994

Leitschuh-Weber, Christine: Gold – Die ewige Faszination. In: Jockenhövel, A. – Kubach, W. (Hrsg.) *Bronzezeit in Deutschland. Archäologie in Deutschland, Sonderheft*, 1994, 93–97.

LEITSCHUH-WEBER 1996

Leitschuh-Weber, Christine: Die urnenfelderzeitlichen Goldscheibenanhänger von Dietzenbach. *Archäologisches Korrespondenzblatt* 26 (1996) 281–291.

LENERZ-DE WILDE 1995

Lenerz-de Wilde, Majolie: Prämonetäre Zahlungsmittel in der Kupfer- und Bronzezeit Mitteleuropas. *Fundberichte aus Baden-Württemberg* 20 (1995) 227–327.

LICHARDUS – VLADÁR 1996

Lichardus, Jan – Vladár, Jozef: Karpatenbecken – Sintašta – Mykene. Ein Beitrag zur Definition der Bronzezeit als historischer Epoche. *Slovenská Archeológia* 44 (1996) 25–93.

MACHT, HERRSCHAFT 1988

Macht, Herrschaft und Gold. Das Gräberfeld von Varna (Bulgarien) und die Anfänge einer neuen europäischen Zivilization. Hrsg. Fol, A. – Lichardus, J. Saarbrücken, Moderne Galerie des Saarland-Museums, 1988.

MAKKAY 2000

Makkay, János: *The early Mycenaean Rulers and the Contemporary Early Iranians of the Northeast*. Budapest, Magánkiadás, 2000.

MAKKAY 2006

Makkay, János: The Late Bronze Age hoard of Nadap. *A nyíregyházi Jósa András Múzeum Évkönyve* XLVIII (2006) 135–184.

MARTIN 2009

Martin, Jens: *Die Bronzegefäße in Mecklenburg-Vorpommern, Brandenburg, Berlin, Sachsen-Anhalt, Thüringen und Sachsen.* Prähistorische Bronzefunde II, 16. Stuttgart, Franz Steiner Verlag, 2009.

MÁRTON 1907

Márton Lajos: A féregyházi őskori aranylelet. *Archaeologiai Értesítő* 27 (1907) 57–68.

MAY – ZUMPE 2003

May, Jens – Zumpe, Reiner: Ein Buckel – ein Tag. Zur Nutzbarkeit buckeldekorierter Schilde, Hängebecken und Amphoren der jüngeren Bronzezeit als Kalender. In: Grebe, A. – Springer, T. et al. (Red.) *Gold und Kult der Bronzezeit.* Ausstellungskatalog. Nürnberg, Verlag des Germanischen Nationalmuseums, 2003, 252–265.

MAYER 1977

Mayer, E. Friedrich: *Die Äxte und Beile in Österreich.* Prähistorische Bronzefunde IX, 9. München, Verlag C. H. Beck, 1977.

MEDELEŢ 1995

Medeleţ, Florin: Ein urnenfelderzeitlicher Depotfund von bronzenen Werkzeugen in Fratelia, bei Timişoara, Kr. Timiş. In: Soroceanu, T. (Red.) *Bronzefunde aus Rumänien.* Prähistorische Archäologie in Südosteuropa 10. Berlin, Wissenschaftsverlag Volker Spiess, 1995, 229–236.

MEDOVIĆ 1995

Medović, Predrag: Die Waage aus der frühhallstattzeitlichen Siedlung Bordjoš (Borjas) bei Novi Bečej (Banat). In: Hänsel, B. (Hrsg.) *Handel, Tausch und Verkehr im bronze- und früheisenzeitlichen Südosteuropa.* Prähistorische Archäologie in Südosteuropa 11. München–Berlin, Südosteuropa-Gesellschaft – Seminar für Ur- und Frühgeschichte der Freien Univ. Berlin, 1995, 209–218.

MELLER 2010

Meller, Herald: Nebra: Vom Logos zum Mythos – Biographie eines Himmelsbildes. In: Meller, H. – Bertemes, F. (Hrsg.) *Der Griff nach den Sternen.* Internationales Symposium in Halle (Saale) 16.-21. Februar 2005.

Halle, Landesamt für Denkmalpflege und Archäologie Sachsen-Anhalt – Landesmuseum für Vorgeschichte Halle (Saale), 2010, 23–73.

MENGHIN 2003
Menghin, Wilfried: Goldene Kegelhüte – Manifestationen bronzezeitlicher Kalenderwerke. In: Grebe, A. – Springer, T. et al. (Red.) *Gold und Kult der Bronzezeit.* Ausstellungskatalog. Nürnberg, Verlag des Germanischen Nationalmuseums, 2003, 221–237.

MENGHIN – SCHAUER 1983
Menghin, Wilfried – Schauer, Peter: *Der Goldkegel von Ezelsdorf. Kultgerät der späten Bronzezeit.* Die vor- und frühgeschichtlichen Altertümer im Germanischen Nationalmuseum, Heft 3. Nürnberg, Konrad Theiβ Verlag, 1983.

METZNER-NEBELSICK 2009
Metzner-Nebelsick, Carola: Symbole der Macht in der Bronze- und Eisenzeit Europas. *Beiträge zur Vorgeschichte Nordostbayerns* 7. Nürnberg, 2009, 13–26.

MISKE 1896
Miske Kálmán: Velemi (Vasm.) régiségekről. *Archaeologiai Értesítő* 16 (1896) 250.

MISKE 1897
Miske, Kálmán: Der Bronzefund von Velem–St. Veit bei Güns in Ungarn. *Mitteilungen der Antropologischen Gesellschaft in Wien* VII (1897) 13–17.

MISKE 1903
Miske, Kálmán: Funde aus Velem-St. Veit. *Mitteilungen der Antropologischen Gesellschaft in Wien* XIII (1903) 33–35.

MISKE 1904
Miske, Kálmán: Bericht über die im Jahre 1903 in Velem – St. Veit gefundenen Machrocephalen. *Mitteilungen der Antropologischen Gesellschaft in Wien* XIV (1904) 62–63.

MISKE 1907
Miske Kálmán: A Velem Szent Vidi őstelep. I. A harácsolt leletek leírása. Wien, Konegen Károly kiadása, 1907.

MISKE 1908
Miske, Kálmán: *Die prähistorische Ansiedelung Velem St. Vid. Band I. Beschreibung der Raubbaufunde.* Wien, Verlagsbuchhandlung Carl Konegen, 1908.

MISKE 1909
Miske Kálmán: A statigraphikus beszerzésekről. *Múzeumi és Könyvtári Értesítő,* III: 2–3 (1909) 66–75.

MISKE 1925
Miske Kálmán: A Vasvármegyei Múzeum. Das Museum des Komitates Vas (Eisenburg) in Szombathely. *Vasvármegye és Szombathely Város Kulturegyesülete és a Vasvármegyei Múzeum I. Évkönyve* (1925) 45–63.

MISKE 1928
Miske, Kálmán: Bergbau, Verhüttung und Metallbearbeitungswerkzeuge aus Velem St. Veit (Westungarn). *Wiener Prähistorische Zeitschrift*, 1928. 81–94.

MONTAG 2000
Montag, Miriam: Das Problem der süddeutschen Spiral- und Vogelornamentik. In Mühldorfer, B. – Zeitler, P. J. (Hrsg.) *Mykene – Nürnberg - Stonehenge. Handel und Austausch in der Bronzezeit. Begleitbuch zur Ausstellung.* Nürnberg, Naturhistorische Gesellschaft Nürnberg e. V., 2000, 95–108.

MOZSOLICS 1942
Mozsolics Amália: A magyarkeresztesi (Vas megye) bronzlelet. Der Bronzefund von Magyarkeresztes. *Archaeologiai Értesítő* 69 (1942) 155–161.

MOZSOLICS 1945
Mozsolics Amália: Őskori bronzkalapácsok. Marteaux préhistoriques en bronze. *Magyar Múzeum* 1 (1945) 53–57, 95.

MOZSOLICS 1950
Mozsolics, Amália: *Der Golfund von Velem–Szentvid. Ein Beitrag zur Metallkunst der älteren Hallstattzeit.* Praehistorica I. Basel, Prometheus, 1950.

MOZSOLICS 1963
Mozsolics, Amália: Der Bronzefund von Ópályi. *Acta Archaeologica Academiae Scientiarum Hungaricae* 15 (1963) 65–82.

MOZSOLICS 1966
Mozsolics, Amália: Goldfunde von Nyíregyháza und von Szarvasszó. *Acta Archaeologica Academiae Scientiarum Hungaricae* 18 (1966) 15–33.

MOZSOLICS 1968
Mozsolics, Amália: Goldfunde des Depotfundhorizontes von Hajdúsámson. *Bericht der Römisch-Germanischen Kommission* 46–47 (1968) 2–62.

MOZSOLICS 1973
Mozsolics, Amália: *Bronze- und Goldfunde des Karpatenbeckens. Depotfundhorizonte von Forró und Ópályi.* Budapest, Akadémiai kiadó, 1973.

MOZSOLICS 1981
Mozsolics, Amália: Der Goldfund von Várvölgy–Felsőzsid. In: Lorenz, H. (Hrsg.) *Studien zur Bronzezeit. Festschrift für Wilhelm Albert v. Brunn.* Mainz/Rhein, Verlag Philipp von Zabern, 1981, 299–308.

MOZSOLICS 1984
Mozsolics, Amália: Ein Beitrag zum Metallhandwerk der ungarischen *Bronzezeit. Bericht der Römisch-Germanischen Kommission* 65 (1984) 20–72.

MOZSOLICS 1985
Mozsolics, Amália: *Bronzefunde aus Ungarn. Depotfundhorizonte von Aranyos, Kurd und Gyermely*. Budapest, Akadémiai kiadó, 1985.

MOZSOLICS 1987
Mozsolics, Amália: Verwahr- oder Opferfunde? *Acta Archaeologica Academiae Scientiarum Hungaricae* 39 (1987) 93–98.

MOZSOLICS 2000
Mozsolics, Amália: *Bronzefunde aus Ungarn. Depotfundhorizonte Hajdúböszörmény, Románd und Bükkszentlászló.* Kiel, Verlag Oetker/Voges, 2000.

MÜLLER 1972
Müller Róbert: A pötrétei későbronzkori kincslelet. Der spätbronzezeitliche Schatzfund von Pötréte. *Veszprém Megyei Múzeumok Közleményei* 11 (1972) 59–74.

MÜLLER 2006a
Müller Róbert: Várvölgy, Kis-Lázhegy. In: Kisfaludi J. (ed.) *Régészeti Kutatások Magyarországon 2005 – Archaeological Investigations in Hungary*

2005. Budapest, Kulturális Örökségvédelmi Hivatal – Magyar Nemzeti Múzeum, 2006, 334–335.

MÜLLER 2006b
Müller Róbert: Várvölgy–Nagy-Lázhegy késő bronzkori földvár kutatása. Die Erforschung des spätbronzezeitlichen Burgwalles von Várvölgy–Nagy-Lázhegy. In: Kovács Gy. – Miklós Zs. (Red.) *Tanulmányok a 80 éves Nováki Gyula tiszteletére* (*Burgenkundliche Studien zum 80. Geburstag von Gyula Nováki*). Budapest, Castrum Bene Egyesület – Historiaantik Könyvesház kiadó, 2006, 227–236.

MÜLLER 2007
Müller Róbert: Késő bronzkori magaslati település kutatása Várvölgy, Nagyláz-hegyen (2003-2006). Investigation of a hill settlement from the Late Bronze Age at Várvölgy, Nagyláz-hegy (2003-2006). – In: Kisfaludi J. (Ed): *Régészeti kutatások Magyarországon – Archaeological Investigations in Hungary 2006*. Budapest, Kulturális Örökségvédelmi Hivatal – Magyar Nemzeti Múzeum, 2007, 5–26.

MÜLLER 2011
Müller Róbert: Keménységvizsgálatok a Várvölgy–Nagy-Lázhegy-i késő bronzkori eszközökön. – In: Kővári K. – Miklós Zs. (szerk): *„Fél évszázad terepen" Tanulmánykötet Torma István tiszteletére 70. születésnapja alkalmából.* Budapest, Magyar Tudományos Akadémia Régészeti Intézete, 2011, 211–224.

MÜLLER 2013
Müller Róbert: A második késő bronzkori aranykincs Várvölgyről. Der zweite spätbronzezeitliche Goldschatz von Várvölgy (Kom. Zala). *Archaeologiai Értesítő*, 138. (2013) 81–103.

MÜLLER-KARPE 1959
Müller-Karpe, Hermann: *Beiträge zur Chronologie der Urnenfelderzeit nördlich und südlich der Alpen. II.* Tafeln. Römisch-Germanische Forschungen, Band 22. Berlin, 1959.

MÜLLER-KARPE 1969
Müller-Karpe, Hermann: Das urnenfelderzeitliche Toreutengrab von Steinkirchen, Niederbayern. *Germania* 47 (1969) 86–91.

Müller-Karpe 1975
Müller-Karpe, Hermann: Neuere Forschungen zur Geschichte des 13. und 12. Jh. in Zentraleuropa. *Jahresbericht des Instituts für Vorgeschichte der Univ. Frankfurt a.M.* 1975. München, Verlag C. H. Beck, 1975, 7–23.

Müller-Karpe 1978–79
Müller-Karpe, Hermann: Bronzezeitliche Heilzeichen. *Jahresbericht des Instituts für Vorgeschichte der Universität Frankfurt a.M.* 1978–79. München, Verlag C. H. Beck, 1979, 9–28.

Müller-Karpe 1980
Müller-Karpe, Hermann: *Handbuch der Vorgeschichte. Vierter Band: Bronzezeit. Dritter Teilband: Tafeln.* München, C. H. Beck`she Verlagsbuchhandlung, 1980.

Müller-Karpe 2003
Müller-Karpe, Hermann: Zur religiösen Symbolik von bronzezeitlichem Trachtschmuck aus Mitteleuropa. *Anodos. Studies of the Ancient World 3.* Trnava, Fakulta humanistiky Trnavskej university v Trnave, 2003, 145–154.

Nagy 2011
Nagy Marcella: A korai urnamezős időszak kronológiai vázlata a Kárpát-medence nyugati felében. Urnamezős kori temető- és településrészlet Sárvár–Felsőmezőn. Die chronologische Skizze der frühen Urnenfelderzeit in dem westlichen Teil des Karpatenbeckens. Friedhof und Siedlungsteil aus der frühen Urnenfelderzeit in Sárvár–Felsőmező. *Savaria, A Vas Megyei Múzeumok Értesítője* 34:1 (2011) 67–94.

Nagy – Ilon – Révész 2008
Nagy Marcella – Ilon Gábor – Révész József: *„Kincs" A velemi Szent Vid hegy bronzkori kincsei. Időszaki kiállítás báró Miske Kálmán halálának 65. évfordulója és nemzetközi hírű monográfiájának centenáriuma alkalmából.* Pannonkör Füzetek, 3. Kőszeg, Pannon Kulturális Örökség Egyesület, 2008.

Nagy – Sümegi – Persaits – Gulyás – Törőcsik 2012
Nagy, Marcella – Sümegi, Pál – Persaits, Gergő – Gulyás, Sándor – Törőcsik Tünde: Iron Age Hoard Found at Ikervár (Vas County, Hungary) in the Western Region of the Carpathian Basin. A Study in the Reconstruction of the Cultic Life of the Hallstatt Period in the Light of Archaeological and Scientific Analyses. In: Berecki S. (ed.) *Iron Age rites and rituals in the Carpathian basin.* Proceedings of the International Colloquium from Târgu Mureş 7–9 October 2011. Târgu Mureş, Editura MEGA, 2012, 31– 64.

NEBELSICK 1997

Nebelsick, D. Louis: Auf Biegen und Brechen. Ekstatische Elemente bronzezeitlicher Materialopfer – Ein Deutungsversuch. In: Menghin, W. – Hänsel, B. (Hrsg.) *Gaben an die Götter. Schätze der Bronzezeit Europas.* Berlin, Seminar für Ur- und Frühgeschichte der Freien Univ. – Museum für Vor- und Frühgeschichte,1997, 35–41.

NEBELSICK 2000

Nebelsick, Louis: Rent asunder: ritual violence in Late Bronze Age hoards. In: Pare, E. F. C. (ed.) *Metals Make The World Go Round. The Supply and Circulation of Metal in Bronze Age Europe.* Oxford, Oxbow Books, 2000, 160–175.

NESSEL 2008

Nessel, Bianka: Zu Gliederung und Verwendungsmöglichkeiten bronzener Tüllenhämmer der jüngeren Bronzezeit im Karpatenbecken. *Mitteilungen der Berliner Gesellschaft für Anthropologie, Ethnologie und Urgeschichte* 29 (2008) 71–82.

NESSEL 2010

Nessel, Bianka: Schmiede und Toreuten in den urnenfelderzeitlichen Depotfunden des Karpatenbeckens? – Funktionsanalyse von Handwerksgerät un soziale Implikationen. In: Horejs, B. – Kienlin, T. L. (Hrsg.) *Siedlung und Handwerk. Studien zu sozialen Kontexten in der Bronzezeit.* Universitätsforschungen zur Prähistorischen Archäologie, 194. Bonn, Verlag Dr. Rudolf Habelt GmbH, 2010, 373–386.

NESSEL 2012a

Nessel, Bianka: Metallurgen im Grab – Überlegungen zur sozialen Einstufung handwerklicher Spezialisten. In: Kienlin, T. L. – Zimmermann, A. (Hrsg.) *Beyond Elites.* Teil 2. Universitätsforschungen zur Prähistorischen Archäologie , 215. Bonn, Verlag Dr. Rudolf Habelt GmbH, 2012, 423–432.

NESSEL 2012b

Nessel, Bianka: Hervorgehobene oder verborgene Identität? Zu Ausstattungsmustern von Metallhandwerkergräbern. In: Heske, I. – Horejs, B. (Hrsg.) *Bronzezeitliche Identitäten und Objekte.* Universitätsforschungen zur Prähistorischen Archäologie , 221. Bonn, Verlag Dr. Rudolf Habelt GmbH, 2012, 55–74.

NESSEL 2013

Nessel, Bianka: The 'Absence' of Smiths and Founders – Why Tools are Rare in Bronze Age Burials. In: Rezi B. – Németh R. – Berecki S. (eds): *Bronze Age Crafts and Craftsmen in the Carpathian Basin.* Proceedings of the International Colloquium from Târgu Mureş 5–7 October 2012. Bibliotheca Mvsei Marisiensis Ser. Archaeologica VI. Târgu Mureş, Editura MEGA, 2013, 139–147.

NEUGEBAUER 1994

Neugebauer, Johannes-Wolfgang: *Bronzezeit in Ostösterreich.* St. Pölten-Wien, Niederösterreichisches Pressehaus Druck- und Verlagsgesellschaft mbH, 1994.

NEUGEBAUER – NEUGEBAUER 1997

Neugebauer, Christine – Neugebauer, Johannes-Wolfgang: *Franzhausen das Frühbronzezeitliche Gräberfeld I.* Bd. 1–2. Fundberichte aus Österreich Materialhefte A 5:1–2, Wien, Verlag Ferdinand Berger & Söhne Ges. M. b. h. Horn, 1997.

NICOLARDOT – VERGER 1998

Nicolardot, Jean-Perre – Verger, Stéphane: Le dépôt des Granges-sous-Grignon (Commune de Grignon, Côte-d'Or). In: Mordant, C. – Pernot, M. – Rychner, V. (eds): *L'Atelier du bronzier en Europe du XXe au VIIIe siècle avant notre ère. Actes du colloque international „Bronze 96" Neuchtel et Dijon Tom. III. Production, circulation et consommation du bronze.* Paris, Comité des travaux historiques et scientifiques, 1998, 9–32.

NØRGAARD 2009

Nørgaard, W. Heide: Die Halskragen der Nordischen Bronzezeit. *Mitteilungen der Berliner Gesellschaft für Antropologie, Ethnologie und Urgeschichte* 30 (2009) 95–114.

NØRGAARD 2011

Nørgaard, W. Heide: *Die Halskragen der Bronzezeit im nördlichen Mitteleuropa und Südskandinavien.* Universitätsforschungen zur Prähistorischen Archäologie, 200. Bonn, Verlag Dr. Rudolf Habelt GmbH, 2011.

NORTHOVER 1995

Northover, Peter: Late Bronze Age Drawplates in the Isleham hoard. In: Schmid-Sikimić, B. – Della Casa, Ph. (Hrsg.) *Trans Europam. Beiträge zur*

Bronze- und Eisenzeit zwischen Atlantik und Altai. Festschrift für Margarita Primas. Bonn, Dr. Rudolf Habelt GmbH, 1995, 15–22.

NOVÁKI 1966
Nováki Gyula: Koravaskori sarlólelet Kőszegről. Sichelfunde aus der Frühen Eisenzeit in Kőszeg. *Magyar Mezőgazdasági Múzeum Közleményei*, 1965–66 (1966) 67–72.

NOVOTNÁ 1970
Novotná, Maria: *Die Äxte und Beile in der Slowakei.* Prähistorische Bronzefunde IX, 3. München, C. H. Beck`sche Verlagsbuckhhandlung, 1970.

NOVOTNÁ 1984
Novotná, Mária: *Halsringe und Diademe in der Slowakei.* Prähistorische Bronzefunde XI, 4. München, C. H. Beck`sche Verlagsbuckhhandlung, 1984.

OBERFRANK 1986
Oberfrank Ferenc: *Az aranyművesség története.* Budapest, Műszaki könyvkiadó, 1986.

OŽĎÁNI 2009
Ožďáni, Ondrej: Depoty bronzových predmetov z Hradiska pri Nemeckej. *Slovenská Archeológia* 57 (2009) 1–56.

PABST 2011
Pabst, Sabine: Die großräumige Ausbreitung der Brillenfibeln am Übergang von der Bronze- zur Eisenzeit – Kommunikationswege und Soziale Hintergründe. In: Dietz, U. E – Jockenhövel, A. (Hrsg.) *Bronzen im Spannungsfeld zwischen Nutzung und symbolischer Bedeutung. Beiträge zum internationalen Kolloquium am 9. und 10. Oktober 2008 in Münster.* Prähistorische Bronzefunde XX, 13. Stuttgart, Franz Steiner Verlag, 2011. 199–234.

PARE 1999
Pare, Christopher: Weights and Weighing in Bronze Age Central Europe. In: *Eliten in der Bronzezeit. Teil 2. Ergebnisse zweier Kolloquien in Mainz und Athen. 2.* Römisch-Germanisches Zentralmuseum Monographien, Band 43. Mainz, Verlag des Römisch-Germanischen Zentralmuseums – Dr. Rudolf Habelt GMBH, 1999, 421–514.

PARE 2013

Pare, Christopher: Weighing, Commodification, and Money. In: Fokkens, H. – Harding, A. (eds): *The Oxford Handbook of the European Bronze Age.* Oxford, Oxford University Press, 2013, 508–527.

PÁSZTHORY – MAYER 1998

Pászthory, Katharine – Mayer, Friedrich Eugen: *Die Äxte und Beile in Bayern.* Prähistorische Bronzefunde IX, 20. Stuttgart, Franz Steiner Verlag, 1998.

PÁSZTOR 2012

Pásztor, Emília: Magical Signs in Prehistory: Near Eastern Celestial Symbols in the Ancient Carpathian Basin. In: Rountree, K. – Morris, Ch. – Peatfield, A. A. D. (eds): *Archaeology of Spriritualities.* One World Archaeology Series. New York, Springer, 2012, 185–203.

PÁSZTOR – ROSLUND 2007

Pásztor, Emília – Roslund, Curt: An interpretation of the Nebra disc. *Antiquity* 81 (2007) 267–278.

PATAY 1967

Patay Pál: Egy miniatür bronz diadém. Miniature bronze diadem. *Archaeologiai Értesítő,* 94 (1967) 53–57.

PAULÍK 1984

Paulík, Jozef: Bronzový diadém z Dedinky. In: *Zborník prác Ľudmile Kraskovskej životnému jubilen.* Bratislava, Slovenské národné múzeum, 1984, 39–48.

PAULÍK 1986

Paulík, Jozef: Čačianska mohyla v Dedinke, okres Nové Zamky (IV). *Zborník Slovenského národného múzea* LXXX (1986) 69–112.

PENNER 1998

Penner, Silvia: *Schliemanns Schachtgräberrund und der europäische Nordosten. Studien zur Herkunft der frühmykenischen Streitwagenausstattung.* Saarbrücker Beiträge zur Altertumskunde, 60. Bonn, Dr. Rudolf Habelt Verlag GMBH, 1998.

PEREA – ARMBRUSTER – DEMORTIER – MONTERO 2003

Perea, Alicia – Armbruster, Bárbara – Demortier, Guy – Montero, Ignacio: Tecnología atlántica para dioses mediterráneos. Los 'candelabros' de oro tipo Lebrija. Atlantic technology for Mediterranean gods. The Lebrija type gold 'candelabra'. *Trabajos de prehistoria* 60:1 (2003) 99–114.

PERNICKA – BÜHLER – LEUSCH – MEHOFER 2008

Pernicka, Ernst – Bühler, Birgit – Leusch, Verena – Mehofer, Mathias: Chemische und technologische Untersuchungen an den Goldobjekten vom Arikogel und aus dem Koppental. In: *schätze.gräber.opferplätze traunkirchen.08 Archäologie im Salzkammergut.* Katalog zur Ausstellung im ehemaligen Kloster Traunkirchen 29. April bis 2. November 2008. *Fundberichte aus Österreich Materialhefte A, Sonderheft* 6, Wien, 2008, 78–81.

PERNOT 1991

Pernot, Michel: Procédés de formage de quelques objets de bronze et d' or. In: Thevenot, Jean-Paul*: L' Âge du bronze en Bourgogne. Le dèpôt de Blanot (Côte-d' Or).* 11ème Supplément à la Revue archaeologique de l'Est. Dijon, Ministère de la Cultura et de la Communication et de la Ville de Dijon, 1991. 123–134.

PERONI 1998

Peroni, Renato: Bronzezeitliche Gewichtssysteme im Metallhandel zwischen Mittelmeer und Ostsee. In: Hänsel, B. (Hrsg.) *Mensch und Umwelt in der Bronzezeit Europas*. Kiel, Oetker-Voges Verlag, 1998, 217–224.

PETRES 1990

Petres F. Éva: Anhang. Die Bronzegefässe aus dem Depotfund von Nadap. In: Patay Pál: *Die Bronzegefäße in Ungarn.* Prähistorische Bronzefunde II, 10. München, Verlag C. H. Beck, 1990, 87–93.

PETRUSO, 1978

Petruso, M. Karl: *Systems of weight in the Bronze Age Europe.* Doctoral Dissertation Indiana Univ. Indiana, 1978.

PIETTE 1998

Piette, Jacques: Les pectoraux du Bronze final: les découvertes récentes de la Saulsotte (Aube, France). In: Mordant, C. – Pernot, M. – Rychner, V. (eds): *L' Atelier du bronzier en Europe du XXe au VIIIe siècle avant notre ère. Actes du colloque international „Bronze 96" Neuchtel et Dijon Tom. III. Production, circulation et consommation du bronze.* Paris, Comité des travaux historiques et scientifiques, 1998,129–140.

PITTIONI 1952

Pittioni, Richard: Der Goldfund von Rothengrub (N.-Ö.) und seine wirtschaftsgeschichtliche Verankerung. *Archaeologia Austriaca* 11 (1952) 89–99.

PITTIONI 1954

Pittioni, Richard: *Urgeschichte des österreichischen Raumes.* Wien, Franz Deuticke, 1954.

PRIMAS 1971

Primas, Margarita: Der Beginn der Spätbronzezeit im Mittelland und Jura. In: Drack, W. (Red.) *Ur- und frühgeschichtliche Archäologie der Schweiz. Band III. Die Bronzezeit.* Basel, Verlag Schweizerische Gesellschaft für Ur- und Frühgeschichte, 1971, 55–70.

PRIMAS 1997

Primas, Margarita: Der frühbronzezeitliche Depotfund von Arbedo – Castione (Kanton Tessin, Schweiz). In: Becker, C. – Dunkelmann, M-L. – Metzner-Nebelsick, C. et al. (Hrsg.) Χρόνος. *Beiträge zur prähistorischen Archäologie zwischen Nord- und Südosteuropa. Festschrift für Bernhard Hänsel.* Espelkamp, Verlag Marie Leidorf GmbH, 1997, 287–296.

PRIMAS 1998

Primas, Margarita: Gesellschaft. In: Hochuli, S. – Niffeler, U. – Rychner, V. (Hrsg.) *Die Schweiz vom Paläolothikum bis zum frühen Mittelalter. III.* Basel, Verlag Schweizerische Gesellschaft für Ur- und Frühgeschichte, 1998, 337–346.

PRIMAS 2008

Primas, Margarita: *Bronzezeit zwischen Elbe und Po. Strukturwandel in Zentraleuropa 2200–800 v. Chr.* Universitätsforschungen zur Prähistorischen Archäologie, 150. Bonn, Verlag Dr. Rudolf Habelt GmbH, 2008.

PRIMAS – PERNICKA 1998

Primas, Margarita – Pernicka, Ernst: Der Depotfund von Oberwilflingen. *Germania* 76 (1998) 25–65.

PULAK 2000

Pulak, Cemal: The balance weights from the Late Bronze Age shipwreck at Uluburun. In: Pare, E. F. C. (ed.) *Metals Make the World Go Round. The Supply and Circulation of Metal in Bronze Age Europe.* Oxford, Oxbow Books, 2000, 247–266.

RAHMSTORF 2011

Rahmstorf, Lorenz: Re-integrating 'Diffusion': the Spread of Innovations among the Neolithic and Bronze Age Societies. In: Wilkinson, T. C. – Sherratt, S. – Bennet, J. (eds): *Interweaving Worlds. Systematic Interactions in Eurasia 7th to 1st Millenia BC. Papers from a conference in memory of Professor Andrew Sherratt.* Oxford, Oxbow Books, 2011, 100–119.

RAHMSTORF – PARE 2007

Rahmstorf, Lorenz – Pare, Christopher: Zu Gewichtssteinen der Späthallstatt- und Latènezeit. *Jahrbuch des Römisch-Germanischen Zentralmuseums* 54 (2007) 265–295.

REMÉNYI 2005

Reményi, László: Early Bronze Age Idol from Budapest, Kőérberek. In: *XIX. International Early Bronze Age Symp.* Levice, 2005. In Print

RUIZ-GÁLVEZ 2000

Ruiz-Gálvez, Marisa: Weight systems and exchange networks in Bronze Age Europe. In: Pare, E. F. C. (ed.) *Metals Make the World Go Round. The Supply and Circulation of Metal in Bronze Age Europe.* Oxford, Oxbow Books, 2000, 267–279.

RUTTKAY 1988/1989

Ruttkay, Elizabeth: Zwei verzierte Goldplättchen aus dem frühbronzezeitlichen Gräberfeld von Hainburg-Teichtal. *Mitteilungen der Antropologischen Gesellschaft in Wien* 118/119 (1988/1989) 135–150.

RYCHNER 1998

Rychner, Valentin: Weitere Metalle. Gold. In: Hochuli, S. – Niffeler, U. – Rychner, V. (Hrsg.) *Die Schweiz vom Paläolithikum bis zum frühen Mittelalter III.* Basel, Verlag Schweizerische Gesellschaft für Ur- und Frühgeschichte, 1998, 253–254.

RYCHNER-FARAGGI 1993

Rychner-Faraggi, Anne-Marie: *Métal et parure au Bronze final. Hauterive-Champréveyres 9.* Archéologie neuchâteloise, 17. Neuchâtel, Musée cantonal d'archéologie Nauchâtel, 1993.

SALAŠ 2005

Salaš, Milan: *Bronzové depoty středulní až doby bronzové na Moravě a ve Slezsku II.* Brno, Moravské zemské muzeum, 2005.

SCHLOSSER 2010

Schlosser, Wolfhard: Die Himmelscheibe von Nebra – Astronomische Untersuchungen. In: Meller, H. – Bertemes, F. (Hrsg.) *Der Griff nach den Sternen.* Internationales Symposium in Halle (Saale) 16.–21. Februar 2005.

Halle, Landesamt für Denkmalpflege und Archäologie Sachsen-Anhalt – Landesmuseum für Vorgeschichte Halle (Saale), 2010, 913–933.

SCHMIDTOVÁ – BAXA – PAULÍK 2002
Schmidtová, Jaroslava – Baxa, Peter – Paulík, Josef: Der Bronzehortfund aus Bratislava-Rusovce. *Anodos. Studies of the Ancient World 2*. Trnava, Fakulta humanistiky Trnavskej university v Trnave, 2002, 277–294.

SCHMOTZ 1985
Schmotz, Karl: Zum Stand der Forschung im bronzezeitlichen Gräberfeld von Deggendorf–Fischerdorf. *Archäologisches Korrespondenzblatt* 15 (1985) 313–323.

SCHUMACHER-MATTHÄUS 1985
Schumacher-Matthäus, Gisela: *Studien zu bronzezeitlichen Schmucktrachten im Karpatenbecken. Ein Beitrag zur Deutung der Hortfunde im Karpatenbecken.* Marburger Studien zur Vor- und Frühgeschichte, Band 6. Mainz am Rhein, 1985.

SOMMERFELD 1994
Sommerfeld, Christoph: *Gerätegeld Sichel.* Vorgeschichtliche Forschungen, 19. Berlin – New York, Walter de Gruyter, 1994.

SOMMERFELD 2010
Sommerfeld, Christoph: …nach Jahr und Tag – Bemerkungen über die Trundholm-Scheiben. *Praehistorische Zeitschrift* 85 (2010) 207–242.

SOMOGYI 2004
Somogyi Krisztina: A kisapostagi kultúra birituális temetője Ordacsehi–Csereföldön. Das birituelle Gräberfeld der Kisapostag-Kultur in Ordacsehi–Csereföld. In: Ilon Gábor (szerk.): *ΜΟΜΩΣ III. Őskoros kutatók III. összejövetelének konferenciakötete. Halottkultusz és temetkezés.* Szombathely–Bozsok, 2002. október 7–9. Szombathely, Vas Megyei Múzeumok Igazgatósága, 2004. 349–381.

SOROCEANU 1995
Soroceanu, Tudor: Die Fundumstände bronzezeitlicher Deponierungen – Ein Beitrag zur Hortdeutung beiderseits der Karpaten. In: Hänsel, B. – Soroceanu, T. (Hrsg.) *Bronzefunde aus Rumänien.* Prähistorische Archäologie in Südosteuropa, 10. Berlin, Wissenschaftsverlag Volker Spiess, 1995, 15–80.

SOROCEANU 2005

Soroceanu, Tudor: Zu den Fundumständen der europäischen Metallgefäβe bis in das 8. Jh. v. Chr. Ein Beitrag zu deren religionsgeschichtlicher Deutung. In: Soroceanu, T. (Hrsg.) *Bronzefunde aus Rumänien II.* Biblioteca Muzeului Bistriţa 11. Cluj-Napoca, Complexul Muzeal Bistriţa-Năsăud, 2005, 387–428.

SOROCEANU 2011

Soroceanu, Tudor: Zweigeteilte Einheit oder geeinte Zweiheit? Zur Frage der Dualität in der bronzezeitlichen Deponierungen. In: Berecki, S. – Németh, R. – Rezi. B. (eds): *Bronze Age Rites and Rituals in the Carpathian Basin.* Bibliotheca Mvsei Marisiensis Ser. Archaeologica IV. Târgu Mureş, Editura MEGA, 2011, 269–294.

SPERBER 1993

Sperber, Erik: Establishing weight systems in Bronze Age Scandinavia. *Antiquity* 87 (1993) 613–619.

SPERBER 1992

Sperber, Lothar: Bemerkungen zur sozialen Bewertung von Goldenem Trachtschmuck und Schwert in der Urnenfelderkultur. *Archäologisches Korrespondenzblatt* 22 (1992) 63–77.

SPERBER 1999

Sperber, Lothar: Zu den Schwertträgern im westlichenkreis der Urnenfelderkultur: Profane und Religiöse Aspekte. In: *Eliten in der Bronzezeit. Teil 2. Ergebnisse zweier Kolloquien in Mainz und Athen. 2.* Römisch-Germanisches Zentralmuseum Monographien, 43. Mainz, Verlag des Römisch-Germanischen Zentralmuseums – Dr. Rudolf Habelt GMBH, 1999, 605–659.

SPERBER 2000

Sperber, Lothar: Zum Grab eines spätbronzezeitlichen Metallhandwerkers von Lachen–Speyerdorf, Stadt Neustadt A. D. Weinstrasse. *Archäologisches Korrespondenzblatt* 30 (2000) 383–402.

SPERBER 2003

Sperber, Lothar: Wer trug den goldenen Hut? – Überlegungen zur gesellschaftlichen Einbindung der Goldkegel vom Typus Schifferstadt. In: Grebe, A. – Springer, T. et al. (Red.) *Gold und Kult der Bronzezeit.* Ausstellungskatalog. Nürnberg, Verlag des Germanischen Nationalmuseums, 2003, 204–219.

SPRINGER 2003

Springer, Tobias: Gold und Kult der Bronzezeit. In: Grebe, A. – Springer, T. et al. (Red.) *Gold und Kult der Bronzezeit.* Ausstellungskatalog. Nürnberg, Verlag des Germanischen Nationalmuseums, 2003, 10–25.

SPROCKHOFF – HÖCKMANN 1979

Sprockhoff, Ernst – Höckmann, Olaf: *Die gegossenen Bronzebecken der jüngeren nordischen Bronzezeit.* Kataloge Vor- und Frühgeschichtlicher Altertümer, Band 19. Mainz, Verlag des Römisch-Germanischen Zentralmuseums – Dr. Rudolf Habelt GMBH, 1979.

STEINRÜCKEN 2010

Steinrücken, Burkard: Die Dynamische Interpretation der Himmelscheibe von Nebra. In: Meller, H. – Bertemes, F. (Hrsg.) *Der Griff nach den Sternen.* Internationales Symposium in Halle (Saale) 16.–21. Februar 2005. Halle, Landesamt für Denkmalpflege und Archäologie Sachsen-Anhalt – Landesmuseum für Vorgeschichte Halle (Saale), 2010, 935–945.

SÜMEGI – BODOR 2000

Sümegi, Pál – Bodor, Elvira: Sedimentological, pollen and geoarcheological analysis of core sequence at Tököl. In: Poroszlai, I. – Vicze, M. (eds) *Százhalombatta Archaeological Expedition.* Budapest, Archaeolingua, 2000, 83–96.

SZABÓ 1995

Szabó Géza: Adatok a késő bronzkori pénzforgalom kérdéséhez. In: Újváry Z. (szerk.): *Tanulmányok és Közlemények.* Debrecen – Szolnok, Etnica, 1995, 49–56.

SZABÓ 1996

Szabó, Géza: The manufacture and usage of Late Bronze Age rings: two new ring hoards. In: Kovács, T. (Hrsg.) *Studien zur Metallindustrie im Karpatenbecken und den benachbarten Regionen. Festschrift für Amália Mozsolics zum 85. Geburtstag.* Budapest, Magyar Nemzeti Múzeum, 1996, 207–230.

SZABÓ 1998

Szabó, Géza: Evaluation of late Bronze Age Carpathian tinbronzes based on the alloying content. In: Költő, L. –Bartosiewicz, L. (eds) *Archaeometrical Research in Hungary II.* Budapest – Kaposvár – Veszprém, Hungarian National Museum – Dir. of Somogy Museums – Archaeocomp Ass. and the

Working Group of Industrial Archaeology and Archaeometry of the Veszprém Reg. Comm. of the HAS, 1998, 159–173.

SZABÓ 2012
Szabó Géza: A Kárpát-medencei archaeometallurgiai kutatások eredményei, aktuális kérdései a 21. század elején, különös tekintettel a bronz- és vasgyártás társadalmi hátterének változásaira. Recent advances and new questions of archaeometallurgical research in the Carpathian basin at the social backgroung of bronze and iron artefacts. *Archeometriai Műhely* IX:2 (2012) 75–96.

SZABÓ 2013a
Szabó, Géza: What Archaeometallurgy Tells Us about the Changes of Bronze Craftwork in the Carpathian Basin at the Transition of the Bronze Age into Iron Age. In: Rezi B. – Németh R. – Berecki S. (eds): *Bronze Age Crafts and Craftsmen in the Carpathian Basin.* Proceedings of the International Colloquium from Târgu Mureş 5–7 October 2012. Bibliotheca Mvsei Marisiensis Ser. Archaeologica VI. Târgu Mureş, Editura MEGA, 2013, 291–312.

SZABÓ 2013b
Szabó Géza: *A dunántúli urnamezős kultúra fémművessége az archeometallurgiai vizsgálatok tükrében.* The metallurgy of the Transdanubian Urnfield Culture in light of archaeometallurgical investigations. Pécs, Pécsi Tudományegyetem BTK Történettudományi Intézete Ókortörténeti Tanszék, 2013.

TERŽAN 2004
Teržan, Biba: 'Obolos – mediterrane Vorbilder einer prämonetären "Währung" der Hallstattzeit?" In: Hänsel, B. (ed): *Parerga Praehistorica. Jubilaumsschrift zur Prähistorischen Archaologie – 15 Jahre UPA.* Universitätsforschungen zur Prähistorischen Archäologie, 100. Bonn, Verlag Dr. Rudolf Habelt GmbH, 2004. 161–202.

TERŽAN 2005
Teržan, Biba: Metamorphose – eine Vegetationsgottheit in der Spätbronzezeit. In: Horejs, B. – Jung, R. – Kaiser, E. – Teržan, B. (Hrsg.) *Interpretationsraum Bronzezeit. Bernhard Hänsel von seinem Schülern gewidmet.* Universitätsforschungen zur Prähistorischen Archäologie, 121. Bonn, Verlag Dr. Rudolf Habelt GmbH, 2005, 241–261.

THEOPHILUS 1986

Theophilus Presbyter: *A különféle művességekről*. Budapest, Műszaki kiadó, 1986.

THEVENOT 1991

Thevenot, Jean-Paul: *L' Âge du bronze en Bourgogne. Le dèpôt de Blanot (Côte-d' Or).* 11ème Supplément à la Revue archaeologique de l'Est. Dijon, Ministère de la Cultura et de la Communication et de la Ville de Dijon, 1991.

THEVENOT 1998

Thevenot, Jean-Paul: Un outillage de bronzier: le dépôt de la Petite Laugère, Génelard (Saône-et-Loire, France). In: Mordant, C. – Pernot, M. – Rychner, V. (eds): *L' Atelier du bronzier en Europe du XXe au VIIIe siècle avant notre ère. Actes du colloque international „Bronze 96" Neuchtel et Dijon Tom. II. Du minerai au métal, du métal à l' objet.* Paris, Comité des travaux historiques et scientifiques, 1998, 123–144.

TOMEDI 1998

Tomedi, Gerhard: Eine vorgeschichtliche Wanderung im Raum Wörgl. In: Zangerl, J. (Hrsg.) *Wörgl, ein Heimatbuch.* Wörgl, Edition Josef Zangerl, 1998, 39–52.

TOMEDI 2005

Tomedi, Gerhard: Grenzen der Kunst. In: Grabherr, G. – Kainrath, B. – Larcher, A. – Welte, W. (Hrsg.) *VIS IMAGINVM. Festschrift für Elisabeth Walde zum 65. Geburtstag.* Innsbruck, Institut für Klassische und Provinzialrömische Archäologie Universität Innsbruck, 2005, 518–526.

TOMPA 1928

Tompa Ferenc: Újabb szerzemények a Nemzeti Múzeum őskori gyűjteményében. II. A felsőzsidi lelet. Der Fund von Várvölgy. *Archaeologiai Értesítő* 42 (1928) 204–207.

TOMPA 1934–35

Tompa, Ferenc: 25 Jahre Urgeschichtsforschung in Ungarn 1912–1936. *Bericht der Römisch-Germanischen Kommission* 24–25 (1934–35) 27–127.

TOMPA 1937

Tompa Ferenc: Adatok az őskori aranykereskedelemhez. *Archaeologiai Értesítő* 40 (1937) 49–56.

TOMPA 1943

Tompa Ferenc: Báró Miske Kálmán. *Dunántúli Szemle* X:7–8 (1943) 257–261.

TOPÁL 1973

Topál Judit: Bronzkori lemezdiadém Ócsáról. Bronze age plate diadem from Ócsa. *Studia Comitatensia* 2 (1973) 3–11.

TÓTH 2009

Tóth Kálmán: A szombathelyi kultúrpalota építéstörténete (1900–1910). History of the construction of Szombathely palace of culture (1900–1910). *Savaria, A Vas Megyei Múzeumok Értesítője* 32:2 (2009) 15–35.

TURK 2012a

Turk, Peter: Die Horte der Bronzezeit und ihre Fundplätze im „Kreuzungsbereich der Welten". In: Hansen, S. – Neumann, D. – Vachta, T. (Hrsg.) *Hort und Raum. Aktuelle Forschungen zu bronzezetlichen Deponierungen in Mitteleuropa.* Topoi. Berlin Studies of the Ancient World. Berlin – Boston, De Gruyter, 2012, 209–226.

TURK 2012b

Turk, Peter: Drugi poznobronastodobni depo z Bleda. Second Late Bronze Age hoard from Bled. In: *Potopljena preteklost: arheologija vodnih okolij in raziskovanje podvodne kulturne dediščine v Sloveniji: zbornik ob 128-letnici Dežmanovih raziskav Ljubljanice na Vrhniki (1884–2012.)* Didakta d.o.o. Radovljica, 2012, 305–308.

UENZE 1993

Uenze, Hans Peter: Die Schlange, ein Kultsymbol der Urnenfelder und Hallstattzeit. *Acta Praehistorica et Archaeologica* 25 (1993) 132–136.

UZSOKI 1984

Uzsoki András: Aranymosási módszerek és aranykinyerő eljárások. Methods of Gold Washing and Extraction. In: Gömöri J. (ed.) *Iparrégészeti és archaeometriai kutatások Magyarországon II. Research in Industrial Archaeology and Archaeometry in Hungary II.* Veszprém, MTA veszprémi Akadémiai Bizottsága, 1984, 73–81.

UZSOKI 1985.

Uzsoki, András: Gold Panning in the Carpathian Basin. In: *Neogene mineral resources in the Carpathian Basin. Historical studies on their utilization.* VIIIth RCMNS Congress – Hungary. Budapest, Hungarian Geological Survey, 1985. 285–303.

UZSOKI 2004

Uzsoki András: Adalékok az aranymosás történetéhez és technikájához. *Érc- és Ásványbányászati Múzeumi Füzetek* 31. Rudabánya, Érc- és Ásványbányászati Múzeum, 2004.

VÁGUSZ 2010

Vágusz Anina: Magyarcsesztvei báró Miske Kálmán (1860–1943) élete és tudományos tevékenysége. Das Leben und die wissenschaftliche Tätigkeit des Barons Kálmán Miske von Magyarcsesztve (1860–1943). *Savaria, A Vas Megyei Múzeumok Értesítője* 33 (2010) 57–67.

VARGYAS 2010

Vargyas Péter: A pénzhasználat és az árak speciális problémái a Kr. e. 2. és 1. évezredben Asszíriában és Babilóniában. In: Csabai Z. (szerk.): *A pénz története Babilóniában a pénzverés előtt és után.* Pécs – Budapest, Pécsi Egyetem Ókortörténeti Tanszéke – L' Harmattan, 2010, 191–215.

VERGER 1998

Verger, Stéphane: Les trois âges de la dame de Blanot. In: Mordant, C. – Pernot, M. – Rychner, V. (eds): *L' Atelier du bronzier en Europe du XXe au VIIIe siècle avant notre ère. Actes du colloque international „Bronze 96" Neuchtel et Dijon Tom. III. Production, circulation et consommation du bronze.* Paris, Comité des travaux historiques et scientifiques, 1998, 33–39.

VERGER – DUMONT – MOYAT – MILLE 2007

Verger, Stéphane – Dumont, Annie – Moyat, Philippe – Mille, Banoît: Le dépôt de bronzes du site fluvial de la Motte à Agde (Hérault). *Jahrbuch des Römisch-Germanischen Zentralmuseums* 54 (2007) 85–171.

VINSKI-GASPARINI 1973

Vinski-Gasparini, Ksenija: *Kultúra polja sa žarama u sjevernoj Hrvatskoj. I-II.* Zadar, 1973.

VISY 2003

Visy, Zsolt (editor-in-chief): *Hungarian Archaeology at the Turn of the Millennium.* Budapest, 2003.

VLADÁR 1973

Vladár, Jozef: Osteuropäische und mediterrane Einflüsse im Gebiet der Slowakei während der Bronzezeit. *Slovenská Archaeológia* 21 (1973) 253–357.

VOSS 1986

Voß, Eberhard: Restauratorische Untersuchungsmethoden und Rekonstruktionsmöglichkeiten am Beispiel urnenfelderzeitlichen Kopfschmucks. *Archäologisches Korrespondenzblatt* 16 (1986) 49–56.

WANZEK 1992

Wanzek, Burger: Der älterurnenfelderzeitliche Hortfund von Lengyeltóti („Lengyeltóti II"), Komitat Somogy, Ungarn. Eine Vorlage. *Acta Praehistorica et Archaeologica* 24 (1992) 249–288.

WELS-WEYRAUCHT 1991

Wels-Weyraucht, Ulrike: *Die Anhänger in Südbayern.* Prähistorische Bronzefunde XI, 5. Stuttgart, Franz Steiner Verlag, 1991.

WELS-WEYRAUCHT 1995

Wels-Weyrauch, Ulrike: Zu dem Gehänge von Aislingen. In: *Festschrift für Hermann Müller-Karpe zum 70. Geburtstag*. Bonn, Dr. Rudolf Habelt GMBH, 1995, 117–130.

WELS-WEYRAUCHT 2008

Wels-Weyrauch, Ulrike: Stachelscheiben-Colliers: Nur zur Zierde? In: Verse, F. – Knoche, B. et al. (Hrsg.) *Durch die Zeiten... Festschrift für Albrecht Jockenhövel zum 65. Geburtstag.* Studia honoraria, 28. Rahden (Westf.), Verlag Marie Leidorf, 2008, 275–289.

WELS-WEYRAUCHT 2011

Wels-Weyrauch, Ulrike: Colliers – Nur zur Zierde? In: Dietz, U. E – Jockenhövel, A. (Hrsg.) *Bronzen im Spannungsfeld zwischen Nutzung und symbolischer Bedeutung. Beiträge zum internationalen Kolloquium am 9. und 10. Oktober 2008 in Münster.* Prähistorische Bronzefunde XX, 13. Stuttgart, Franz Steiner Verlag, 2011, 259–278.

WIRTH 1999

Wirth, Stefan: Auf der Suche nach Eliten der späten Bronzezeit und der Urnenfelderzeit. In: *Eliten in der Bronzezeit. Teil 2. Ergebnisse zweier Kolloquien in Mainz und Athen. 2.* Römisch-Germanisches Zentralmuseum Monographien, 43. Mainz, Verlag des Römisch-Germanischen Zentralmuseums – Dr. Rudolf Habelt GMBH, 1999, 565–604.

WYSS 1971

Wyss, René: Technik, Wirtschaft und Handel. In: Drack, W. (Red.) *Ur- und frühgeschichtliche Archäologie der Schweiz. III. Bronzezeit.* Basel, Verlag Schweizerische Gesellschaft für Ur- und Frühgeschichte, 1971, 123–144.

ZEITLER 2000

Zeitler, P. John: Handel und Austausch in der Bronzezeit Süddeutschlands. In: Mühldorfer, B. – Zeitler, P. J. (Hrsg.) *Mykene – Nürnberg – Stonehenge. Handel und Austausch in der Bronzezeit. Begleitbuch zur Ausstellung.* Nürnberg, Naturhistorische Gesellschaft Nürnberg e. V., 2000, 75–93.

ZOFFMANN 2004

Zoffmann Zsuzsanna: A bronzkori kisapostagi kultúra embertani leletei Ordacsehi–Csereföldön. Die antropologischen Funde der Kisapostag-Kultur aus dem Fundort Ordacsehi–Csereföld. In: Ilon G. (szerk.): *ΜΟΜΩΣ III. Őskoros kutatók III. összejövetelének konferenciakötete. Halottkultusz és temetkezés*. Szombathely–Bozsok, 2002. október 7–9. Szombathely, Vas Megyei Múzeumok Igazgatósága, 2004, 383–389.

ZSIDI 2005

Zsidi Paula (szerk.): *Kincsek a város alatt. Tresaures under the city. Survey of the archaeological heritage of Budapest, 1989–2004.* Budapest, temporary exhibition at the Budapest History Museum 27 May – 20 August 2005. Budapest, Archaeolingua, 2005.

Appendix

1. Ferenc Tompa's letterheaded, typewritten letter to Kálmán Miske on the international archaeological conference

A letter among the uninventoried records of the Department of History of the Savaria Museum, originally filed under no. 70/1929.

Tompa informs Miske of the provisions made for the guests in Szombathely and the change in the date of the conference. Tompa addresses Miske as Uncle Kálmán. The guests would be arriving from Sopron on September 4 and the archaeological field trip to Velem was to be on September 5.

Hungarian National Museum
Department of Archaeology
Archaeologische Abteilung

Dear Uncle Kálmán,

I hastily reply to your dear letter. I am pleased to inform you that the dinner and the accommodations have been managed quite well, with a few more notable guests perhaps being lodged elsewhere too (at the Premonstratensians, prebends). Tóni* can assist you in this. There has been a change in the programme, and one quite favourable for us: on September 4, we will come straight to Szombathely from Sopron, arriving at 14:44. We will make a tour of the museum and the city, with dinner at 20 h, organised courtesy of the town. On September 5, we will take the train to Kőszeg, either at 7:55 or 10:30, as seems best to you. A city tour (perhaps with a short programme), lunch, and excursion to Velemszentvid by either car or bus. Return to Kőszeg to catch the 20:20 train to Szombathely again. [Tompa then requests Miske's assistance on certain matters, for instance, breakfast in Kőszeg, and bus rental for the journey between Kőszeg and Velem. He sent the invitation appended to his letter, and asked Miske to join the conference in Sopron, if he was unable to do so in Vienna. At the same time, he promised that he would forward the list of conference participants on time.]

Hand-kisses to her ladyship, and my own and Lajos Márton's most cordial greetings to you.

Budapest, August 5, 1929.

Your loving lad,

Feri

* Dr. Ágoston Pável, Keeper of the Department of Ethnography of the Museum of Vas County, was Miske's deputy at the time.

2. Ferenc Tompa's letterheaded, typewritten letter to Kálmán Miske regarding funding for the planned conference

A letter among the uninventoried records of the Department of History of the Savaria Museum, originally filed under no. 74/1929.

Miske is requested to petition the Ministry that would be willing to provide 200 *pengő* for an archaeological investigation and 100 *pengő* for refreshments.

Hungarian National Museum
Department of Archaeology
Archaeologische Abteilung

My dear Uncle Kálmán,
I have finally managed to speak with Aladár Haász. The Ministry is willing to grant 200 pengő for the archaeological investigation and 100 pengő for afternoon refreshments. For this reason, I beg you to immediately petition the Ministry. It should be very brief. It should only note that a group of German, Austrian and Hungarian archaeologists will be visiting the prehistoric settlement in Velemszentvid on the occasion of their conference held in September and that the museum would like to conduct an archaeological excavation beforehand and therefore requests funding of 200 Hungarian pengő. The museum would also like to provide refreshments for the excursion's participants, for which it requests funding of 100 Hungarian pengő. The petition should be addressed to the Minister. If the funds are not received in time, the Cultural Society will advance it to you because the requested funds will quite certainly be granted.
Hand-kisses to her ladyship and with loving greetings to you.
Budapest, August 16, 1929.
Your lad,
Feri
NB. You should write a formal petition, not an ordinary letter!

3. Kálmán Miske's letter with a list of the conference's participants

A letter among the uninventoried records of the Department of History of the Savaria Museum, originally filed under no. 75/1929.

The letter is addressed to an unknown person with regard to the guests' accommodation.

My Dear Friend,
Feri has become a reliable lad and has sent the list of participants to me and Ujváry too. Of these attendees, the big-shots are as follows:
Dr. Seger,[**] Breslau
Dr. Bersu, Frankfurt a/M.

Dr. Berens, Mainz
Dr. Beltz, Schwerin
Dr. Menghin, Wien
Dr. Láng, Debrecen
Dr. Alföldy, Debrecen
Dr. Lajos Márton, Bpest
The above eight notabilities should be lodged in private residences. Of them, if possible, Seger as the Chairman, should be accommodated at [indecipherable word]. Or even Menghin or ad libitum Márton or Alföldy could be lodged there.
Thirty-two [participants] have been registered.
In order to avoid any hitches in Kőszeg, in my letter, which I will send to Jambrics,[***] I will include an additional foreigner and myself as the thirty-fourth participant, and should you want to come along, you should specify yourself as the thirty-fifth guest.
Until we see each other
Kind regards,
Kőszeg, August 22, 1929 Your Uncle Kálmán
It would do no harm, if it can be managed without too many complications, to lodge
Dr. Schultz, Halle
Dr. Fremersdorf, Cologne
Dr. Franz, Wien
and perhaps Aggházy as lesser big-shots in private residences too.

[**] Hans Seger (1864–1943): From 1892, he was director of the Museum of Breslau, and from 1907, a professor at the local university. His book, *Schlesische Funde der vorrömischen Eisenzeit. Aus Schlesiens Vorzeit in Bild und Wort* (Bd. VI) was quoted by Miske in his monograph. Gerhard Bersu (1889–1964): In 1928, together with Tompa, he excavated the ramparts in Lengyel. From 1929, he was director of the Römisch-Germanische Kommission (RGK), and from 1935, the principal director of the same institution. From 1937, he relocated to England because of his Jewish origins. From 1950, he was director of the RGK again. Robert Beltz (1854–1942): He was the head of department at the Landesmuseum of Schwerin between 1910 and 1930; he published major studies on the typology of brooches from the Bronze Age, the Hallstatt period and the Celtic Age found in Germany (1911, 1913). His book, *Die Gräbefelder der älteren Eisenzeit in Mecklenburg* (Jahrbuch des Vereins für Mecklenburgische Geschichte. 1906), was quoted by Miske in his monograph. Oswald Menghin (1888–1973): In 1918, he was professor at the Department of Prehistory at the University of Vienna, and later rector of the university. He was a guest lecturer at the University of Cairo in the winter semesters between 1930 and 1933. He was a professor at several South American universities after World War 2.

[***] Mayor of Kőszeg.

4. Miske's hand-written letter to Ferenc Tompa about the treasure

Academician András Mócsy gave this letter to Mária Fekete, in whose possession it is today.

Miske urges Tompa to lobby at the Ministry for the payment of the compensation as stipulated by law, as soon as possible, to the owner of the land where the treasure trove was discovered. The amount of compensation should be fair, in order to avoid illegal treasure hunting and looting generated by the greed of the landowners. At the same time, Miske requests funding for himself as well.

I would be very, very much obliged if you were so kind as to urge the Ministry to pay the funding requested for the excavation on the St. Vid Hill of Velem and if it could ensure, pursuant to Act XI, that a certain amount of compensation be paid to the landowner for the # treasure discovered in Velem. But I beg you to advise them not to pay more than one-third of the value of the # treasure known to you because if the landowner is paid more, we can bid adieu to the other fascinating finds in Velem, because unless we have a gendarme ordered to guard the site, he and his companions will uproot the entire place. Therefore, I believe that the maximum compensation should not exceed 30–35 Pengő.

Also, if you were so kind as to urge the Ministry to grant me some funding to remedy my financial misery quickly, I would be very, and I mean very much, grateful to you. Please do not forget to show my letter to the His Excellency Bálint Hóman, or refer to it, because it reports on preventive actions that might be of interest to both the National Museum and the National Board.

Hand-kisses to your Dear Wife and kisses to your little daughters.

Embracing you in his thoughts, your old loving

Kőszeg, October 3, 1929

Uncle Kálmán

5. Amália Mozsolics's letter to Ferenc Tompa

Academician András Mócsy gave this letter to Mária Fekete, in whose possession it is today.

Mozsolics requests information about the findspot of the treasure. Tompa politely advises her to turn to Miske.

Museum of Vas County
Collection of Coins and Antiquities
35/1941

To His Honour
Dr. Ferenc Tompa
retired university professor

Dear Sir Professor,
I am keen to publish the treasure discovered in Velem, but have not managed to acquire accurate information about the find circumstances. Baron Miske claims that he had sent an excavation report at that time to the Public Collections, but I assume that it was actually sent to the museum because its department was in charge of excavations. I have already asked Nelly to find the relevant documents, but she only found a single file, according to which Sir Professor had determined the excavation costs.
This archaeological excavation took place in 1929, before the archaeological conference.
I hereby kindly request, Sir Professor, to tell me about what else was discovered at the time and I would be also curious to learn about the find circumstances.
[The rest of the letter is concerned with offprints and specialist books.]
The grateful admirer of Sir Professor, with the greatest respect
Szombathely, April 23, 1941
Amália Mozsolics

A handwritten remark by Ferenc Tompa on the margin of Amália Mozsolics's typewritten letter, obviously for his secretary, on how to respond:
"I know nothing about this report. As far as I can remember, there was an embossed golden belt and a ball of golden wires. Only Miske can provide further information. Thank you for the offprints."

6. Amália Mozsolics's typewritten letter to Ágoston Pável
A letter among the uninventoried records of the Department of History of the Savaria Museum, originally filed under no. 1944/13.
The manuscript of the book describing the golden treasure, funded by the Hungarian National Museum, has been completed. It would be unwise for the golden treasure to be mentioned in Jenő Lázár's planned publication because she (Mozsolics) would find herself in a very embarrassing situation.

Dear Sir Professor,
Jenő Lázár has recently sent me a letter inquiring about the golden treasure discovered in Velem. I provided the relevant information, but I would not like to see him publish it before my book comes out because, as I have already mentioned, my book will be published by the National Museum, and the entire

book was written because of this treasure. [...] it would be very embarrassing for me towards the National Museum if Lázár's book came out earlier with the first publication of the treasure. [...] the National Museum has provided substantial funding, reimbursed my travel costs, the expenses of the conservation and restoration procedure, and the photographs, etc., and the publishing costs of the book add up to a considerable amount too, as will its translation, and so I would insist on this point.

I would like to see the book already published, but I was sick so often, and I had so many other troubles that I was unable to work as I would have liked. Moreover, I have several new plans – only heaven knows whether they can be realised. I have little hope of anything.

With many cordial regards to Sir Professor
February 21, 1944
Amália Mozsolics

List of Figures

Fig. 1. A: Location of Velem in Hungary, B: The archaeological sites in Velem on a 1:10,000 topographical map, showing the findspot of the diadem (made by István Eke)

Fig. 2. Bronze Age sites in the Velem area and the palaeoenvironmental sampling locations on the administrative boundary between Velem and Dozmat (made by István Eke, based on JAKAB *et al.* 2007, complemented with new information from the author)

Legend: ● settlement; ▲ cemetery, burial site; hoards; □ Kalapos-kő of Bozsok; ★ Palaeoenvironmental sampling location (on the administrative boundary between Dozmat and Velem); diadem

Abbreviations of archaeological periods and cultures: B = Bronze Age (unspecified); FB = Early Bronze Age; MB = Middle Bronze Age; SB = Late Bronze Age; HK = Tumulus culture; UK = Urnfield culture; FE = Early Iron Age

1. Bozsok–Kalapos-kő:[636] religious-ritual-ceremonial site, Late Bronze Age/Early Iron Age; 2. Bucsu–Szabad erdő: Early Bronze Age settlement and Urnfield cemetery (2003–2004, author's excavation, unpublished); 3. Dozmat–Csompatka dűlő:[637] Late Bronze Age settlement; 4. Dozmat–nyugati nagy Völgy-dűlő:[638] Late Bronze Age settlement traces; 5. Torony–Másfeles földek:[639] settlement of the Makó culture with a stone axe manufacturing workshop and Vučedol finds; 6. Torony–Nemesszer-dűlő: Early or Middle Bronze Age settlement traces and burial (2004, author's excavation, unpublished); 7. Northern side of Torony–Malom-patak: Bronze Age settlement traces (1984, field survey); 8. Sé–Malomoldal:[640] late Vučedol and Early Somogyvár–Vinkovci settlement traces; 9. Sé area:[641] Early Bronze Age fragments collected by an unknown collector, west-southwest of the settlement:

---

[636] ILON 2002c.

[637] ILON – RASZTOVICS 2000, 153.

[638] ILON – RASZTOVICS 2000, 154.

[639] KÁROLYI 2004, Fig. 55, 142–143 and Fig. 38.

[640] ILON – RASZTOVICS 2000, 157–158; KÁROLYI 2004, 142.

[641] KULCSÁR 1999, 125.

partly late Vučedol and partly Somogyvár–Vinkovci finds; 10. Kőszeg–Ördögasztala/Ördögtányér:[642] bronze hoard from the Urnfield period; 11. Lukácsháza–keleti Kertalja-dűlő: Bronze Age settlement traces (1998, field survey); 12. Kőszeg–Kőszegfalvi-rétek I:[643] Middle Bronze Age and Urnfield settlements; 13. Lukácsháza–Csömötei-hegy/Kisrókás-dűlő: Late Bronze Age settlement traces (1998–1999, 2002, 2004, field survey); 14. Lukácsháza–Pap-földek: Late Bronze Age settlement traces (2002–2003, field survey); 15. Kőszegdoroszló–Delece: Bronze Age settlement traces (1974, 2000, 2003, field survey); 16. Kőszegdoroszló–Berekalja I: Bronze Age settlement traces (unknown date, field survey); 17. Kőszegdoroszló–Kisrét dűlő: Late Bronze Age settlement traces (1970, field survey); 18. Kőszegszerdahely–Belső-Vidráb: Late Bronze Age settlement traces (2002, field survey); 19. Gyögyösfalu–Hegyalja dűlő: Late Bronze Age settlement traces (2002–2003, field survey); 20. Gyöngyösfalu–Pöse, Gátmellék: Late Bronze Age stray finds (2002, field survey); 21. Perenye–Zsellérföld: Late (?) Bronze Age settlement traces (1971, 2004, field survey); 22. Perenye–kaszálórét I: Late (?) Bronze Age settlement traces (2002, field survey); 23. Gencsapáti–Besenyő-sziget: Early Bronze Age settlement (2004, author's excavation, unpublished); 24. Gencsapáti–Urasági táblák I: Late Bronze Age settlement traces (1998, field survey); 25. Gencsapáti–Kápolnadomb: Late Bronze Age settlement traces (1999, field survey); 26. Gencsapáti–Hosszú-rész mellett: Late Bronze Age settlement traces (unknown date, field survey); 27. Gencsapáti, outskirts of:[644] grip-tongue sword (*Griffzungenschwert*) from a hoard (?) of the Urnfield period; 28. Szombathely–Kőszeri-dűlő:[645] Urnfield period settlement; 29. Szombathely–Olad-Reiszig-erdő alatti dűlő:[646] stray Middle Bronze Age arrowhead, Urnfield settlement; 30. Szombathely–Oladi plató: Late Bronze Age settlement traces (1984, field survey); 31. Szombathely–Alsómező-dűlő:[647] Tumulus settlement traces (2000, Csilla Farkas's excavation); 32. Szombathely–

[642] Nováki 1966.
[643] Ilon 2010, 39.
[644] Károlyi 2004, Fig. 154, 209.
[645] Ilon 2004, 65–68.
[646] Ilon 2004, 46–47, 68.
[647] Ilon 2004, 50.

Kámon, Távhő:[648] Tumulus settlement with Litzen pottery, Urnfield settlement; 33. Szombathely–Senyefa, 129 Szent Imre herceg út:[649] Makó settlement; 34. Szombathely–Újperinti kavicsbánya:[650] Makó settlement; 35. Szombathely–Metró dept. store, Minerva apartments and Motel:[651] Early Bronze Age settlement; 36. Szombathely–Jáki út cemetery:[652] bronze hoard of the Urnfield period; 37. Szombathely–44 Táncsics Mihály utca:[653] Urnfield cemetery; 38. Szombathely–Zanat:[654] Urnfield cemetery and settlement

Fig. 3. The findspot of Hoard Ia-b of bronze artefacts (triangle) and of the golden treasure (encircled) discovered in 1896 shown on the 1857 cadastral map of St. Vid Hill and the Szentkút Spring (arrow sign) (made by Magdolna Mátyus, after CZAJLIK 1993, Fig. 1, complemented with new information from the author)

Fig. 4. The findspot of Hoard Ia-b of bronze artefacts (triangle) and of the golden treasure (encircled) discovered in 1896 shown on the contour map of the hill. The Szentkút Spring is marked by an arrow (made by Magdolna Mátyus, based on Karácsony Eőry's survey, after Balázs Holl, Zoltán Czajlik, Ádám Marton, and CZAJLIK 1993. Fig. 2, complemented with new information from the author)

Fig. 5. One of the archaeological sites in Velem excavated by Kálmán Miske (photographer and date of photograph unknown)

Fig. 6. 1. Kálmán Miske; 2. Ferenc Tompa; 3. Amália Mozsolics; 4. Gábor Bándi

Fig. 7. The first page of Miske's letter written at the end of 1929 (with the section on the visit of the foreign archaeologists highlighted)

Fig. 8. Page 3 of Miske's letter (with the section on the location of the trial trench highlighted)

Fig. 9. Page 6 of Miske's letter (with the section on the golden treasure found underneath the upright slab of stone highlighted)

---

648 ILON 2004, 48–50; KÁROLYI 2004, 150–151 and Figs 141–142.

649 ILON – RASZTOVICS 2000, 168.

650 KÁROLYI 2004, 142 and Fig. 126.

651 ILON 2004, 45.

652 ILON 2002b.

653 NAGY 2011, Fig. 28.

654 ILON – SÜMEGI – TÓTH *et al.* 2011.

Fig. 10. 1. The Szent Vid Hill; 2. The chapel; 3. The Szentkút Spring with the ruins of the scout camp; 4. Tourist path to the spring; 5. Terrace with the pit above the spring; 6. Szilveszter Katona standing on the assumed findspot of the treasure (author's photographs, 2012–2013)

Fig. 11. 1.a-b. Entry on the gold artefacts found in Velem in the inventory book dated March 27, 1941. The diadem is described as a belt. 2. Receipt of the golden treasure returned in August 1943, after conservation and restoration

Fig. 12. The condition of the diadem in 1943 (after MOZSOLICS 1950, Taf. 1) and a drawing made prior to its restoration (Csaba E. Kiss, 2004)

Fig. 13. The first page of the inventory of precious metal artefacts of the Museum of Vas County drawn up in 1944 (with Item 1 of Section 7 describing the diadem "mounted onto a circular base", i.e. onto a copper plate, highlighted)

Fig. 14. The diadem before its conservation and restoration (photo by Gábor Papp, 2002)

Fig. 15. The diadem's copper plate made by István Méri (1943) and details of the diadem during its restoration (photo by Katalin T. Bruder, 2004)

Fig. 16. Details of the diadem: perforations and traces of stamping (photo by Tibor Takács, 2013)

Fig. 17. Domed roundels (Pair I) in 1943–44 and their drawing (after MOZSOLICS 1950, Taf. 2. 1–2, and Csaba E. Kiss's drawing, 2004)

Fig. 18. Domed roundels (Pair I) before and after restoration (photos by Katalin T. Bruder, 2004; Tamás Tárczy, 2008; Tibor Takács, 2013)

Fig. 19. Domed roundels (Pair II) in 1943–44 and their drawing (after MOZSOLICS 1950, Taf. 2. 3–4, and Csaba E. Kiss's drawing, 2004)

Fig. 20. Domed roundels (Pair II) before and after restoration (photos by Katalin T. Bruder, 2004; Tibor Takács, 2013)

Fig. 21. 1–2. Gold tangle of the pectoral (?) and its fragments in 1943–44; 3–5. after the new conservation and restoration, some with bronze wire in them (after MOZSOLICS 1950, Taf. 3. 1, Abb. 5; photos 3, 5 by Tamás Tárczy, 2008; 4 by Tibor Takács, 2013)

Fig. 22. Fragments of the pectoral (wires) after the new conservation and restoration (photo by Tamás Tárczy, 2008)

Fig. 23. Bronze backplates and their drawings before and after restoration (photos by Katalin T. Bruder, 2004; Tibor Takács, 2013; drawing by Csaba E. Kiss, 2004)

Fig. 24. The diadem and the domed roundels of the golden treasure (photo by Tamás Tárczy, 2008)

Fig. 25. The results of the metal analysis of the diadem (sample code: V5, VD)

Fig. 26. The results of the metal analysis of the domed roundels (Pair I, sample codes: V1 and V4)

Fig. 27. The results of the metal analysis of the domed roundels (Pair II, sample codes: V2 and V3)

Fig. 28. 1–2. The results of the metal analysis of the gold spirals (sample codes: Vel4 and Vel5)

Fig. 29. 1. The results of the metal analysis of the gold spiral (sample code: Vel6); 2. The results of the metal analysis of the bronze backplate of the diadem (sample code: Vel1)

Fig. 30. 1–2. The results of the metal analysis of the bronze backplates of the domed roundels 1 and 3 (sample codes: Vel2 and Vel3a)

Fig. 31. Metalworking tools. Punches: 1. Génelard (after THEVENOT 1998, Fig. 5. 11–13); 2. Murnau (after GOLD UND KULT 2003, Kat. Nr. 7a); Punch with cable motif: 3. Murnau (after GOLD UND KULT 2003, Kat. Nr. 7b); Anvil: 4. Jevičko (after SALAŠ 2005, II: Tab. 179. 30); Anvils for drawing wire: 5. Keranfinit, 6. Bardouville, 7. Fresné-la-Mère (after THEVENOT 1998, Fig. 9. 3–5), 8. Venarey-les-Laumes (NICOLARDOT–VERGER 1998, Fig. 11. 10). The drawings are not to the same scale (drawing by Magdolna Mátyus)

Fig. 32. Goldsmithing and smithing tools as well as golden sheet objects ("crowns", vessels mounts, jewellery) of the Late Bronze Age from Central Europe (after KOSSACK 1995, Abb. 1; LEHRBERGER 1995, Fig. 1; ARMBRUSTER 2012, Abb. 1; GERLOFF 2003, Abb. 7; SPERBER 2003, Abb. 2, complemented by the author; made by Tibor Takács)

Findspots of goldsmithing and smithing tools, according to countries:

Stamps/punches

France: 2. Arbois–Grotte des Planches; 5. Génelard, Saône-et-Loire; 8. Larnaud, hoard

Switzerland: 15. Hauterive-Champréveyres
Germany: 23. Marnau (Bavaria); 24. Nürnberg–Mögeldorf (Bavaria); 25. unprovenanced, in the Nürnberg Museum; 29. Stockheim (Bavaria)
Czech Republic: 41. Přestavlký
Hungary: 89. Velem–Szent Vid (?)

Goldsmithing tools (hammers and anvils)
France: 1. Alise-Sainte-Reine, Côte d' Or:[655] anvil (horned, cross-shaped); 2. Arbois–Grotte des Planches cave:[656] bone stamp/punch; 3. Bardouville, Seine-Maritime:[657] anvil, also suitable for drawing wire (cf. *Fig. 31. 6*); 4. Fresné-la-Mère Calvados, hoard (Ha B1):[658] anvil resembling the previous one (cf. *Fig. 31. 7*), found together with gold objects; 5. Génelard, Saône-et-Loire, hoard (Ha A1, 13th–12th centuries BC):[659] anvil (horned, cross-shaped, with three work surfaces), four socketed hammers (one with a domed face), five chisels (graver) with one or two faces, bronze sheet with hooked end, five punches/stamps, polishing stone, bronze mould, bronze nugget, three bronze tuyères, clay funnel; 6. Gray, Haute-Saône:[660] anvil (horned, cross-shaped); 7. Keranfinit, hoard:[661] anvil, suitable for drawing wire (cf. *Fig. 31, 5*); 8. Larnaud, hoard:[662] bronze punch/stamp; 9. unprovenanced, in the Museum of Lyon:[663] anvil (horned, cross-shaped); 10. Porcieu–Amblagnieu, hoard (close of the Middle Bronze Age):[664] anvil (horned, rectangular work surface), socketed hammer, punch and other small tools, whetstone; 11. Trégorf-en-Surzur, Morbihan, hoard:[665] anvil suitable for drawing wire; 12. Venarey-les-Laumes (Côte-d'Or, Bourgogne), stray find discovered when digging the Bourgogne

[655] THEVENOT 1998, Fig. 8. 3.
[656] JOCKENHÖVEL 2003, 111, Abb. 5. 7.
[657] THEVENOT 1998, Fig. 9. 4.
[658] HANSEN 1994, 144–145; THEVENOT 1998, Fig. 9. 5.
[659] HANSEN 1994, 413, Nr. 165; THEVENOT 1998, 124–133, Figs 1–4, Fig. 5. 9–13, 15–16, Fig. 6. 1–4; JOCKENHÖVEL 2003, 111, Abb. 5. 1–5.
[660] THEVENOT 1998, Fig. 8. 2.
[661] THEVENOT 1998, Fig. 9. 3.
[662] JOCKENHÖVEL 2003, 111, Abb. 5. 9.
[663] THEVENOT 1998, Fig. 8. 4.
[664] HANSEN 1994, 142, 144, 418, Nr. 320, Abb. 78.
[665] THEVENOT 1998, Fig. 4. 2.

canal (*bronze final*):[666] anvil with a perforation for drawing wire (cf. *Fig. 31. 8*)

Switzerland: 13. Auvernier:[667] anvil, two socketed chasing hammers (*Treibhammer*), shaft-hole hammer; 14. Domat–Ems, hoard (Ha B):[668] hammer; 15. Hauterive-Champréveyres, settlement:[669] bronze stamps/punches; 16. Niedau–Steinberg, settlement:[670] hammer (unknown type); 17. Riddes:[671] anvil; 18. Zürich–Alpenqui:[672] antler hammer; 19. Zürich–Haumesser:[673] anvil, socketed chasing hammers (*Treibhammer*)

Germany: 20. Bad Buchau–Wasserburg (Baden-Württemberg), settlement:[674] socketed hammers, copper ore, tin, lead, and bronze raw materials, tuyère and moulds; 21. Großer Knetzberg (Bavaria), hoard:[675] socketed hammer; 22. Lachen–Speyerdorf (Rhein-Pfalz), Ha B1 burial:[676] anvil (prismatic, *Steckamboss* type, with two grooves at each end), bronze pick-ingot; 23. Marnau (Bavaria), metalworker's hoard of twenty-seven artefacts (Bz D–Ha B1):[677] two bronze stamps/ punches; 24. Nürnberg–Mögeldorf (Bavaria), hoard (Ha A1):[678] bronze stamps/punches; 25. unprovenanced, in the Nürnberg Museum (13th–8th centuries BC):[679] bronze stamp/punch; 26. Schornweißah (Bavaria), hoard:[680] socketed hammer; 27. Schwabthal (Bavaria), hoard:[681] socketed hammer; 28. Steinkirchen (Bavaria), Grave 10

666 Nicolardot – Verger 1998, 26, Fig. 11. 10.
667 Wyss 1971, 129, Abb. 4. 5–7.
668 Hansen 1994, II: 434. Kat. Nr. 83.
669 Rychner-Faraggi 1993, 43, Fig. 40, Pl. 41/35; Jockenhövel 2003, Abb. 5. 10.
670 Miske 1908, 23. I was unable to acquire the literature cited by him. When the findspot (Nidau) was published by Hansen 1994, II: 438. Kat. Nr. 234, the hammer was not mentioned.
671 Wyss 1971, 129, Abb. 4. 2.
672 Wyss 1971, 129, Abb. 4. 9.
673 Wyss 1971, 129, Abb. 4. 1, 3–4.
674 Kossack 1995, 27, Abb. 26.
675 Pászthory – Mayer 1998, 175–176, Taf. 76. 1171.
676 Sperber 2000, 386–392, 395, Abb. 2–3, Abb. 10; Jockenhövel 2003, 107, Abb. 1. 1.
677 Gold und Kult 2003, Kat. Nr. 7a.
678 Jockenhövel 2003, 111, 283, Abb. 5. 11, Kat. Nr. 10.
679 Gold und Kult 2003, 281, Kat. Nr. 8a.
680 Pászthory – Mayer 1998, 175–176, Taf. 76. 1172.
681 Pászthory – Mayer 1998, 175–176, Taf. 76. 1170.

(later Ha A):[682] anvil (prismatic, *Steckamboss* type), suitable for drawing wire; 29. Stockheim (Bavaria), hoard (Bz D):[683] bronze stamp/punch; 30. Schinna (Lower Saxony), hoard (Period V):[684] socketed chasing hammer, double-sided bronze mould for an axe and a sickle; 31. Waibling (Bavaria):[685] socketed hammer; 32. Welze (Lower Saxony), pit of a fireplace in the settlement:[686] socketed chasing hammer; 33. Zornheim, hoard (?):[687] socketed hammer

Czech Republic: 34. Blučina, Hoard 2 (Bz D1):[688] socketed hammer; 35. Borotín, hoard (Bz D2–Ha A1):[689] shaft-hole hammer; 36. Boskovice, Hoard 4 (Ha B2):[690] strongly worn socketed hammer; 37. Drslavice, Hoard 2 (Bz D2–Ha A1):[691] socketed hammer, winged axe reworked into a hammer; 38. Hrdlořezy, hoard (Ha B1):[692] blacksmith's hammer-axe (*Hammeraxt*); 39. Jevičko, hoard (Ha A1):[693] socketed horned anvil (cf. *Fig. 31. 4*); 40. Nová Ves, hoard (Bz C-D):[694] horned anvil with rectangular face, three bronze moulds, three pairs of gold wire jewellery (32.06 g) + vessel; 41. Přestavlký, hoard (Ha A1):[695] bronze stamp/punch; 42. Prague–Rýdeč, hoard (Bz D–Ha A1):[696] broken chasing hammer, resembling the piece from the Szombathely area, socketed hammer, saw; 43. Skalička, hoard (Bz A1–2):[697] chasing

[682] MÜLLER-KARPE 1969; HANSEN 1994, 145.

[683] MÜLLER-KARPE 1959, 148–149, 288, Taf. 156. 52; HANSEN 1994, 147, Abb. 80; JOCKENHÖVEL 2003, 111, Abb. 5. 8.

[684] LAUX 2005, 86, Taf. 29. 429–430.

[685] PÁSZTHORY – MAYER 1998, 175, Taf. 76. 1173A.

[686] LAUX 2005, 86, Taf. 58/A/6–7.

[687] HANSEN 1994, Abb. 77; II: 480. Kat. Nr. 1169.

[688] SALAŠ 2005, I: 286, 288, Obr. 24, II: Tab. 45. 9.

[689] SALAŠ 2005, I: 62, 308–309, Obr. 24, Obr. 33, II: Tab. 93. 40.

[690] SALAŠ 2005, I: 415, Obr. 24, 33, II: Tab. 331. 17.

[691] SALAŠ 2005, I: 334, 342, II: Tab. 148. 50–51.

[692] KYTLICOVÁ 2007, 266, Nr. 61. Taf. 182. D/3.

[693] SALAŠ 2005, I: 347–348, Obr. 24, II: Tab. 179. 30.

[694] HANSEN 1994, 144, 497, Nr. 448; KYTLICOVÁ 2007, 312, Nr. 251, Taf. 160. A/8, specified as having been found in Velím. This misunderstanding is clarified in the original publication. FELCMAN (1910–12) [1913], 375–382, Taf. XIX.

[695] JOCKENHÖVEL 2003, 111, Abb. 5. 6.

[696] KYTLICOVÁ 2007, 300–302, Nr. 207, Taf. 88. 95, Taf. 94/A.

[697] KYTLICOVÁ 2007, 303, Nr. 212, Taf. 174/D.

hammer; 44. Štramberk, Hoard 4 (Ha B1):[698] socketed hammer; 45. Ujezd, hoard (Bz C2):[699] conical anvil, two socketed hammers, two awls; 46. Žárovice–Hamry, Hoards 3 and 7 (Ha B1):[700] one socketed hammer in each

Austria: 47. Augsdorf (Carinthia), hoard:[701] anvil; 48. Draßburg (Burgenland), hoard (Ha A1):[702] socketed thinning/stretching hammer (*Schweifhammer*); 49. Mannersdorf (Lower Austria), stray find:[703] socketed hammer (*Ausschlich-* or *Polierhammer*); 50. Oberleis–Oberleisberg (Lower Austria):[704] stretching hammer (*Schweifhammer*); 51. Schiltern (Lower Austria), hoard (Ha A2):[705] anvil (socketed, adze-shaped, upward-curving edge), socketed hammers (one is a stretching hammer, *Schweifhammer*), casting wedges, wires; 52. Volders (Tyrol), Grave 370:[706] small, atypical chasing hammer (*Treibhammer)*

Slovakia: 53. Brvnište/Boronás, hoard (Jászkarajenő period):[707] socketed hammer; 54. Somotor/Szomotor, settlement, from a house (Gáva culture, later than the piece from Zvolen):[708] socketed hammer; 55. Trenčianske Bohuslavice/Bogoszló, hoard (Jászkarajenő period):[709] socketed hammer; 56. Zvolen/Zólyom, Hoard 2 (later Piliny period):[710] socketed hammer

Ukraine, Zakarpattia Oblast: 57. Makarevo (Lazy I series, Ha A1):[711] socketed hammer; 58. Mužievo/Nagymuzsaj, Hoard II (Suskovo

---

698 Salaš 2005, I: 458, 461, Obr. 24, II: Tab. 439. 13.

699 Hansen 1994, 128, 506, Abb. 68, Abb. 77; Kytlicová 2007, 311–312, Nr. 245, Taf. 1/B.

700 Salaš 2005, I: 472–474, Obr. 24, II: Tab. 475. 8, 476. B/4.

701 Hansen 1994, Abb. 77, II: 510, Kat. Nr. 22.

702 Mayer 1977, 223, Taf. 89. 1330–1331.

703 Mayer 1977, 223–224, Taf. 90. 1334.

704 Mayer 1977, 223, Taf. 90. 1333.

705 Mayer 1977, 224, Taf. 90. 1338–1339, Taf. 123/C; Lauermann – Rammer 2013, 168, Taf. 70.

706 Sperber 2000, 395.

707 Novotná 1970, 80, 99, Taf. 43. 804.

708 Novotná 1970, 99, Taf. 43. 805.

709 Novotná 1970, 68, 99, Taf. 43. 803.

710 Novotná 1970, 43–44, 99, Taf. 43. 802; Hansen 1994, Abb. 77.

711 Kobaľ 2000, 50, 85.

series, Ha A2):[712] socketed hammer; 59. Mužievo/Nagymuzsaj, Hoard I (Kriva series, Bz C–D):[713] socketed hammer; 60. Podmonastyr, today part of Munkács/Mukacheve, Hoard II (Bz C–D):[714] socketed hammer; 61. Velikie Lučki/Nagylucska, hoard (Bz C–D):[715] socketed hammer

Hungary: 62. Balsa, hoard (Kurd horizon):[716] socketed hammer; 63. Beremend (Gyermely horizon):[717] two or three socketed hammers; 64. Bihar County, hoard:[718] shaft-hole hammer; 65. Dévaványa, hoard (Hajdúböszörmény horizon):[719] hammer; 66. Esztergom–Szentgyörgymező, hoard (Kurd horizon):[720] socketed hammer; 67. Gemzse, hoard (Ópályi horizon):[721] hammer; 68. Gyermely, hoard (Gyermely horizon):[722] socketed hammer; 69. Gyöngyössolymos, hoard (Kurd horizon):[723] socketed hammer; 70. Hajdúnánás, hoard (Kurd horizon):[724] socketed hammer; 71. Kenderes, Hoard I (Kurd horizon):[725] socketed hammer; 72. Keszőhidegkút, hoard (Kurd horizon):[726] socketed hammer; 73. Lengyeltóti, Hoards II and III (Kurd horizon):[727] three socketed hammers in one, four in the other hoard; 74. Lovasberény, hoard (Gyermely horizon):[728] two or three socketed hammers; 75. Ménfőcsanak–Széles-földek, settlement, found with a metal detector:[729] socketed hammer; 76. Mohács, hoard, later lost

712 Kobaľ 2000, 50, 89.
713 Kobaľ 2000, 50, 89.
714 Kobaľ 2000, 93–94, Taf. 36. 34.
715 Kobaľ 2000, 50, 99, Taf. 28. B5
716 Mozsolics 1985, 39, 93.
717 Mozsolics 1985, 40, 95–96, Taf. 253. 8–10.
718 Hampel 1896, Taf. CCXXVI. 10.
719 Mozsolics 2000, 40–41, Taf. 24. 11.
720 Mozsolics 1985, 40, 117, Taf. 138. 6.
721 Mozsolics 1973, 138–139, Taf. 33. 6; Hansen 1994, 539, Nr. 255.
722 Mozsolics 1985, 40, 82–83, 121, Taf. 240. 3.
723 Mozsolics 1985, 39, 122, Taf. 144. 10.
724 Mozsolics 1945, 53–57, 95 and note 9.
725 Mozsolics 1985, 134.
726 Mozsolics 1985, 39, 135, Taf. 31. 16.
727 Wanzek 1992, 261–262, Taf. 8. 5–7; Hansen 1994, II: 544, Nr. 391; Mozsolics 1985, 142, Taf. 109. 36–39; Hansen 1994, II: 544, Nr. 392.
728 Mozsolics 1985, 40, 145, Taf. 245. 6–7, 12.
729 Author's excavation in 2009–2011, unpublished.

(Gyermely horizon):[730] socketed hammer; 77. Nadap, metalworker's hoard (Ha A1 or A2):[731] five socketed hammers; 78. Nagydém, hoard (Gyermely horizon):[732] socketed hammer and broken shaft-hole hammer; 79. Öreglak, hoard (Kurd horizon):[733] socketed axe reworked into a socketed hammer; 80. Peterd, hoard (Kurd horizon):[734] socketed hammer; 81. Regöly–Birkás, later lost:[735] socketed hammer; 82. Rinyaszentkirály, hoard (Kurd horizon):[736] winged axe reworked into a hammer, shaft-hole hammer suitable for gold-working according to Mozsolics; 83. Celldömölk–Ság-hegy, Urnfield settlement, stray find (Románd horizon):[737] hammers;[738] 84. Szentpéterszeg, hoard (Kurd horizon):[739] two socketed hammers; 85. Tiszaszőlős, hoard, later lost (Kurd horizon):[740] socketed hammer; 86. Torvaj, hoard (Gyermely horizon):[741] small socketed hammer (*Tüllenhammer*); 87–88. Várvölgy–Felsőzsid, Hoards 4 and 10 (Ha A2–B1):[742] seven socketed hammers in one and six in the other hoard, chisels; 89. Velem–Szent Vid, Urnfield settlement, stray finds:[743] mould for an anvil, anvil (horned, bent at right-angle, cf. *Fig. 35. 5*), cutting anvil (cf. *Fig. 35. 4*), mould for a socketed hammer, socketed hammers (cf. *Fig. 35. 3, 6*), bronze stamp/punch (?), chasing tools with single and double working edge, and Hoard I (Gyermely horizon):[744] socketed hammer

---

730 Hampel 1892, 92; Mozsolics 1985, 40, 150.

731 Mozsolics 1981, 304; Hansen 1994, 546, Nr. 451; Makkay 2006, 141, Pl. XIX. 168–170, Pl. XX. 171–172; Petres 1990, 93.

732 Hampel 1896, Taf. CXCV. 1, 7; Mozsolics 1985, 152; Hansen 1994, 546, Nr. 458.

733 Mozsolics 1985, 163–165, Taf. 77. 1.

734 Mozsolics 1985, 39, 174, Taf. 60. 11.

735 Szabó 2013b, notes 89 and 392.

736 Mozsolics 1985, 39, 183, Taf. 96. 8, Taf. 97. 10.

737 For the hoards assigned to the Románd horizon (BVIb), cf. Mozsolics 2000, 37–39, Taf. 7. 8–13, Taf. 22.

738 Lázár 1943, 280–287, Taf. VII. 70–71.

739 Hampel 1886, Taf. X. 3; Mozsolics 1985, 195; Hansen 1994, 554, Nr. 674.

740 Szabó 2013b, 90 and note 402.

741 Mozsolics 1985, 206, Taf. 271. B/1; Hansen 1994, 556, Nr. 740.

742 Müller 2007, Figs 13–14; Müller 2006b, 234–235, Figs 3–4; Müller 2011, 216, Fig. 1. 2–5, Fig. 2. 6–8, Fig. 3. 15–17, Fig. 4. 18.

743 Miske 1908, Taf. XXII. 3, Taf. XXIV. 2, Taf. XXIX. 1–2, 4–5, 7–8, Taf. XXXVI. 45; Mozsolics 1985, 40.

744 Mozsolics 1985, 40, 212, Taf. 228. 8.

Romania: The list is based on Florian Gogâltan's excellent overview,[745] but I have omitted the tool moulds and the unprovenanced artefacts. I added a single artefact found in Temesvár to his catalogue. 90. Adrian/Görgényadjorján, stray find:[746] socketed hammer; 91. Aiud/Nagyenyed, hoard (Susani horizon, Ha A1):[747] five or six socketed hammers (with elliptical, round and rectangular faces); 92. Arad, Hoard II (Ha B1):[748] socketed hammer; 93. Bicaz/Bikácfalva, Hoard II (Ha A1):[749] socketed hammer; 94. Bogata/Marosbogát, stray find:[750] socketed hammer; 95. Călugăreni/Mikháza, hoard (Ha A1):[751] socketed hammer; 96. Cluj-Napoca/Kolozsvár, Hoard III:[752] socketed hammer; 97. Corneşti Sinfalva, hoard (Ha B1):[753] socketed hammer; 98. Corund/Korond, hoard (Bz D):[754] unique socketed hammer; 99. Dipşa/Dipse/Dürrbach, hoard (Ha A1):[755] six socketed hammers; 100. Domăneşti/Domahida, hoard (Domăneşti horizon, Bz D1):[756] shaft-hole axe hafted with a socketed axe; 101. Drajna de Jos, hoard (Bz D):[757] socketed hammer; 102. Gherla/Szamosújvár/Neuschloss, stray find:[758] socketed hammer; 103. Guşteriţa/Szenterzsébet, Hoard II (Ha A1):[759] three socketed hammers (with different faces: narrow rectangular, broad rectangular, round); 104. Igriţa-Höhle/Kisigrice, hoard (Bz D):[760] socketed hammer; 105. Stray find discovered in Jibou/

[745] Gogâltan 2005, 343–386.

[746] Gogâltan 2005, 346, Taf. 1. 1.

[747] Gogâltan 2005, 346, 365, 377, Taf. 1. 3–4, 2. 5–7.

[748] Gogâltan 2005, 349, 377, Taf. 2. 8.

[749] Gogâltan 2005, 349, 377, Taf. 2. 9.

[750] Gogâltan 2005, 349, Taf. 3. 10.

[751] Gogâltan 2005, 349, 377, Taf. 3. 11.

[752] Gogâltan 2005, 349.

[753] Gogâltan 2005, 349, 377, Taf. III. 14.

[754] Gogâltan 2005, 349, 376, Taf. 3. 15.

[755] Gogâltan 2005, 349, 352, 377, Taf. 3. 16, 4. 17–21.

[756] Hampel 1886, Taf. 123. 7; Bader 1978, 124, Pl. 68; Gogâltan 2005, 352, Taf. 4. 22.

[757] Gogâltan 2005, 352, 376, Taf. 4. 23.

[758] Gogâltan 2005, 352, Taf. 4. 24.

[759] Petrescu-Dîmboviţa 1978, 120, Taf. 105. 58–60; Gogâltan 2005, 353–354, 377, Taf. 5. 25–27.

[760] Gogâltan 2005, 354, 376, Taf. 5. 28; Nessel 2012b, 60, Abb. 6.

Zsibó :[761] socketed hammer; 106. Liubcova, hoard (Ha A1):[762] socketed hammer; 107. Nou Săsesc/Szászújfalva (Ha B1):[763] socketed hammer; 108. Ocna Sibiului/Vízakna, stray find (possibly Ha A):[764] socketed hammer; 109. Plăieşti/Kövend (?),hoard:[765] socketed hammer; 110. Rigmani/Rigmány, stray find:[766] socketed hammer; 111. Sâmbriaş, stray find:[767] socketed hammer or anvil; 112. Seleuş/Nagyszőlős, hoard (Bz D):[768] socketed hammer; 113. Sfăraş/Farnas, hoard (Ha A1):[769] socketed hammer; 114. Şpălnaca/Ispánlaka, Hoard I (Ha B1):[770] socketed hammer; 115. Şpălnaca/Ispánlaka, Hoard II (Ha A1):[771] one shaft-hole and eight socketed hammers (with narrow rectangle and elliptical faces); 116. Şuncuiuş-Höhle/Vársonkolyos, hoard (Ha A1):[772] socketed hammer; 117. Tătărani, hoard (Bz D):[773] socketed hammer; 118. Timişoara/Temesvár II–Fratelia, hoard (Ha B1):[774] anvil, socketed hammer, chisel; 119. Uioara de Sus/Felsőmarosújvár, hoard (Ha A1):[775] nine socketed hammers (narrow rectangular, broader rectangular, elliptical and round faces); 120. Uriu/Felőr, stray find:[776] socketed hammer; 121. Variaş, hoard (Ha A1):[777] socketed hammer; 122. Vărd/Vérd, hoard (Ha B1):[778] socketed hammer

---

761 GOGÂLTAN 2005, 354, Taf. 5. 29.

762 GOGÂLTAN 2005, 354, 377, Taf. 6. 30.

763 GOGÂLTAN 2005, 354, 377, Taf. 6. 31.

764 PETRESCU-DÎMBOVIŢA 1978, 123, Taf. 122. E/3; GOGÂLTAN 2005, 354, 379, Taf. 6. 32.

765 GOGÂLTAN 2005, 354, Taf. 6. 33.

766 GOGÂLTAN 2005, 356, Taf. 6. 36.

767 GOGÂLTAN 2005, 356, Taf. 7. 37.

768 GOGÂLTAN 2005, 356, 376, Taf. 7. 38.

769 GOGÂLTAN 2005, 356, 377, Taf. 7. 39.

770 GOGÂLTAN 2005, 356, 377, Taf. 7. 40.

771 PETRESCU-DÎMBOVIŢA 1978, 127, Nr. 177, Taf. 144. 151–155, Taf. 157. 614; MOZSOLICS 1984, 42, 67, Taf. 21. 4; GOGÂLTAN 2005, 356–359, 377, Taf. 7. 41–43, 8. 44–48.

772 GOGÂLTAN 2005, 359, 377, Taf. 8. 49.

773 GOGÂLTAN 2005, 359, 376, Taf. 9. 50.

774 HANSEN 1994, 592, Nr. 391; MEDELEŢ 1995, 229, Abb. 1–3.

775 GOGÂLTAN 2005, 362–365, 377, Taf. 9. 54–55, 10. 56–60, 11. 61–62.

776 GOGÂLTAN 2005, 365, Taf. 11. 63.

777 GOGÂLTAN 2005, 365, 377, Taf. 12. 64.

778 GOGÂLTAN 2005, 365, 377, Taf. 12. 65.

Bosnia-Herzegovina: 123. Boljanič, hoard (Stufe 2 = Kurd horizon):[779] three anvils (*Steckamboss* type, one is horned and has a rectangular work surface), four socketed hammers, five casting wedges, saw blade; 124. Vidovice, hoard (earlier Gyermely horizon):[780] hammer with platter face (*Tellerhammer*)

Croatia: 125. Brodski Varoš, hoard (Phase II, Ha A1):[781] two socketed hammers; 126. Kloštar Ivanić, hoard (Phase III, Ha A2):[782] socketed hammer

Slovenia: 127. Hudinja, hoard:[783] shaft-hole hammer (*Schaftloch-hammer*)

Fig. 33. Weight unit moulds: 1–2. Gór (drawing by István Ughy, photo by Péter Móricz); 3–4. Vát (drawing by András Radics, photo by Tibor Takács); 5–6. scale weight from Ménfőcsanak (drawing by Magdolna Mátyus, photo by Tibor Takács); 7. Ménfőcsanak, stone weight, *in situ* in Grave 11, during excavation (photo by Tibor Takács). The drawings are not to the same scale

Fig. 34. The results of the XRF analysis of the weight found at Ménfőcsanak

Fig. 35. Metal tools and products from Vas County: 1. the "Szombathely" hammer (drawing by Ágnes Nagy); 2. hammer mould from Gór–Kápolnadomb (drawing by István Ughy); 3–6. hammers found on St. Vid Hill, anvils for cutting and embossing (drawing by Ferenc Gelencsér); 7–10. bronze sheet artefacts (drawing by Magdolna Mátyus, photo by Tibor Takács). The drawings are not to scale

Fig. 36. Goldsmith's pitch from an Early Iron Age bronze hoard found at Ikervár (photo by Gábor Papp)

Fig. 37. The wires of Gold Hoard 2 at Várvölgy, *in situ* and after lifting (photos by Róbert Müller, 2005, 2012)

Fig. 38. Pectorals of the Late Bronze Age in Central Europe (after Kossack 1995, Abb. 1; Lehrberger 1995, Fig. 1, made by Tibor Takács based on the author's data collection)

---

[779] König 2004, 48–50, 191–194, Tab. 2–3, Taf. 17. 36–43, Taf. 18. 44–46, 50.

[780] König 2004, 48–49, 227–228, Tab. 2–3, Taf. 5. 9.

[781] Vinski-Gasparini 1973, I: 212, 202–203, II: Tab. 62. 22–23; Hansen 1994, Abb. 77, II: 561, Kat. Nr. 41.

[782] Vinski-Gasparini 1973, I: 205–206, 215; II: Tab. 96. 10.

[783] Hansen 1994, Abb. 77, II: 564. Kat. Nr. 99.

Legend: ■ grave/burial; ♣ hoard, treasure; ▼? unknwn context

1–2. Várvölgy–Felsőzsid, treasure; 3. Velem, St. Vid Hill, treasure; 4. Rothengrub (Lower Austria), treasure; 5. Koppental (Styria), treasure; 6. Bled (Slovenia), treasure; 7. Aislingen (Bavaria), burial; 8. Grünwald (Bavaria), Grave 1; 9. Straubing (Bavaria); Grave 31; 10. Gammertingen (Baden-Württemberg), double grave; 11. Karlsruhe–Neureut (Baden-Württemberg), hoard (*Einzelfunde*), Rhine; 12. Taumering (Oberpfalz), Grave 51; 13–14. Barbey, Cent Arpents (France), Graves 4, 26; 15–16. Barbuise-Courtavant (France), two pieces from burials; 17. Beaujeu (France), hoard; 18. Beaumont, Crot aux Moines (France), context unknown to the author; 19. Blanot (France), hoard; 20. Champlay-la-Columbine (France), Grave 101; 21. Durrenentzen–Haut-Rhin (France), burial; 22–24. La Saulsotte (France), Graves 38, 43, 52; 25. Rixheim (France), Grave 2; 26. Bienne (Switzerland), context unknown to the author; 27. Binningen (Switzerland), burial; 28. Twann–Petersinsel (Switzerland), context unknown to the author; 29. Vallamand–Les Ferrages (Switzerland), context unknown to the author

Fig. 39. Plate jewellery: 1. Diadem: Museum of Berlin (after HÄNSEL 2003, Abb. 2); 2. Gold plates and bronze backplates of Hoard II from Ság-hegy, pre-restoration condition documented in Lázár's album (SM Archaeologial Archives inv. no. 2378-08); 3. Belt plaque: Budinščina (after KILIAN-DIRLMEIER 1975, Taf. 46-47. 460). Pectorals: 4. Rothengrub (after PITTIONI 1952, Taf. 1); 5. Champlay-la-Columbine, Grave 101 (after PIETTE 1998, Fig.1.1); 6. Aislingen (WELSWEYRAUCHT 1995, Abb. 1. 2–4); 7. Blanot (after THEVENOT 1991, Figs 54 and 63). The drawings are not to the same scale (drawing by Magdolna Mátyus)

Fig. 40. Female headbands and breast ornaments of the Bronze Age: 1. Unterwölbling culture, Franzhausen I, Grave 110 (after NEUGEBAUER 1994, Abb. 40. 4, Abb. 41. 1–2); 2. Ordacsehi, Grave 400, Kisapostag culture (after SOMOGYI 2004, Abb. 16. A–C); 3. Budapest–Kőérberek, Early Bronze Age figurine fragment (after ZSIDI 2005, 84); 4. Ludas–Varjú-dűlő, Late Bronze Age figurine with roundels on the chest (after DOMBORÓCZKI 2012, Fig. 196). The drawings are not to the same scale (drawn by Magdolna Mátyus)

Figures

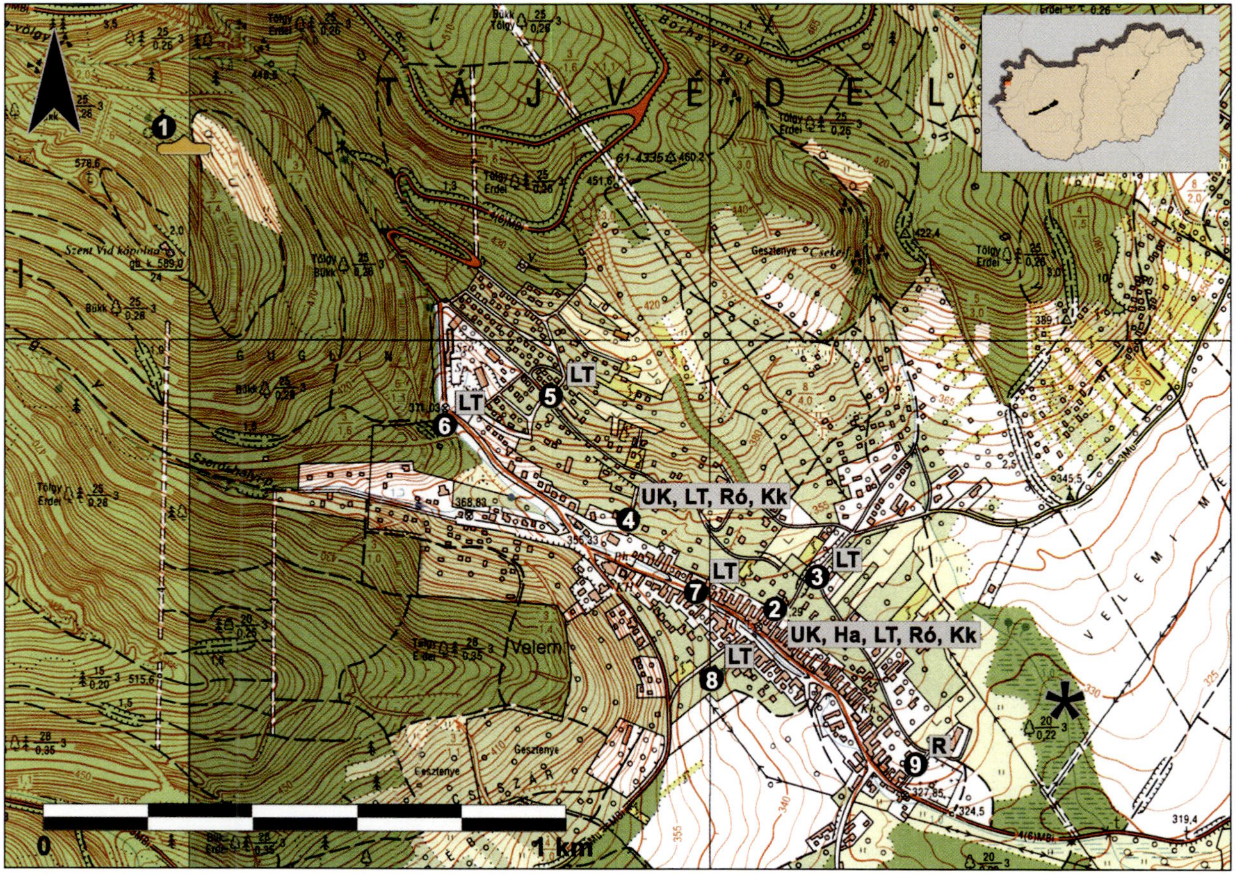

Fig. 1. A: Location of Velem in Hungary, B: The archaeological sites in Velem on a 1:10,000 topographical map, showing the findspot of the diadem (made by István Eke)

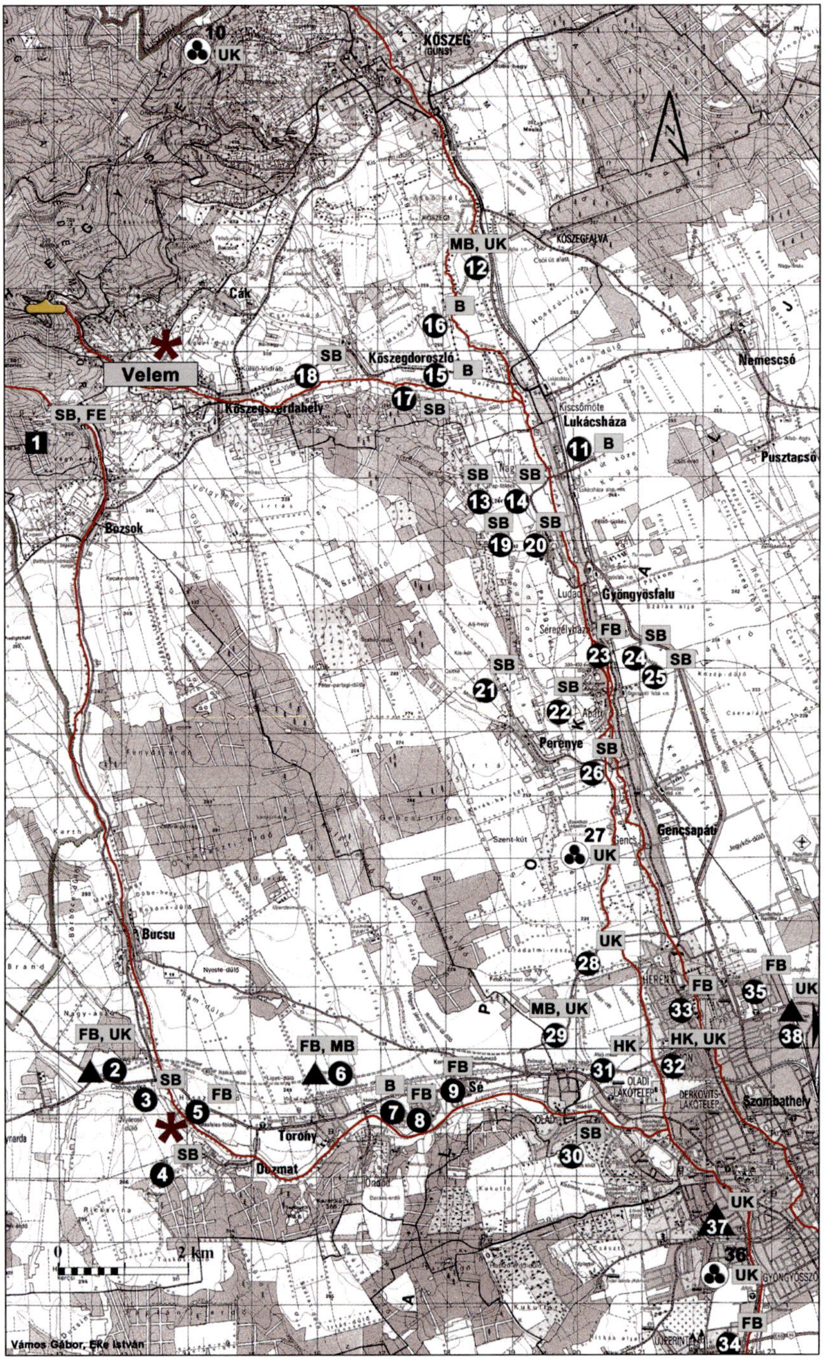
10 UK
KŐSZEG
Velem
SB, FE
1
Cák
SB
18
Kőszegdoroszló
15 B
17 SB
B
16
MB, UK
12
Lukácsháza
11 B
SB SB
13 14
SB SB
19 20
Gyöngyösfalu
FB SB
23 24 SB
25
SB
21
SB
22
Perenye
SB
26
27 UK
Gencsapáti
Bozsok
Bucsu
UK
28
MB, UK
29
FB
33
FB
35
UK
38
HK, UK
32
HK
31
FB, UK
2
SB
3
FB
5
FB, MB
6
B
7
FB
8
FB
9
Sé
Torony
SB
4
Dozmat
SB
30
UK
37
36 UK
FB
34
Szombathely
0 2 km
Vámos Gábor, Ekő István

Fig. 2. Bronze Age sites in the Velem area and the palaeoenvironmental sampling locations on the administrative boundary between Velem and Dozmat (made by István Eke, based on Jakab *et al. 2007, complemented with new information from the author)*

Legend: • settlement; ▲ cemetery, burial site; hoards; □ Kalapos-kő of Bozsok; ★ Palaeoenvironmental sampling location (on the administrative boundary between Dozmat and Velem); diadem

Abbreviations of archaeological periods and cultures: B = Bronze Age (unspecified); FB = Early Bronze Age; MB = Middle Bronze Age; SB = Late Bronze Age; HK = Tumulus culture; UK = Urnfield culture; FE = Early Iron Age

1. Bozsok–Kalapos-kő: religious-ritual-ceremonial site, Late Bronze Age/Early Iron Age; 2. Bucsu–Szabad erdő: Early Bronze Age settlement and Urnfield cemetery (2003–2004, author's excavation, unpublished); 3. Dozmat–Csompatka dűlő: Late Bronze Age settlement; 4. Dozmat–nyugati nagy Völgy-dűlő: Late Bronze Age settlement traces; 5. Torony–Másfeles földek: settlement of the Makó culture with a stone axe manufacturing workshop and Vučedol finds; 6. Torony–Nemesszer-dűlő: Early or Middle Bronze Age settlement traces and burial (2004, author's excavation, unpublished); 7. Northern side of Torony–Malom-patak: Bronze Age settlement traces (1984, field survey); 8. Sé–Malomoldal: late Vučedol and Early Somogyvár–Vinkovci settlement traces; 9. Sé area: Early Bronze Age fragments collected by an unknown collector, west-southwest of the settlement: partly late Vučedol and partly Somogyvár–Vinkovci finds; 10. Kőszeg–Ördögasztala/Ördögtányér: bronze hoard of the Urnfield period; 11. Lukácsháza–keleti Kertalja-dűlő: Bronze Age settlement traces (1998, field survey); 12. Kőszeg–Kőszegfalvi-rétek I: Middle Bronze Age and Urnfield settlements; 13. Lukácsháza–Csömötei-hegy/ Kisrókás-dűlő: Late Bronze Age settlement traces (1998–1999, 2002, 2004, field survey); 14. Lukácsháza–Pap-földek: Late Bronze Age settlement traces (2002–2003, field survey); 15. Kőszegdoroszló–Delece: Bronze Age settlement traces (1974, 2000, 2003, field survey); 16. Kőszegdoroszló–Berekalja I: Bronze Age settlement traces (unknown date, field survey); 17. Kőszegdoroszló Kisrét dűlő: Late Bronze Age settlement traces (1970, field survey); 18. Köszegszerdahely–Belső-Vidráb: Late Bronze Age settlement traces (2002, field survey); 19. Gyögyösfalu–Hegyalja dűlő: Late Bronze Age settlement traces (2002–2003, field survey); 20. Gyöngyösfalu–Pöse, Gátmellék: Late Bronze Age stray finds (2002, field survey); 21. Perenye–Zsellérföld: Late (?) Bronze Age settlement traces (1971, 2004, field survey); 22. Perenye–kaszálórét I: Late (?) Bronze Age settlement traces (2002, field survey); 23. Gencsapáti–Besenyő-sziget: Early Bronze Age settlement (2004, author's excavation, unpublished); 24. Gencsapáti–Urasági táblák I: Late Bronze Age settlement traces (1998, field survey); 25. Gencsapáti–Kápolnadomb: Late Bronze Age settlement traces (1999, field survey); 26. Gencsapáti–Hosszú-rész mellett: Late Bronze Age settlement traces (unknown date, field survey); 27. Gencsapáti, outskirts of: grip-tongue sword (Griffzungenschwert) *of a hoard (?) from the Urnfield period; 28. Szombathely–Kőszeri-dűlő: Urnfield period settlement; 29. Szombathely–Olad-Reiszig-erdő alatti dűlő: stray Middle Bronze Age arrowhead, Urnfield settlement; 30. Szombathely–Oladi plató: Late Bronze Age settlement traces (1984, field survey);*

31. Szombathely–Alsómező-dűlő: Tumulus settlement traces (2000, Csilla Farkas's excavation); 32. Szombathely–Kámon, Távhő: Tumulus settlement with Litzen pottery, Urnfield settlement; 33. Szombathely–Senyefa, 129 Szent Imre herceg út: Makó settlement; 34. Szombathely–Újperinti kavicsbánya: Makó settlement; 35. Szombathely–Metró dept. store, Minerva apartments and Motel: Early Bronze Age settlement; 36. Szombathely–Jáki út cemetery: bronze hoard of the Urnfield period; 37. Szombathely–44 Táncsics Mihály utca: Urnfield cemetery; 38. Szombathely–Zanat: Urnfield cemetery and settlement

Fig. 3. The findspot of Hoard Ia-b of bronze artefacts (triangle) and of the golden treasure (encircled) discovered in 1896 shown on the 1857 cadastral map of St. Vid Hill and the Szentkút Spring (arrow sign) (made by Magdolna Mátyus, after CZAJLIK *1993, Fig. 1, complemented with new information from the author)*

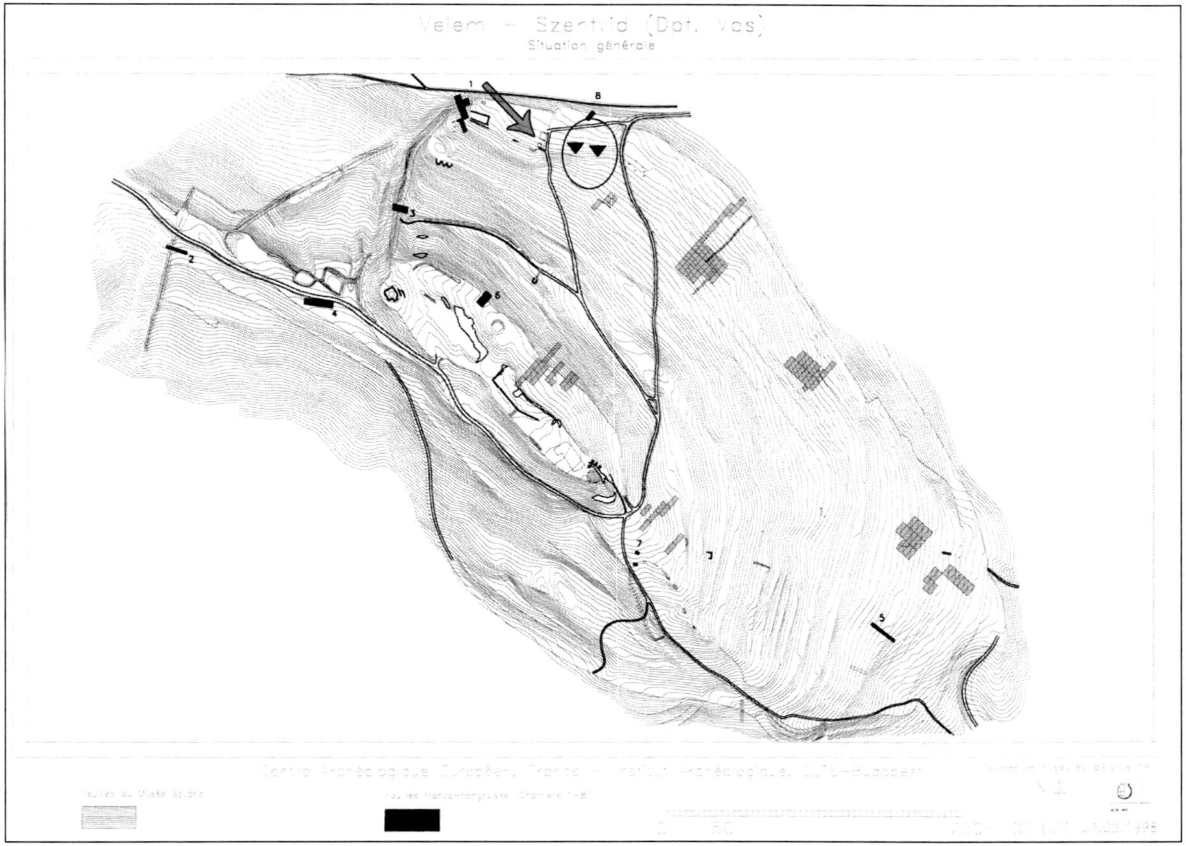

Fig. 4. The findspot of Hoard Ia-b of bronze artefacts (triangle) and of the golden treasure (encircled) discovered in 1896 shown on the contour map of the hill. The Szentkút Spring is marked by an arrow (made by Magdolna Mátyus, based on Karácsony Eőry's survey, after Balázs Holl, Zoltán Czajlik, Ádám Marton, and C*ZAJLIK* *1993. Fig. 2, complemented with new information from the author)*

1

2

3

Fig. 5. One of the archaeological sites in Velem excavated by Kálmán Miske (photographer and date of photograph unknown)

1

2

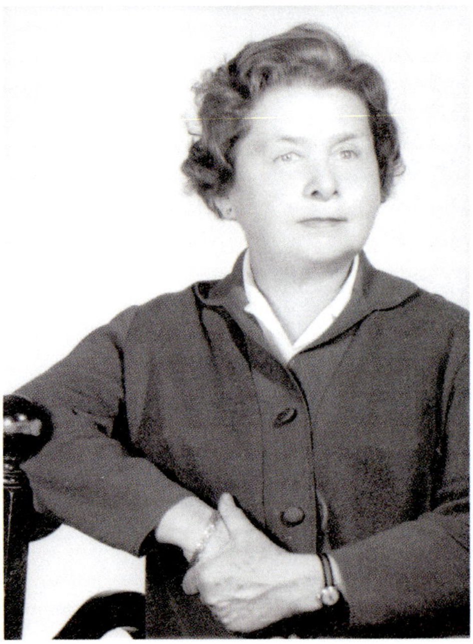

3

4

Fig. 6. 1. Kálmán Miske; 2. Ferenc Tompa; 3. Amália Mozsolics; 4. Gábor Bándi

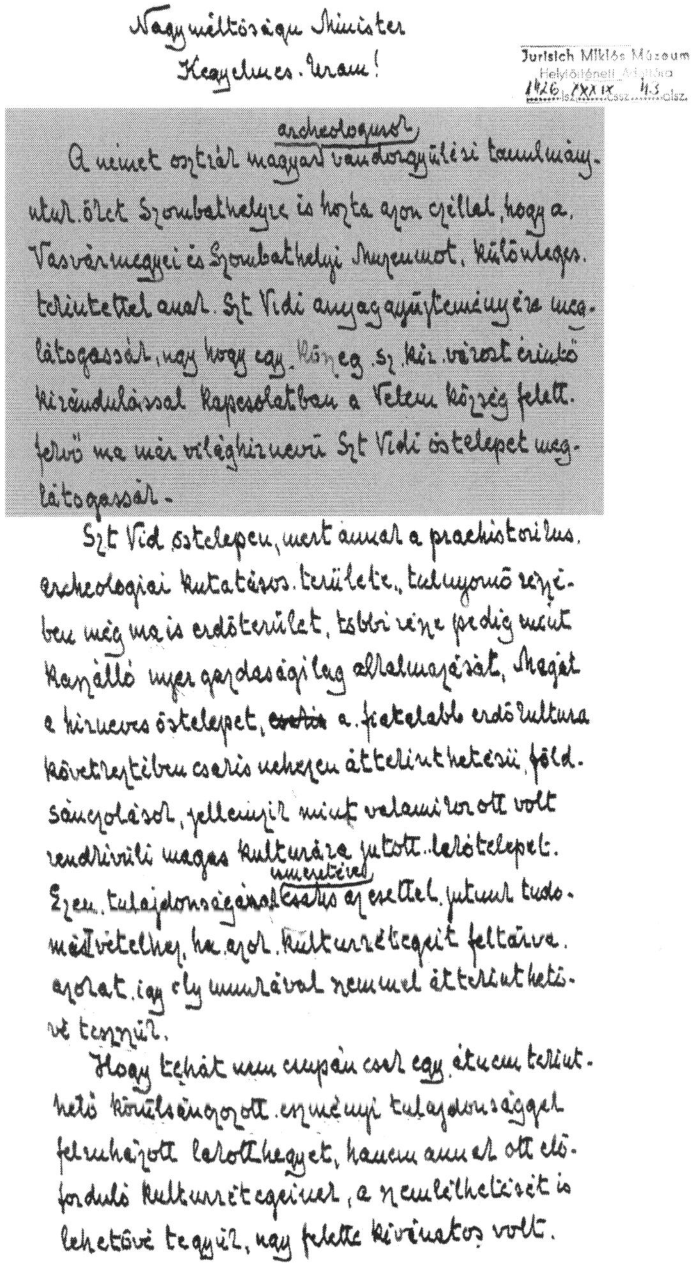

Nagyméltóságu Minister
Kegyelmes Uram!

A német osztrák magyar archeologusok vándorgyülési tanulmányutuk ölet Szombathelyre is hozta azon céllal, hogy a Vasvármegyei és Szombathelyi Muzeumot, különleges tekintettel annak Szt Vidi anyaggyüjteményére meglátogassák, ugy hogy egy Köszeg Sz. kir. várost érintö kirándulással kapcsolatban a Velem község felett fekvö ma már világhirnevü Szt Vidi östelepet meglátogassák.

Szt Vid östelepen, mert annak a praehistorikus archeologiai kutatások területe, tulnyomó részében még ma is erdöterület, többi része pedig mint kaszálló nyer gazdaságilag alkalmazását, magát a hirneves östelepet, a fiatalabb erdökultura következtében csakis nehezen áttekinthetésü, föld-sáncolások, jellemzik mint valamikor ott volt rendkivüli magas kulturára jutott lakótelepet. Ezen tulajdonságának ismereteivel csakis az esettel jutunk tudomásulvételhez, ha azok kulturrétegeit feltárva azokat igy oly munkával nemcsak áttekinthetövé tennük.

Hogy tehát nem csupán csak egy átnem tekinthetö körülsáncozott ezmennyi tulajdonsággal felruházott lakotthegyet, hanem annak ott elöforduló kulturrétegeinek, a szemlélhetését is lehetövé tegyük, ugy felette kivánatos volt.

Fig. 7. The first page of Miske's letter written at the end of 1929 (with the section on the visit of the foreign archaeologists highlighted)

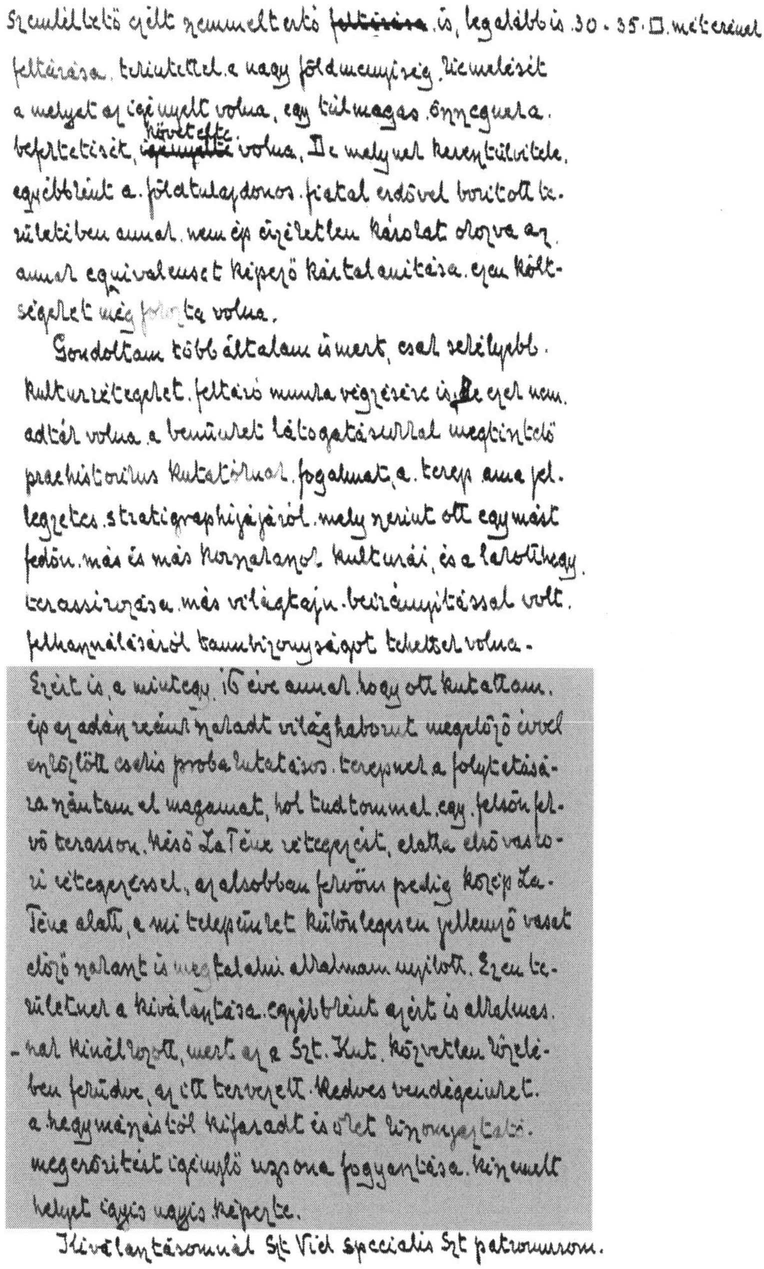

Szemléltető czélt szemmeltartó is, legalább is 30-35 □ méterének
feltárása, tekintettel a nagy földmennyiség kiemelésit
a melyet az igényelt volna, egy túlmagas összegnek a
befektetésit, követelte volna. De melynek keresztülvitele,
egyébbként a földtulajdonos fiatal erdővel borított te-
rületében annak nem épp czélszerű kárát okozva az
annak equivalensét képező kártalanitása, ezen költ-
ségeket még fokozta volna.
Gondoltam több általam ismert, csak selejtebb.
kulturrétegeket feltáró munka végzésére is, de ezek nem
adták volna a bennünket látogatásukkal megtisztelő
praehistorikus kutatóknak fogalmat a terep ama fel-
legzetes stratigraphiájáról, mely szerint ott egymást
fedőn más és más korszakok kulturái, és a Várhegy
terassirozása más világtáju beirányitással volt
felhasználásáról tanubizonyságot tehettek volna.
Ezért is, a mintegy 16 éve annak, hogy ott kutattam,
épp az adány reánk szakadt világháborut megelőző évvel
eszközölt csekis próbakutatásos tereppel a folytatásá-
ra szántam el magamat, hol tudtommal egy felsőn fel-
vő terasson késő La Tène rétegezést, alatta elsővaskó-
ri rétegezéssel, az alsobban fekvőn pedig közép La-
Tène alatt, a mi telepünket különlegesen jellemző vaskort
előző szakaszt is megtalálni alkalmam nyilott. Ezen te-
rületnek a kiválasztása egyébbként azért is alkalmas-
-nak kinálkozott, mert az a Szt. Kut. közvetlen közelé-
ben fekűdve, az itt tervezett kedves vendégeinket
a hegymászástól kifáradt és ölet kinozgatást
megerősitését igénylő uzsona fogyasztása kinevelt
helyet éppis nagyis képezte.
Kiválasztásomnál Szt. Vid speciális Szt. patronusom.

Fig. 8. Page 3 of Miske's letter
(with the section on the location of the trial trench highlighted)

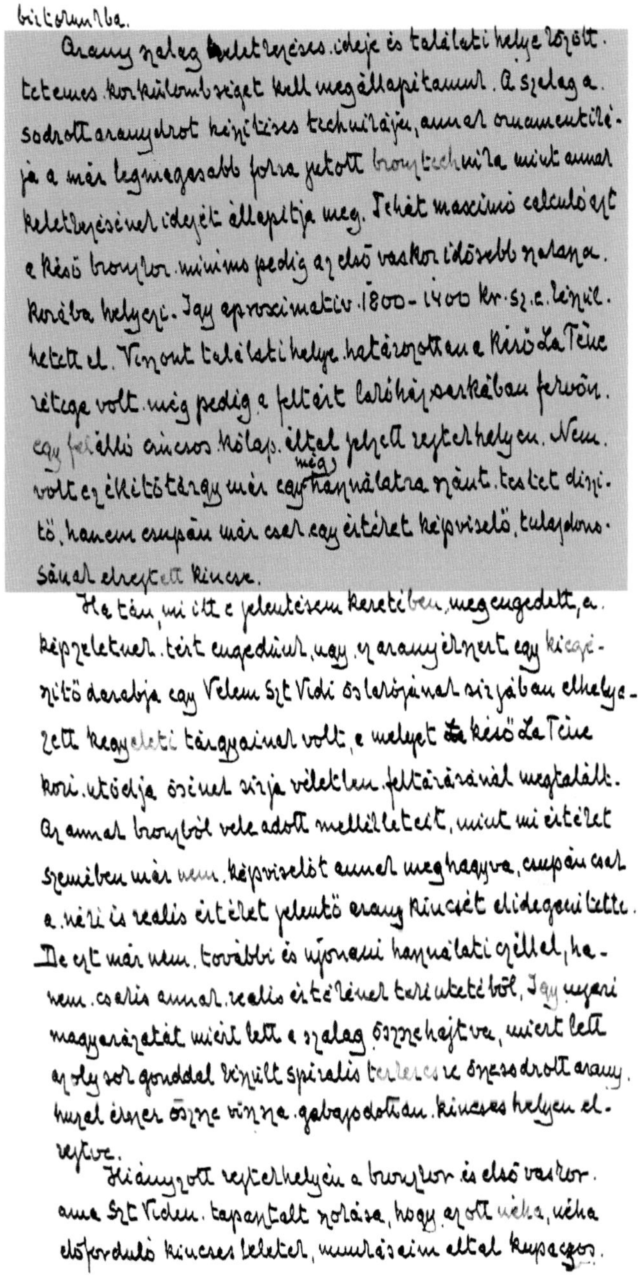

birtokunkba.

Arany szalag [illegible] keletkezéses ideje és találati helye között tetemes korkülömbséget kell megállapitanunk. A szalag a sodrott aranydrot bizitéses technikájú, annak ornamentiké-ja a már legmagasabb fokra jutott bronztechnika mint annak keletkezésének idejét állapitja meg. Tehát maximo calculo ezt a késő bronzkor, minimo pedig az első vaskor idősebb szakaszára korába helyezi. Igy approximativ 1800-1400 Kr. sz. e. kerül tetett el. Viszont találati helye határozottan a késő La Tène rétege volt, még pedig a feltárt lakóház sarkában fenyőn egy felálló cincsos kőlap által jelzett rejtekhelyen. Nem volt ez ékitőtárgy már egy még hanyzálatra szánt testet diszitő, hanem csupán már csak egy értéket képviselő tulajdonosának elrejtett kincse.

Ha tán, mi itt e jelentésem keretében, megengedett, a képzeletnek tért engedünk, úgy ez aranyékszert egy kiegészitő darabja egy Velem Szt Vidi őslakójának sirjában elhelyezett kegyeleti tárgyainak volt, a melyet késő La Tène kori utódja ősének sirja véletlen feltárásánál megtalált. Az annak bronzból vele adott mellékleteit, mint mi értéket szemében már nem képviselőt annak meghagyva, csupán csak a nézi és reális értéket jelentő arany kincsét elidegenitette. De ezt már nem további és ujonani hasznalati czéllal, hanem csakis annak reális értékének tezaurizálásából. Igy ugyani magyarázatát miért lett a szalag összehajtva, miért lett az oly sok gonddal készült spirális tekercsekbe összesodrott aranyhuzal ércnek össze vissza gabalyodottan kincses helyen elrejtve.

Hiányzott rejtekhelyén a bronzkor és első vaskor ama Szt Viden tapasztalt szokása, hogy az ott néha, néha előforduló kincses leletek, munkáim által kupacgos.

Fig. 9. Page 6 of Miske's letter (with the section on the golden treasure found underneath the upright slab of stone highlighted)

Fig. 10. 1. The Szent Vid Hill; 2. The chapel; 3. The Szentkút Spring with the ruins of the scout camp; 4. Tourist path to the spring; 5. Terrace with the pit above the spring; 6. Szilveszter Katona standing on the assumed findspot of the treasure (author's photographs, 2012–2013)

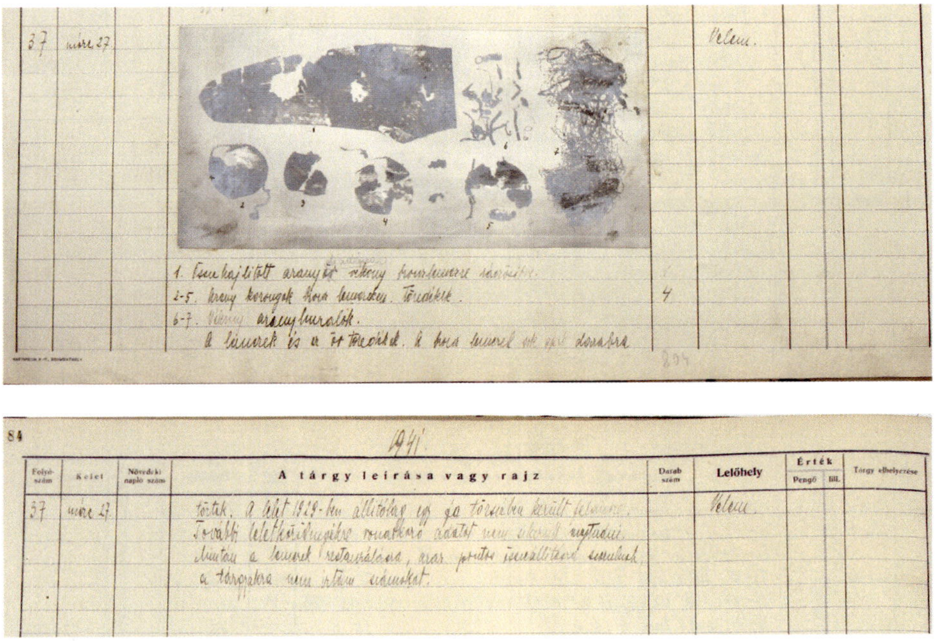

1

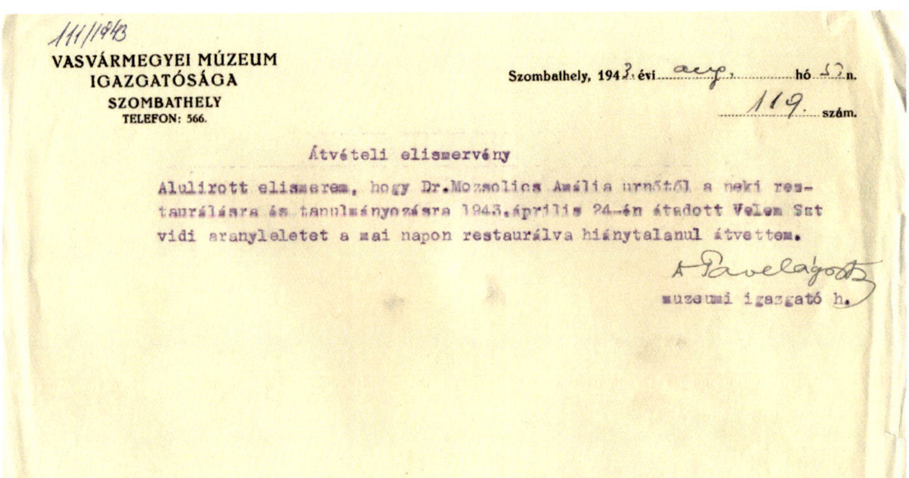
111/1943

VASVÁRMEGYEI MÚZEUM
IGAZGATÓSÁGA
SZOMBATHELY
TELEFON: 566.

Szombathely, 1943. évi aug. hó 5. n.

119. szám.

Átvételi elismervény

Alulirott elismerem, hogy Dr.Mozsolics Amália urnőtől a neki restaurálásra és tanulmányozásra 1943.április 24-én átadott Velem Szt vidi aranyleletet a mai napon restaurálva hiánytalanul átvettem.

muzeumi igazgató h.

2

Fig. 11. 1.a–b. Entry on the gold artefacts found in Velem in the inventory book dated March 27, 1941. The diadem is described as a belt. 2. Receipt of the golden treasure returned in August 1943, after conservation and restoration

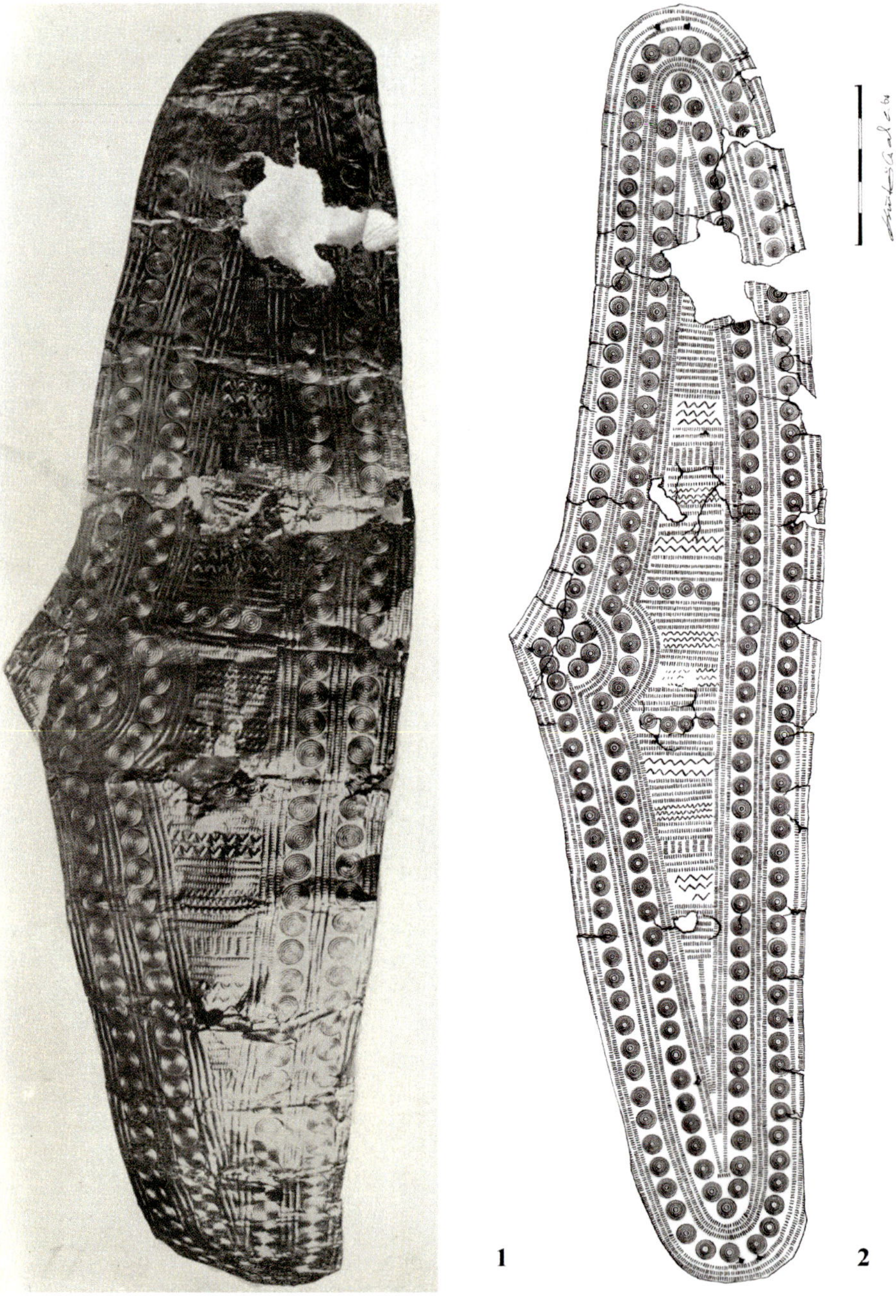

1 2

Fig. 12. The condition of the diadem in 1943 (after MOZSOLICS 1950, Taf. 1) and a drawing made prior to its restoration (Csaba E. Kiss, 2004)

1944/ ad 47/1944.

J e g y z é k

a muzeumi anyagnak biztonságban helyezésével kapcsolatban az ad. 39-1944. sz.főfelügyelőségi rendelet alapján külön elhelyezett tárgyakrólxx az 1941 április 10-én felterjesztett jegyzék kiegészitése képen.

1./ 5 /öt/ darab vett diszitésü aranylemez, állitólag Velemből; három darab trapéz alaku csüngő lemez figurális trébelt mintával; egy darab apró trébelt pontokkal diszitett aranykorong; 1 darab téglalapalaku aranylemez trébelt pontokkal köritve, középen pontozott lóalakkal. Állitólag mind az öt hamisitvány /Tompa F. szerint Mautner Ödön és Niklovits Károly mühelyéből/. Leltári számuk: 40/1941 /1-5.

2./1 /egy/ darab aranyidol /ember alak/ Körmendről; állitólag hamisitvány. Leltári száma: 41/1941.

3./1 /egy/ darab aranyszálból tekercselt gyürü Kőszeg vidékéről. Leltári száma:42/1941.

4./1 /egy/ darab nyitott aranygyürü ismeretlen lelőhellyel. Leltári száma: 43/1941.

5./3 /három/ darab csavart aranykarperec nyitott végekkel állitólag Héderváról. Leltári szám: 38/1941/1-3.

6./1 /egy/ darab csavart aranykarperec, lapos spirálokban végződő /Jánosházáról/. Leltári szám: 39/1941.

7./Az 1941. április 10-i leltárban 37/1941/1-7 szám alatt felvett velemi aranytöredékek az 1943. év folyamán Kolozsvárott Méry István által restauráltattak. A restaurálás után ez az anyag a következő darabokból áll:

1 /egy/ darab köralaku alátételre dolgozott aranyfejdisz /mintás aranyfejlemez/;

41 /negyvenegy/ darab különféle aranytöredék egy kartonlapra feldolgozva /aranykorongok, aranyhuzalok stb./;

egészen apró feldolgozatlan töredékek papirba csomagolva.

8./ 1 /egy/ darab római aranygyürü gemmával. Lelt.sz: 649.

9./ 1 /egy/ darab római aranygyürü, törött, figurális dombormüvü kővel. Lelt. sz: 693.

10/ 1 /egy/ darab római aranygyürü gemmával. Lelt. sz: 650.

11/ 1 /egy/ darab római aranykarikagyürü szám nélkül.

12/ 4 /négy/ darab római aranypénz / Valens, Maxsimianus, Veneri Victrici, Theodosius/.Szám nélkül.

Fig. 13. The first page of the inventory of precious metal artefacts of the Museum of Vas County drawn up in 1944 (with Item 1 of Section 7 describing the diadem "mounted onto a circular base", i.e. onto a copper plate, highlighted)

1

2

3

Fig. 14. The diadem before its conservation and restoration (photo by Gábor Papp, 2002)

1

2

3

4

5

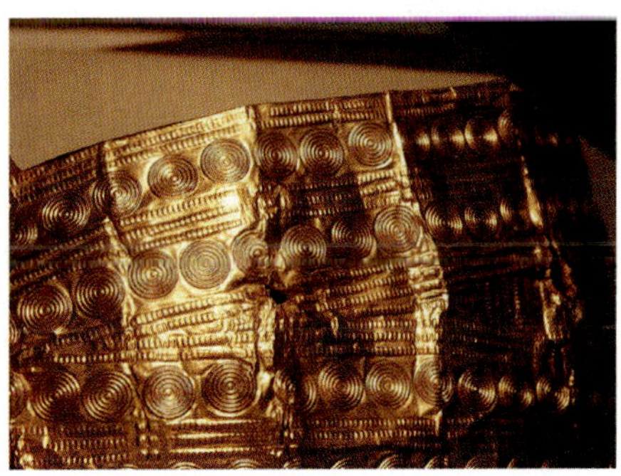

6

Fig. 15. The diadem's copper plate made by István Méri (1943) and details of the diadem during its restoration (photo by Katalin T. Bruder, 2004)

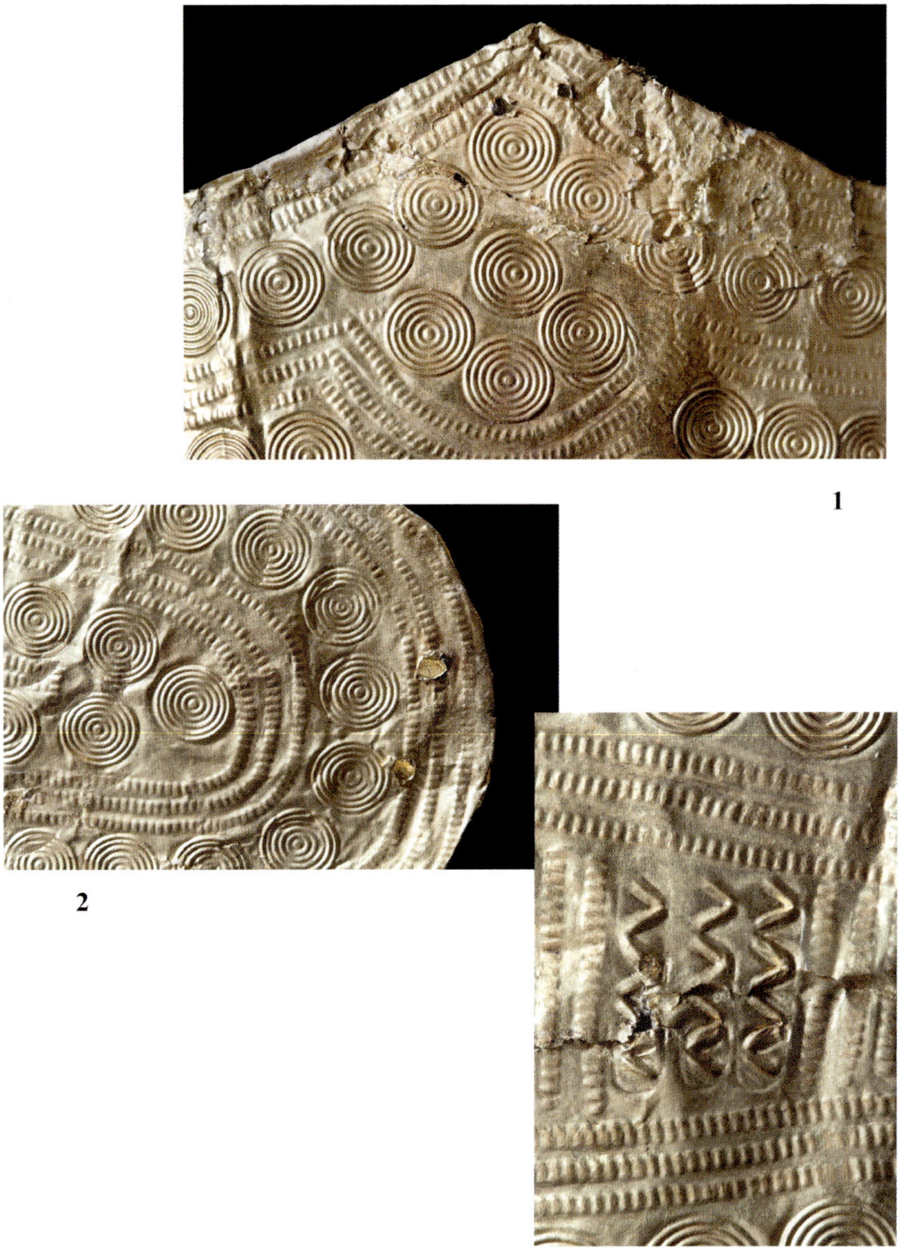

1

2

3

Fig. 16. Details of the diadem: perforations and traces of stamping (photo by Tibor Takács, 2013)

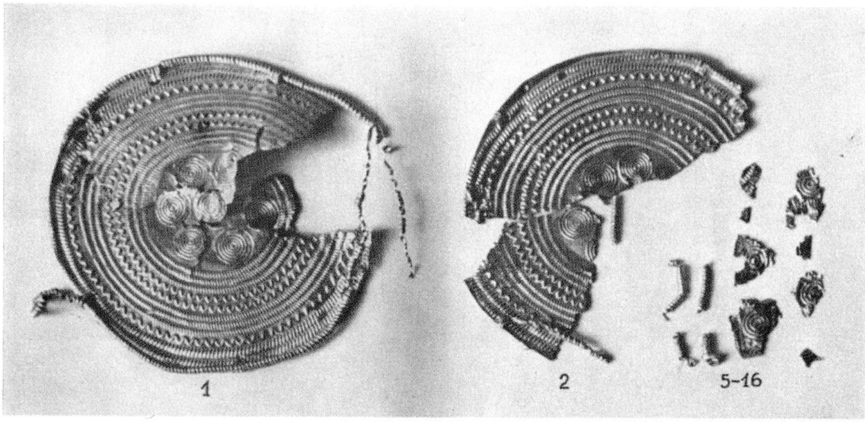

1

2

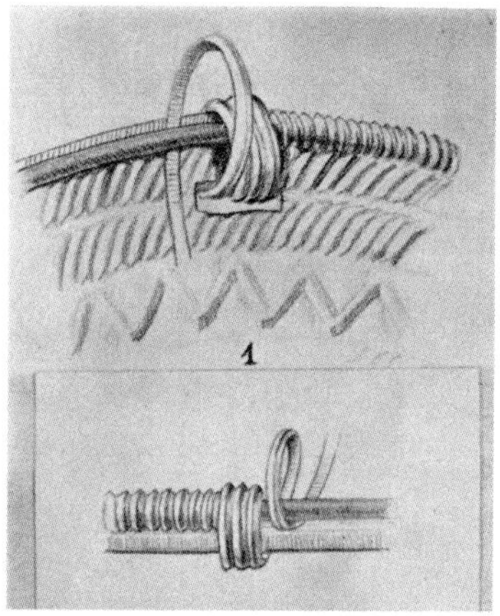

3

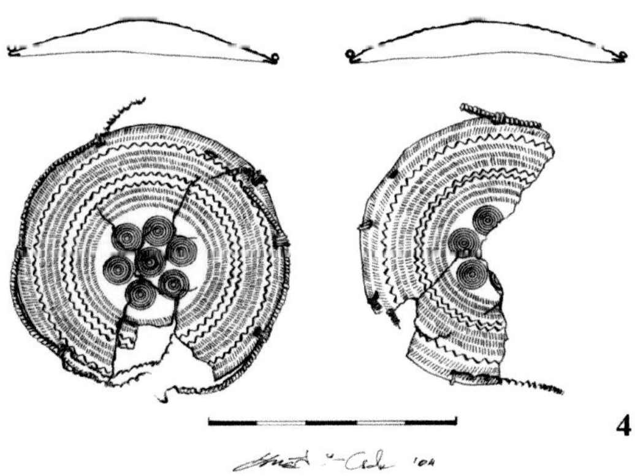

4

Fig. 17. Domed roundels (Pair I) in 1943–44 and their drawing (after MOZSOLICS *1950, Taf. 2. 1–2, and Csaba E. Kiss's drawing, 2004)*

1

2

3

4

Fig. 18. Domed roundels (Pair I) before and after restoration (photos by Katalin T. Bruder, 2004; Tamás Tárczy, 2008; Tibor Takács, 2013)

1

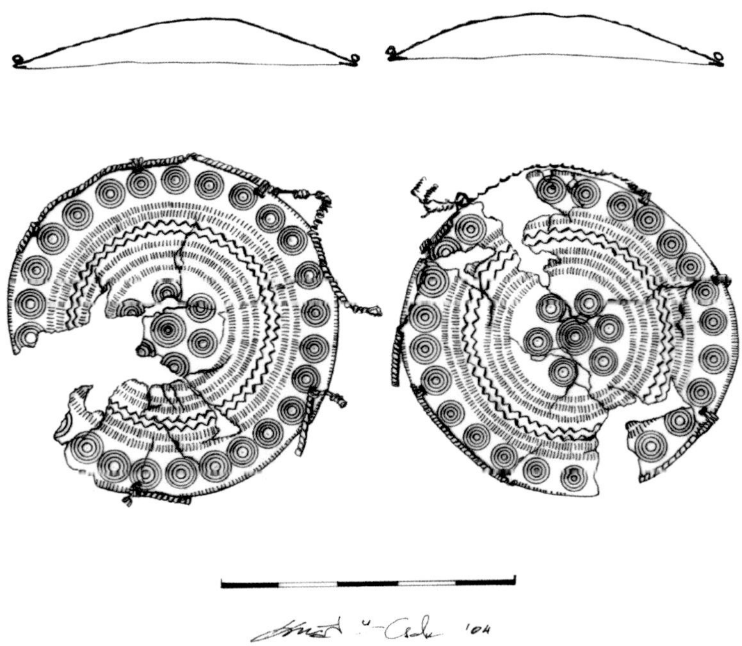

2

Fig. 19. Domed roundels (Pair II) in 1943–44 and their drawing (after MOZSOLICS *1950, Taf. 2. 3–4, and Csaba E. Kiss's drawing, 2004)*

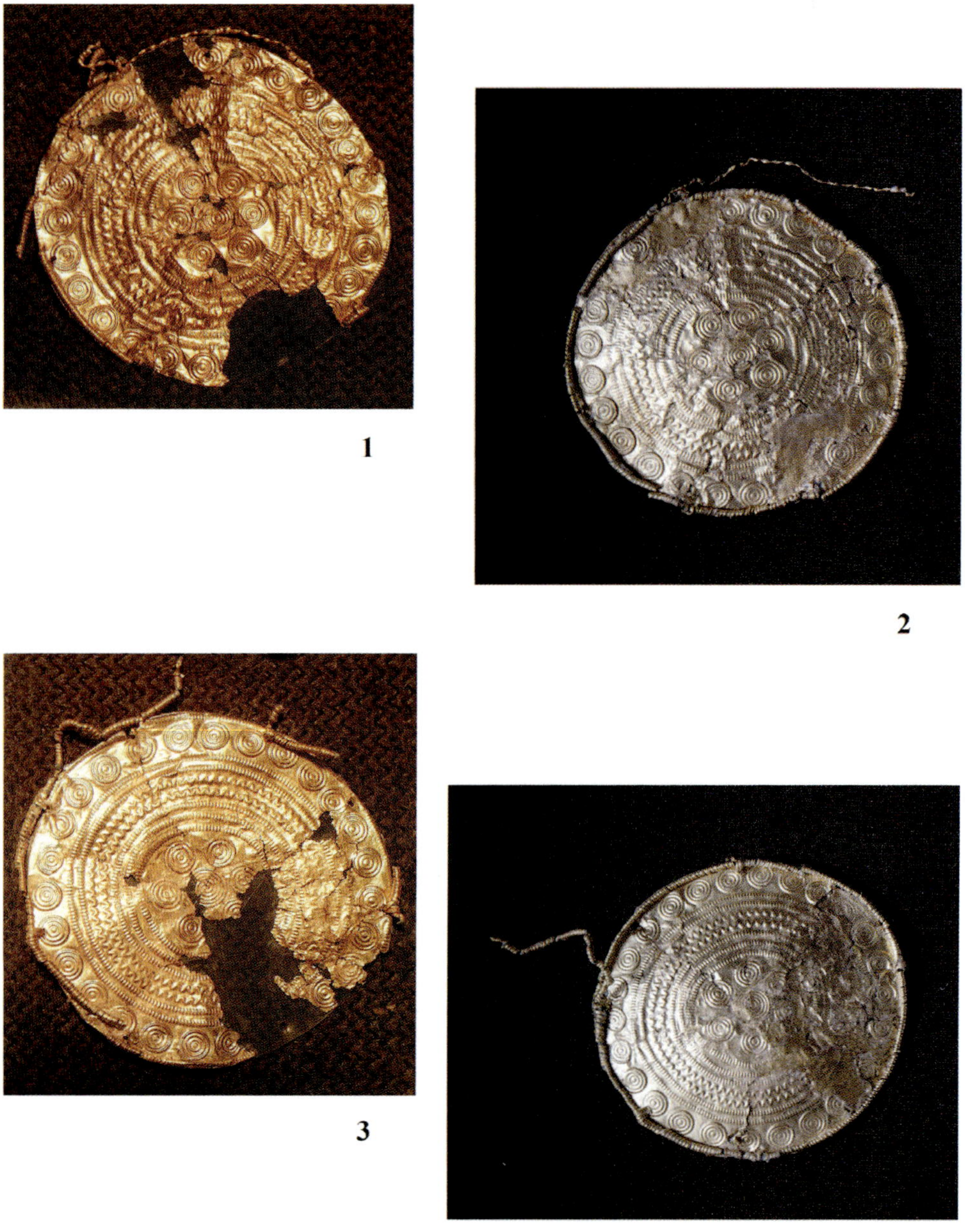

1 2 3 4

Fig. 20. Domed roundels (Pair II) before and after restoration (photos by Katalin T. Bruder, 2004; Tibor Takács, 2013)

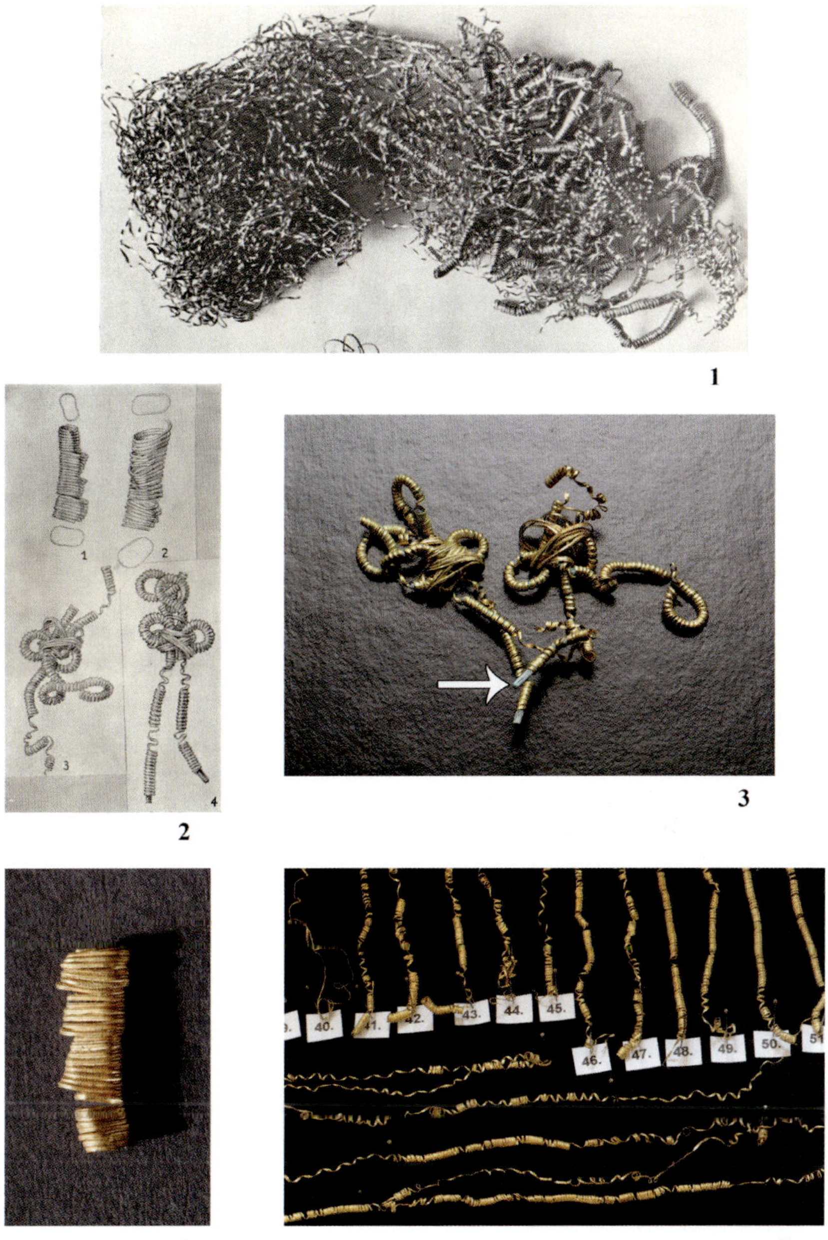

Fig. 21. 1–2. Gold tangle of the pectoral (?) and its fragments in 1943–44; 3–5. after the new conservation and restoration, some with bronze wire in them (after MOZSOLICS *1950, Taf. 3. 1, Abb. 5; photos 3, 5 by Tamás Tárczy, 2008; 4 by Tibor Takács, 2013)*

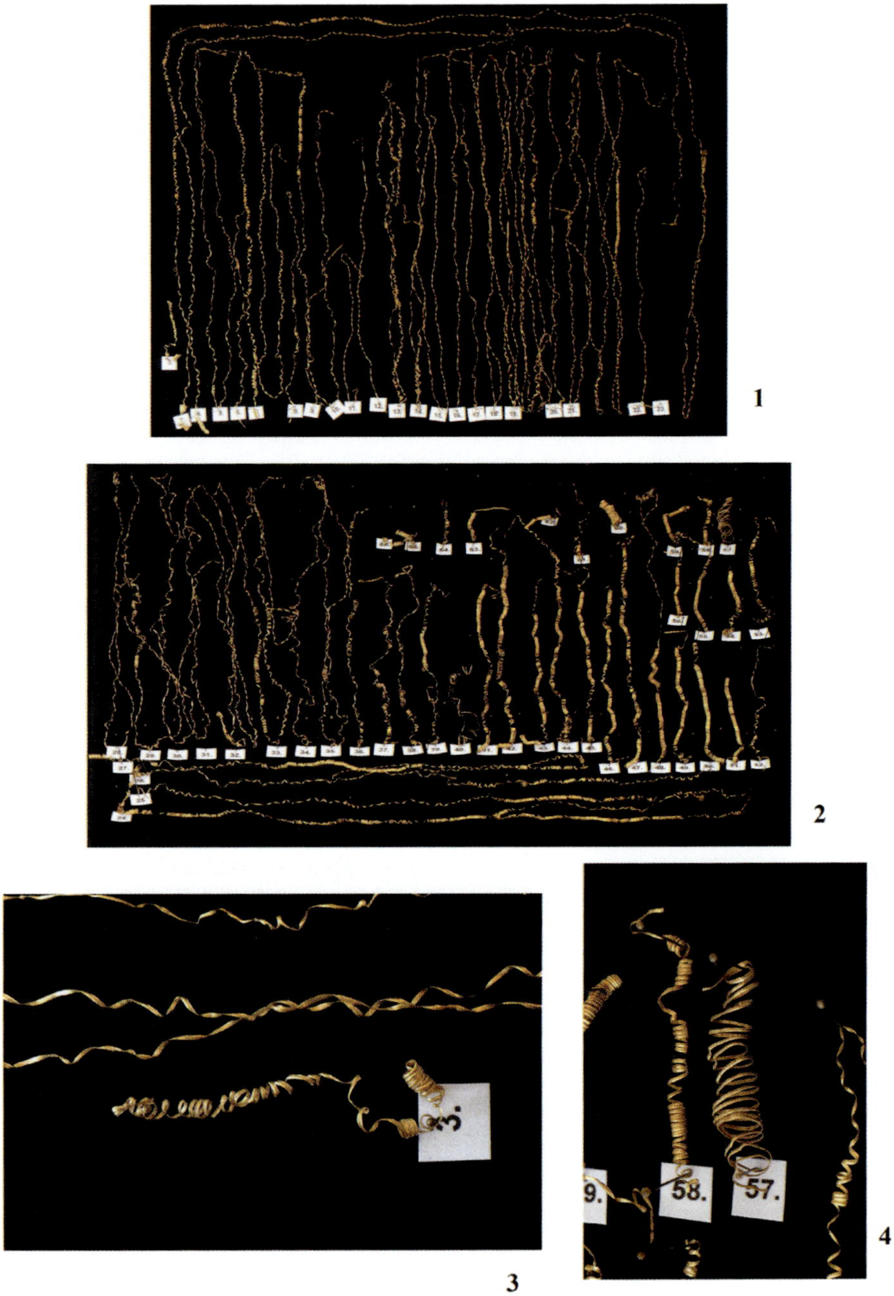

Fig. 22. Fragments of the pectoral (wires) after the new conservation and restoration (photo by Tamás Tárczy, 2008)

Fig. 23. Bronze backplates and their drawings before and after restoration (photos by Katalin T. Bruder, 2004; Tibor Takács, 2013; drawing by Csaba E. Kiss, 2004)

Fig. 24. The diadem and the domed roundels of the golden treasure (photo by Tamás Tárczy, 2008)

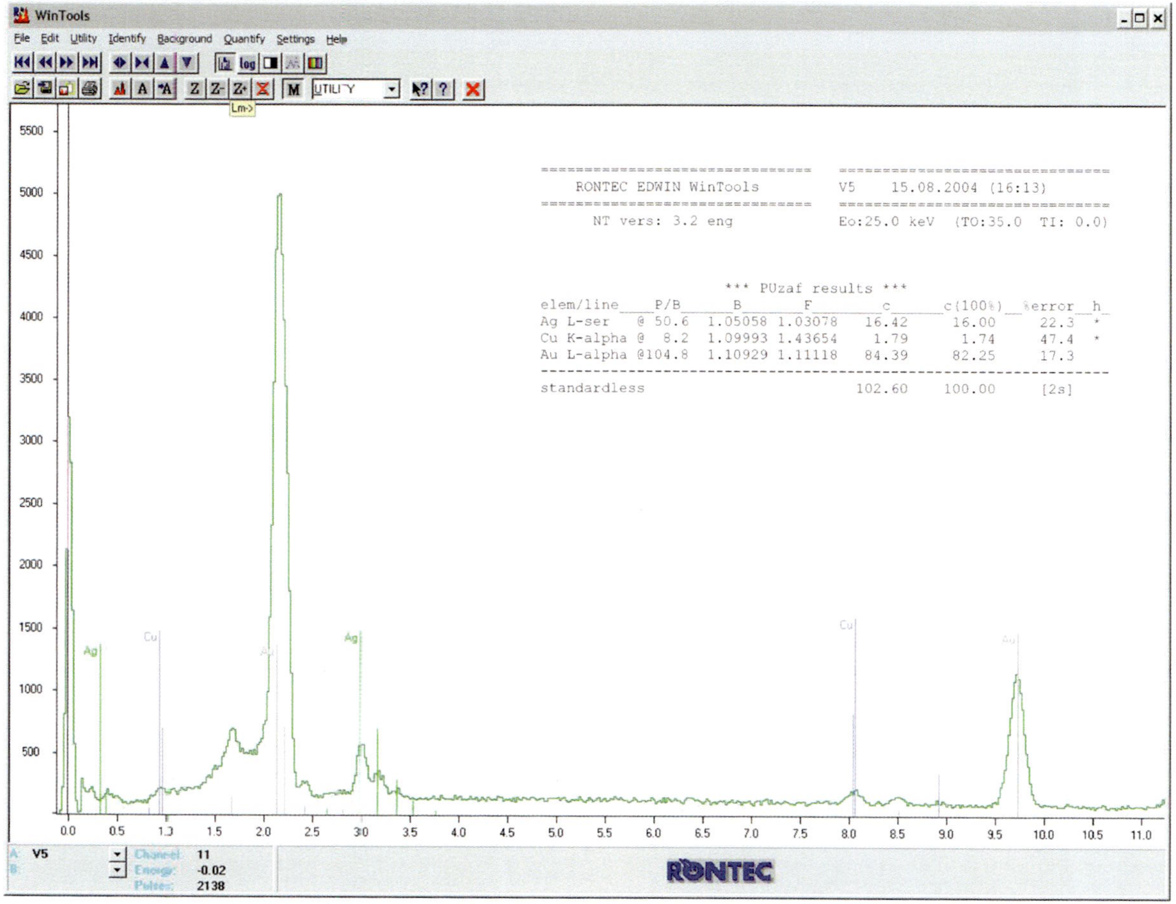

Fig. 25. The results of the metal analysis of the diadem (sample code: V5, VD)

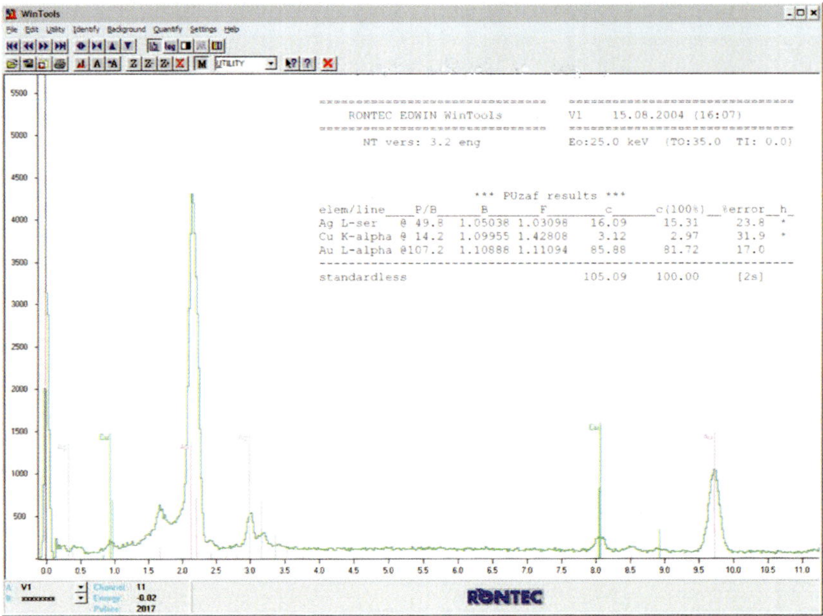

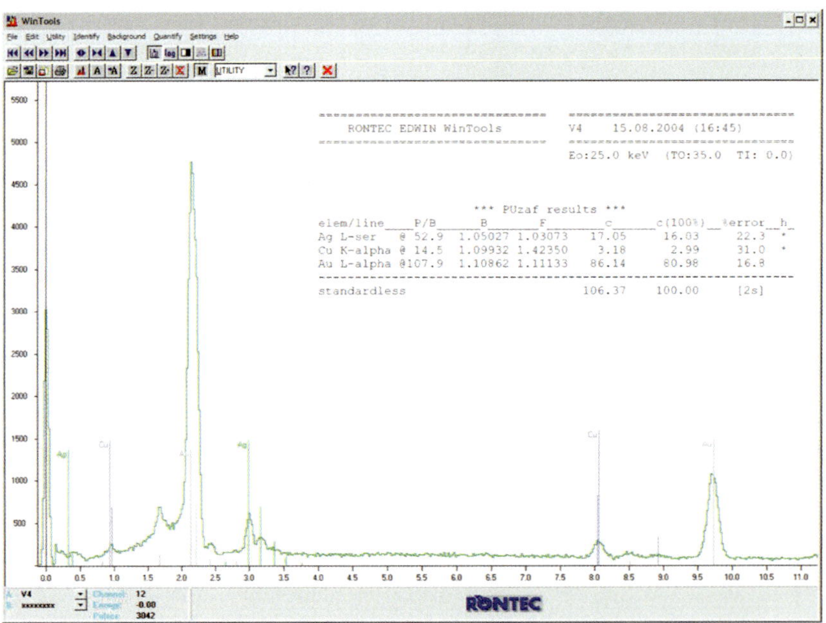

Fig. 26. The results of the metal analysis of the domed roundels (Pair I, sample codes: V1 and V4)

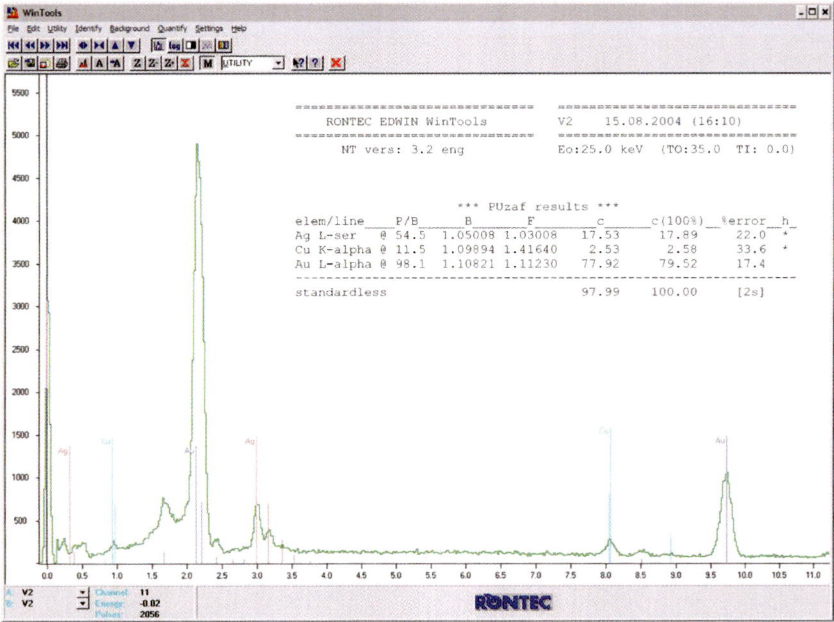

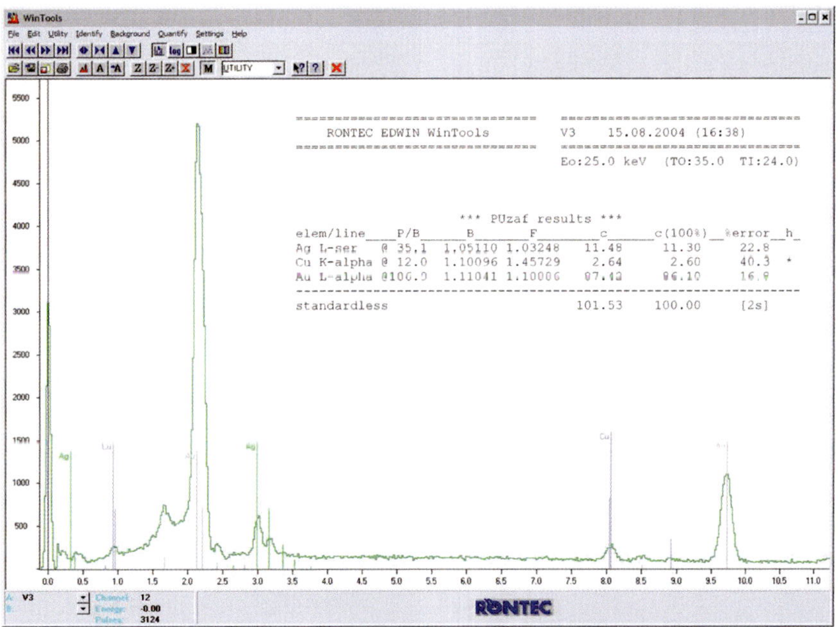

Fig. 27. The results of the metal analysis of the domed roundels (Pair II, sample codes: V2 and V3)

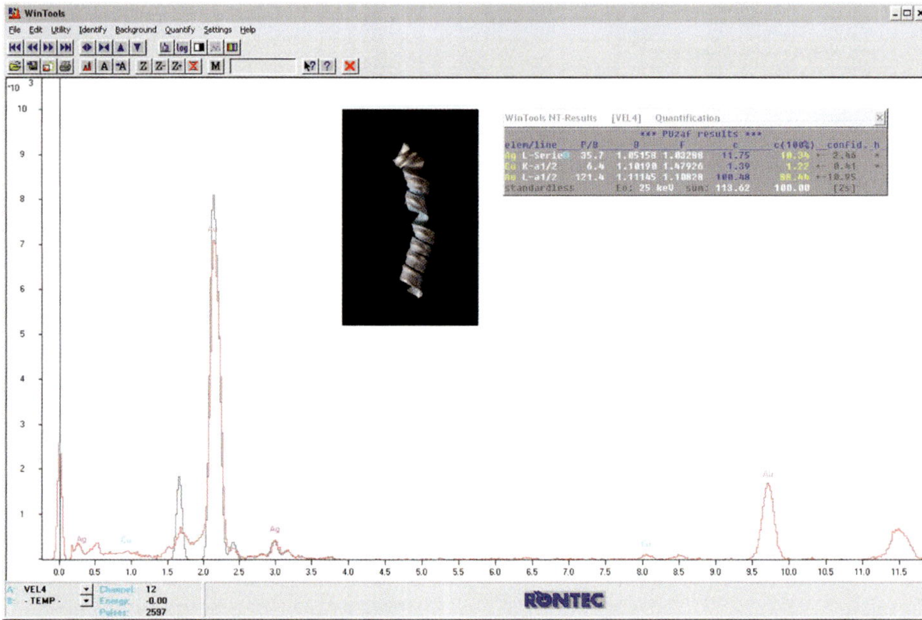

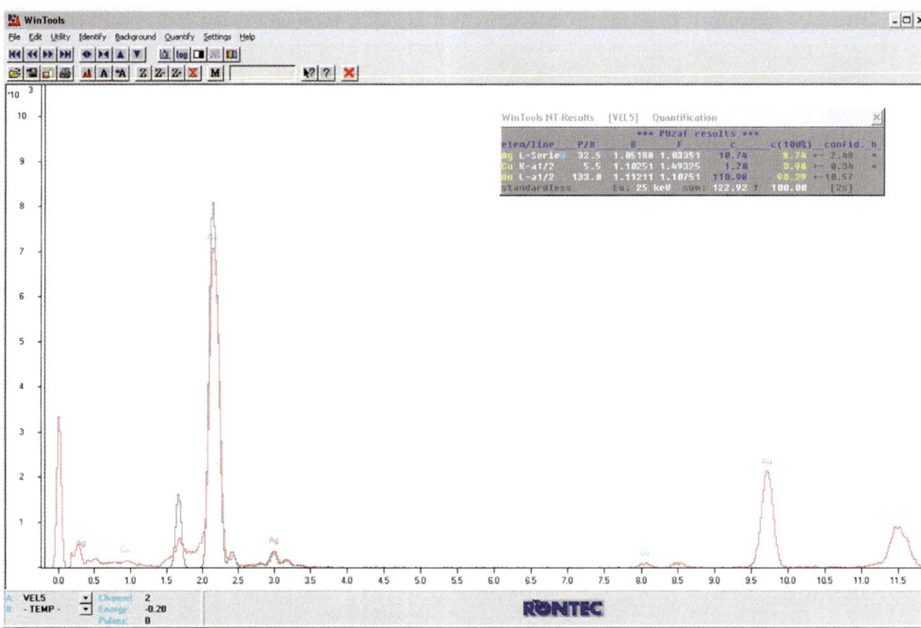

Fig. 28. 1–2. The results of the metal analysis of the gold spirals (sample codes: Vel4 and Vel5)

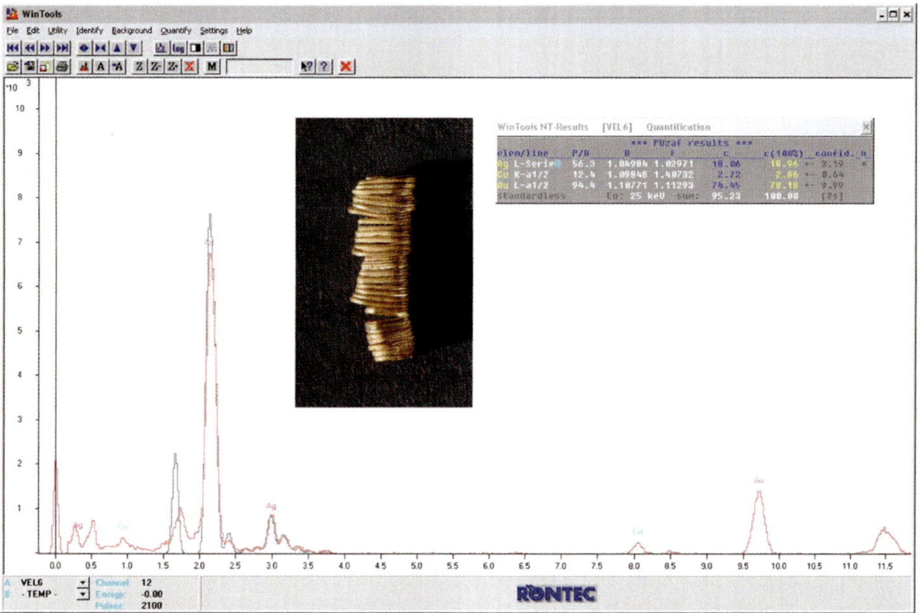

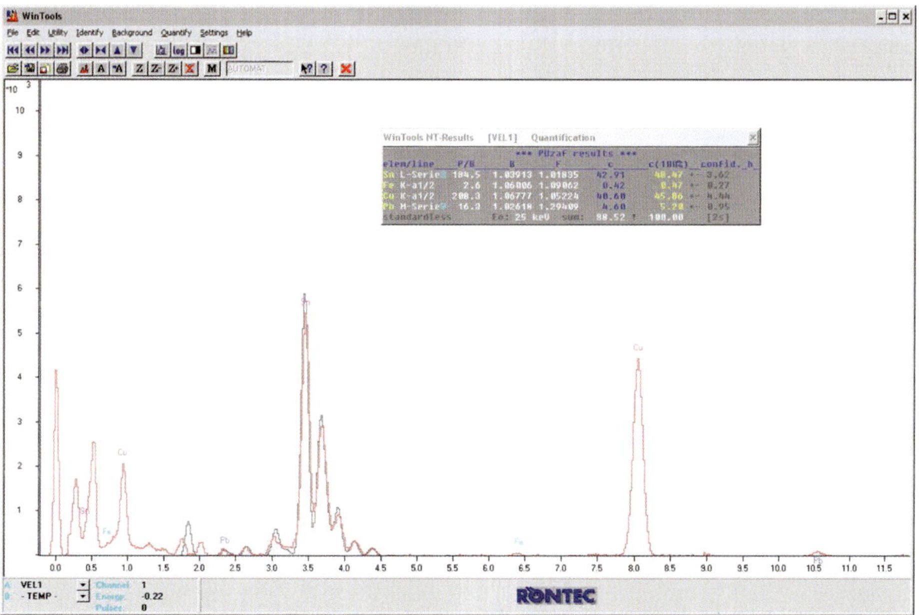

Fig. 29. 1. The results of the metal analysis of the gold spiral (sample code: Vel6); 2. The results of the metal analysis of the bronze backplate of the diadem (sample code: Vel1)

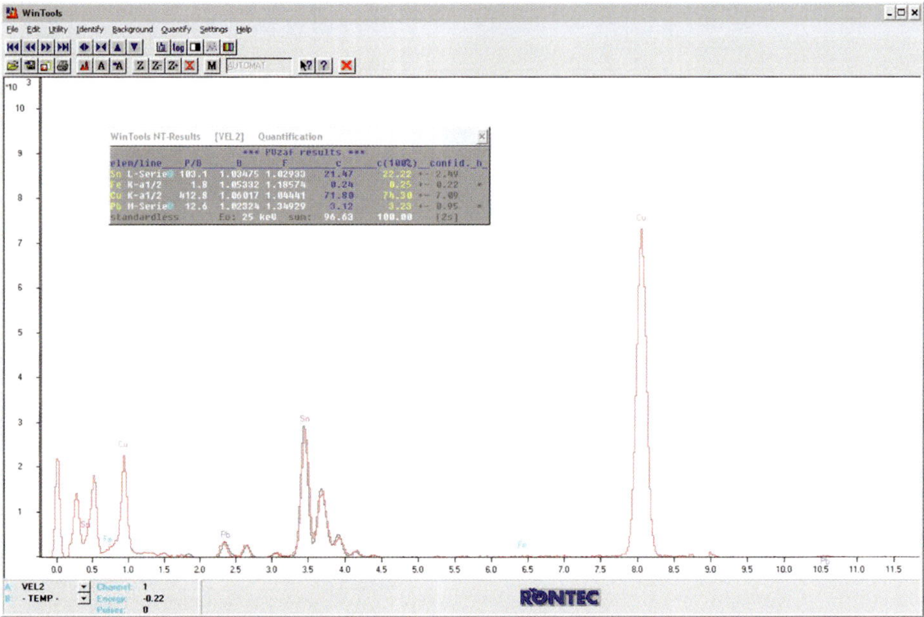

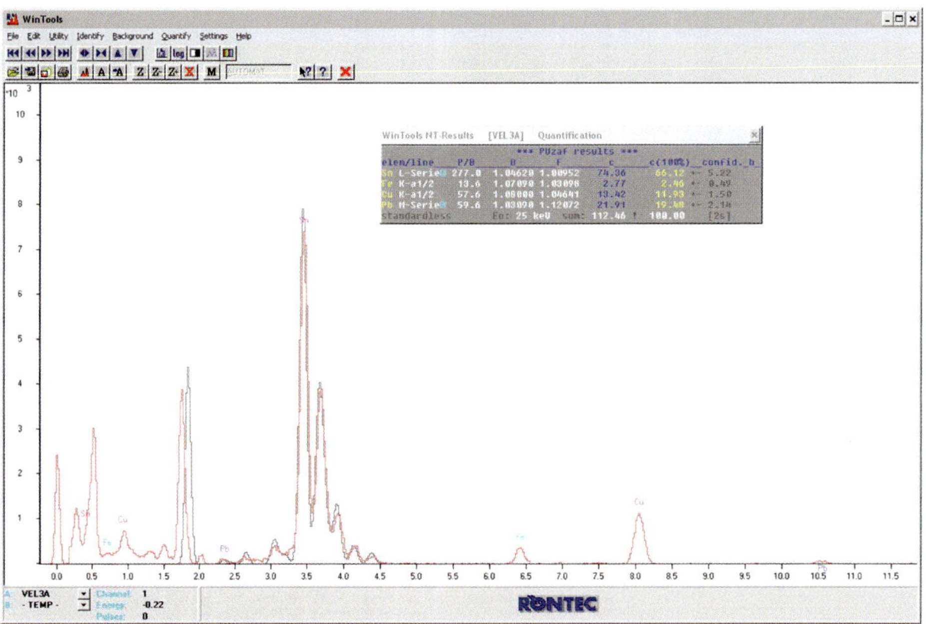

Fig. 30. 1–2. The results of the metal analysis of the bronze backplates of the domed roundels 1 and 3 (sample codes: Vel2 and Vel3a)

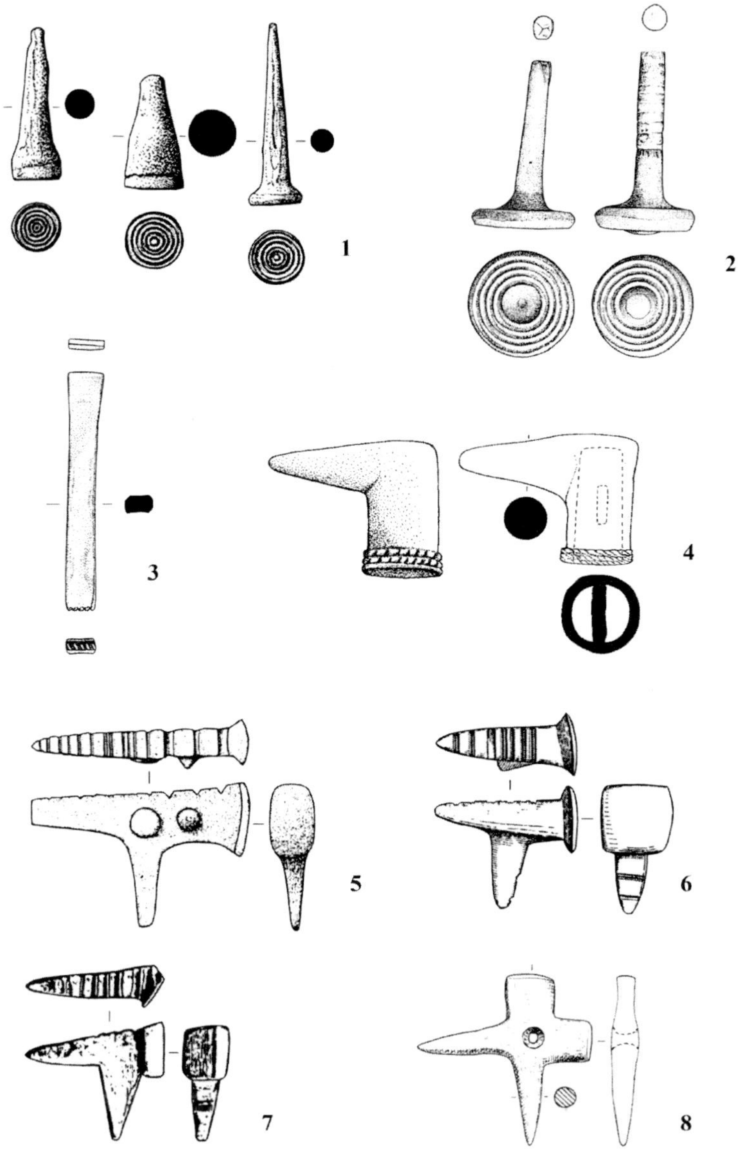

Fig. 31. Metalworking tools. Punches: 1. Génelard (after THEVENOT *1998, Fig. 5. 11–13); 2. Murnau (after* GOLD UND KULT *2003, Kat. Nr. 7a); Punch with cable motif: 3. Murnau (after* GOLD UND KULT *2003, Kat. Nr. 7b); Anvil: 4. Jevičko (after* SALAŠ *2005, II: Tab. 179. 30); Anvils for drawing wire: 5. Keranfinit, 6. Bardouville, 7. Fresné-la-Mère (after* THEVENOT *1998, Fig. 9. 3–5), 8. Venarey-les-Laumes (*NICOLARDOT–VERGER *1998, Fig. 11. 10). The drawings are not to the same scale (drawing by Magdolna Mátyus)*

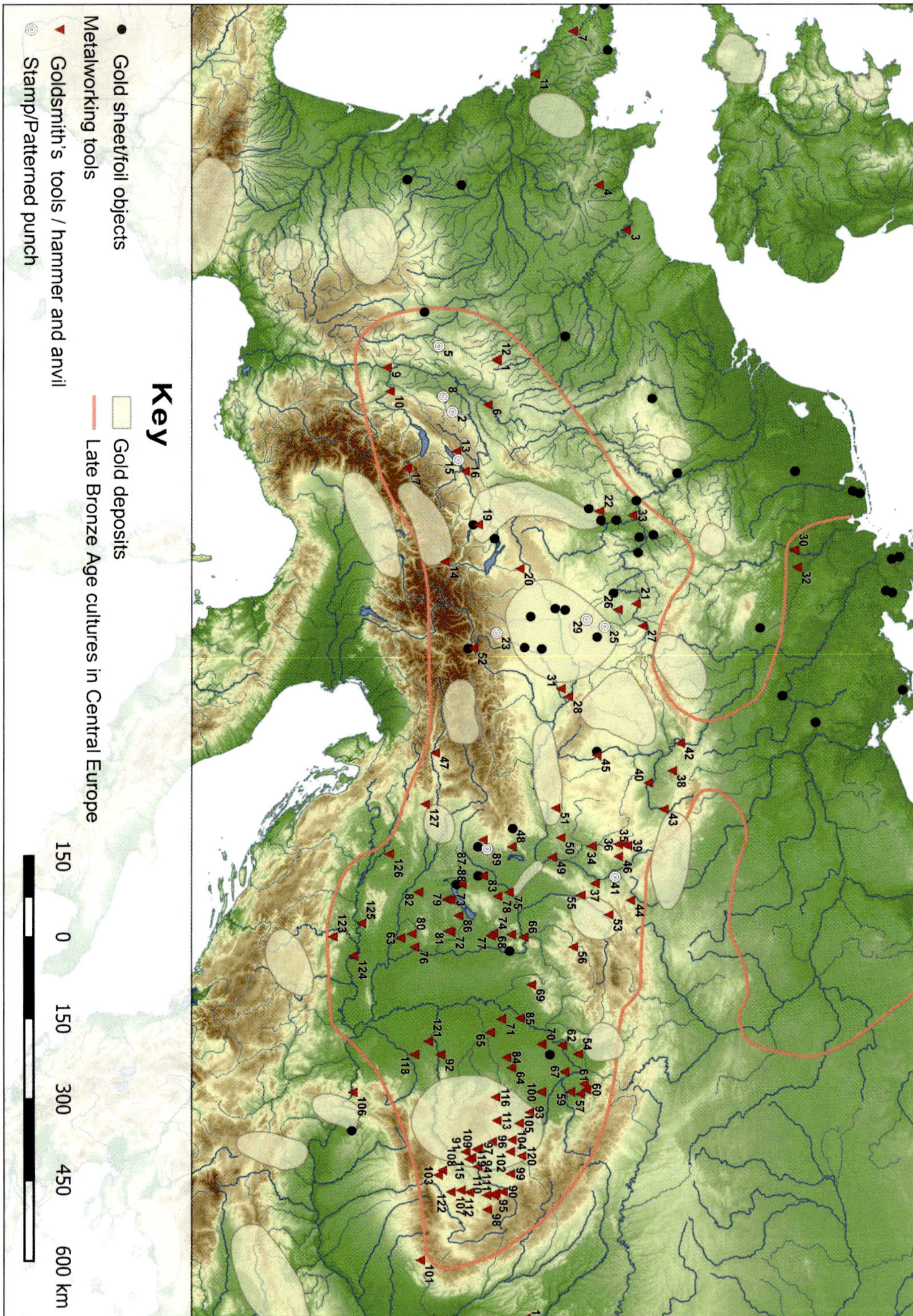
Key
Gold sheet/foil objects
Metalworking tools
Goldsmith's tools / hammer and anvil
Stamp/Patterned punch
Gold deposits
Late Bronze Age cultures in Central Europe
150
0
150
300
450
600 km

Fig. 32. Goldsmithing and smithing tools as well as golden sheet objects ("crowns", vessels mounts, jewellery) of the Late Bronze Age from Central Europe (after KOSSACK *1995, Abb. 1;* LEHRBERGER *1995, Fig. 1;* ARMBRUSTER *2012, Abb. 1;* GERLOFF *2003, Abb. 7;* SPERBER *2003, Abb. 2, complemented by the author; made by Tibor Takács)*

Findspots of goldsmithing and smithing tools, according to countries:

Stamps/punches

France: 2. Arbois–Grotte des Planches; 5. Génelard, Saône-et-Loire; 8. Larnaud, hoard

Switzerland: 15. Hauterive-Champréveyres

Germany: 23. Marnau (Bavaria); 24. Nürnberg–Mögeldorf (Bavaria); 25. unprovenanced, in the Nürnberg Museum; 29. Stockheim (Bavaria)

Czech Republic: 41. Přestavlký

Hungary: 89. Velem–Szent Vid (?)

Goldsmithing tools (hammers and anvils)

France: 1. Alise-Sainte-Reine, Côte d' Or: anvil (horned, cross-shaped); 2. Arbois–Grotte des Planches cave: bone stamp/punch; 3. Bardouville, Seine-Maritime: anvil, also suitable for drawing wire (cf. Fig. 31. 6*); 4. Fresné-la-Mère Calvados, hoard (Ha B1): anvil resembling the previous one (cf.* Fig. 31. 7*), found together with gold objects; 5. Génelard, Saône-et-Loire, hoard (Ha A1, 13th–12th* centuries *BC): anvil (horned, cross-shaped, with three work surfaces), four socketed hammers (one with a domed face), five chisels (graver) with one or two faces, bronze sheet with hooked end, five punches/stamps, polishing stone, bronze mould, bronze nugget, three bronze tuyères, clay funnel; 6. Gray, Haute-Saône: anvil (horned, cross-shaped); 7. Keranfinit, hoard: anvil, suitable for drawing wire (cf.* Fig. 31, 5*); 8. Larnaud, hoard: bronze punch/stamp; 9. unprovenanced, in the Museum of Lyon: anvil (horned, cross-shaped); 10. Porcieu–Amblagnieu, hoard (close of the Middle Bronze Age): anvil (horned, rectangular work surface), socketed hammer, punch and other small tools, whetstone; 11. Trégorf-en-Surzur, Morbihan, hoard: anvil suitable for drawing wire; 12. Venarey-les-Laumes (Côte-d'Or, Bourgogne), stray find discovered when digging the Bourgogne canal (bronze final): anvil with a perforation for drawing wire (cf.* Fig. 31. 8*)*

Switzerland: 13. Auvernier: anvil, two socketed chasing hammers (Treibhammer), shaft-hole hammer; 14. Domat–Ems, hoard (Ha B): hammer; 15. Hauterive-Champréveyres, settlement: bronze stamps/punches; 16. Niedau–Steinberg, settlement: hammer (unknown type); 17. Riddes: anvil; 18. Zürich–Alpenqui: antler hammer; 19. Zürich–Haumesser: anvil, socketed chasing hammers (Treibhammer)

Germany: 20. Bad Buchau–Wasserburg (Baden-Württemberg), settlement: socketed hammers, copper ore, tin, lead, and bronze raw materials, tuyère and moulds; 21. Großer Knetzberg (Bavaria), hoard: socketed hammer; 22. Lachen–Speyerdorf (Rhein-Pfalz), Ha B1 burial: anvil (prismatic, Steckamboss type, with two grooves at each end), bronze pick-ingot; 23. Marnau (Bavaria), metalworker's hoard of twenty-seven artefacts (Bz D–Ha B1): two bronze stamps/punches; 24. Nürnberg–Mögeldorf (Bavaria), hoard (Ha A1): bronze stamps/punches; 25. unprovenanced, in the Nürnberg Museum (13th–8th centuries

BC): bronze stamp/punch; 26. Schornweißah (Bavaria), hoard: socketed hammer; 27. Schwabthal (Bavaria), hoard: socketed hammer; 28. Steinkirchen (Bavaria), Grave 10 (later Ha A): anvil (prismatic, Steckamboss type), suitable for drawing wire; 29. Stockheim (Bavaria), hoard (Bz D): bronze stamp/punch; 30. Schinna (Lower Saxony), hoard (Period V): socketed chasing hammer, double-sided bronze mould for an axe and a sickle; 31. Waibling (Bavaria): socketed hammer; 32. Welze (Lower Saxony), pit of a fireplace in the settlement: socketed chasing hammer; 33. Zornheim, hoard (?): socketed hammer

Czech Republic: 34. Blučina, Hoard 2 (Bz D1): socketed hammer; 35. Borotín, hoard (Bz D2–Ha A1): shaft-hole hammer; 36. Boskovice, Hoard 4 (Ha B2): strongly worn socketed hammer; 37. Drslavice, Hoard 2 (Bz D2–Ha A1): socketed hammer, winged axe reworked into a hammer; 38. Hrdlořezy, hoard (Ha B1): blacksmith's hammer-axe (Hammeraxt); 39. Jevičko, hoard (Ha A1): socketed horned anvil (cf. Fig. 31. 4*); 40. Nová Ves, hoard (Bz C-D): horned anvil with rectangular face, three bronze moulds, three pairs of gold wire jewellery (32.06 g) + vessel; 41. Přestavlký, hoard (Ha A1): bronze stamp/punch; 42. Prague–Rýdeč, hoard (Bz D–Ha A1): broken chasing hammer, resembling the piece from the Szombathely area, socketed hammer, saw; 43. Skalička, hoard (Bz A1–2): chasing hammer; 44. Štramberk, Hoard 4 (Ha B1): socketed hammer; 45. Ujezd, hoard (Bz C2): conical anvil, two socketed hammers, two awls; 46. Žárovice–Hamry, Hoards 3 and 7 (Ha B1): one socketed hammer in each*

Austria: 47. Augsdorf (Carinthia), hoard: anvil; 48. Draßburg (Burgenland), hoard (Ha A1): socketed thinning/stretching hammer (Schweifhammer)*; 49. Mannersdorf (Lower Austria), stray find: socketed hammer* (Ausschlich- *or* Polierhammer)*; 50. Oberleis–Oberleisberg (Lower Austria): stretching hammer* (Schweifhammer)*; 51. Schiltern (Lower Austria), hoard (Ha A2): anvil (socketed, adze-shaped, upward-curving edge), socketed hammers (one is a stretching hammer, Schweifhammer), casting wedges, wires; 52. Volders (Tyrol), Grave 370: small, atypical chasing hammer* (Treibhammer)

Slovakia: 53. Brvnište/Boronás, hoard (Jászkarajenő period): socketed hammer; 54. Somotor/Szomotor, settlement, from a house (Gáva culture, later than the piece from Zvolen): socketed hammer; 55. Trenčianske Bohuslavice/Bogoszló, hoard (Jászkarajenő period): socketed hammer; 56. Zvolen/Zólyom, Hoard 2 (later Piliny period): socketed hammer

Ukraine, Zakarpattia Oblast: 57. Makarevo (Lazy I series, Ha A1): socketed hammer; 58. Mužievo/Nagymuzsaj, Hoard II (Suskovo series, Ha A2): socketed hammer; 59. Mužievo/Nagymuzsaj, Hoard I (Kriva series, Bz C–D): socketed hammer; 60. Podmonastyr, today part of Munkács/Mukacheve, Hoard II (Bz C–D): socketed hammer; 61. Velikie Lučki/Nagylucska, hoard (Bz C–D): socketed hammer

Hungary: 62. Balsa, hoard (Kurd horizon): socketed hammer; 63. Beremend (Gyermely horizon): two or three socketed hammers; 64. Bihar County, hoard: shaft-hole hammer; 65. Dévaványa, hoard (Hajdúböszörmény horizon): hammer; 66. Esztergom–Szentgyörgymező, hoard (Kurd horizon): socketed hammer; 67. Gemzse, hoard (Ópályi horizon): hammer; 68. Gyermely, hoard (Gyermely horizon): socketed hammer;

69. Gyöngyössolymos, hoard (Kurd horizon): socketed hammer; 70. Hajdúnánás, hoard (Kurd horizon): socketed hammer; 71. Kenderes, Hoard I (Kurd horizon): socketed hammer; 72. Keszőhidegkút, hoard (Kurd horizon): socketed hammer; 73. Lengyeltóti, Hoards II and III (Kurd horizon): three socketed hammers in one, four in the other hoard; 74. Lovasberény, hoard (Gyermely horizon): two or three socketed hammers; 75. Ménfőcsanak–Széles-földek, settlement, found with a metal detector: socketed hammer; 76. Mohács, hoard, later lost (Gyermely horizon): socketed hammer; 77. Nadap, metalworker's hoard (Ha A1 or A2): five socketed hammers; 78. Nagydém, hoard (Gyermely horizon): socketed hammer and broken shaft-hole hammer; 79. Öreglak, hoard (Kurd horizon): socketed axe reworked into a socketed hammer; 80. Peterd, hoard (Kurd horizon): socketed hammer; 81. Regöly–Birkás, later lost: socketed hammer; 82. Rinyaszentkirály, hoard (Kurd horizon): winged axe reworked into a hammer, shaft-hole hammer suitable for gold-working according to Mozsolics; 83. Celldömölk–Ság-hegy, Urnfield settlement, stray find (Romànd horizon): hammers; 84. Szentpéterszeg, hoard (Kurd horizon): two socketed hammers; 85. Tiszaszőlős, hoard, later lost (Kurd horizon): socketed hammer; 86. Torvaj, hoard (Gyermely horizon): small socketed hammer (Tüllenhammer)*; 87–88. Várvölgy–Felsőzsid, Hoards 4 and 10 (Ha A2–B1): seven socketed hammers in one and six in the other hoard, chisels; 89. Velem–Szent Vid, Urnfield settlement, stray finds: mould for an anvil, anvil (horned, bent at right-angle, cf.* Fig. 35. 5*), cutting anvil (cf.* Fig. 35. 4*), mould for a socketed hammer, socketed hammers (cf.* Fig. 35. 3. 6*), bronze stamp/punch (?), chasing tools with single and double working edge, and Hoard I (Gyermely horizon): socketed hammer*

Romania: The list is based on Florian Gogâltan's excellent overview, but I have omitted the tool moulds and the unprovenanced artefacts. I added a single artefact found in Temesvár to his catalogue. 90. Adrian/Görgényadjorján, stray find: socketed hammer; 91. Aiud/Nagyenyed, hoard (Susani horizon, Ha A1): five or six socketed hammers (with elliptical, round and rectangular faces); 92. Arad, Hoard II (Ha B1): socketed hammer; 93. Bicaz/Bikácfalva, Hoard II (Ha A1): socketed hammer; 94. Bogata/Marosbogát, stray find: socketed hammer; 95. Călugăreni/Mikháza, hoard (Ha A1): socketed hammer; 96. Cluj-Napoca/Kolozsvár, Hoard III: socketed hammer; 97. Corneşti Sînfalva, hoard (Ha B1): socketed hammer; 98. Corund/Korond, hoard (Bz D): unique socketed hammer; 99. Dipşa/Dipse/Dürrbach, hoard (Ha A1): six socketed hammers; 100. Domăneşti/Domahida, hoard (Domăneşti horizon, Bz D1): shaft-hole axe hafted with a socketed axe; 101. Drajna de Jos, hoard (Bz D): socketed hammer; 102. Gherla/Szamosújvár/Neuschloss, stray find: socketed hammer; 103. Guşteriţa/Szenterzsébet, Hoard II (Ha A1): three socketed hammers (with different faces: narrow rectangular, broad rectangular, round); 104. Igriţa-Höhle/Kisigrice, hoard (Bz D): socketed hammer; 105. Stray find discovered in Jibou/Zsibó : socketed hammer; 106. Liubcova, hoard (Ha A1): socketed hammer; 107. Nou Săsesc/Szászújfalva (Ha B1): socketed hammer; 108. Ocna Sibiului/Vízakna, stray find (possibly Ha A): socketed hammer; 109. Plăieşti/Kövend (?),hoard:socketed hammer; 110. Rigmani/Rigmány, stray find: socketed hammer; 111. Sâmbriaş, stray find: socketed hammer or anvil; 112. Seleuş/Nagyszőlős, hoard (Bz D): socketed hammer; 113. Sfăraş/Farnas, hoard (Ha A1): socketed hammer; 114. Şpălnaca/Ispánlaka, Hoard I (Ha B1):

socketed hammer; 115. Şpălnaca/Ispánlaka, Hoard II (Ha A1): one shaft-hole and eight socketed hammers (with narrow rectangle and elliptical faces); 116. Şuncuiuş-Höhle/ Vársonkolyos, hoard (Ha A1): socketed hammer; 117. Tătărani, hoard (Bz D): socketed hammer; 118. Timişoara/Temesvár II–Fratelia, hoard (Ha B1): anvil, socketed hammer, chisel; 119. Uioara de Sus/Felsőmarosújvár, hoard (Ha A1): nine socketed hammers (narrow rectangular, broader rectangular, elliptical and round faces); 120. Uriu/Felőr, stray find: socketed hammer; 121. Variaş, hoard (Ha A1): socketed hammer; 122. Vărd/ Vérd, hoard (Ha B1): socketed hammer

*Bosnia-Herzegovina: 123. Boljanič, hoard (Stufe 2 = Kurd horizon): three anvils (*Steckamboss *type, one is horned and has a rectangular work surface), four socketed hammers, five casting wedges, saw blade; 124. Vidovice, hoard (earlier Gyermely horizon): hammer with platter face* (Tellerhammer)

Croatia: 125. Brodski Varoš, hoard (Phase II, Ha A1): two socketed hammers; 126. Kloštar Ivanić, hoard (Phase III, Ha A2): socketed hammer

Slovenia: 127. Hudinja, hoard: shaft-hole hammer (Schaftlochhammer)

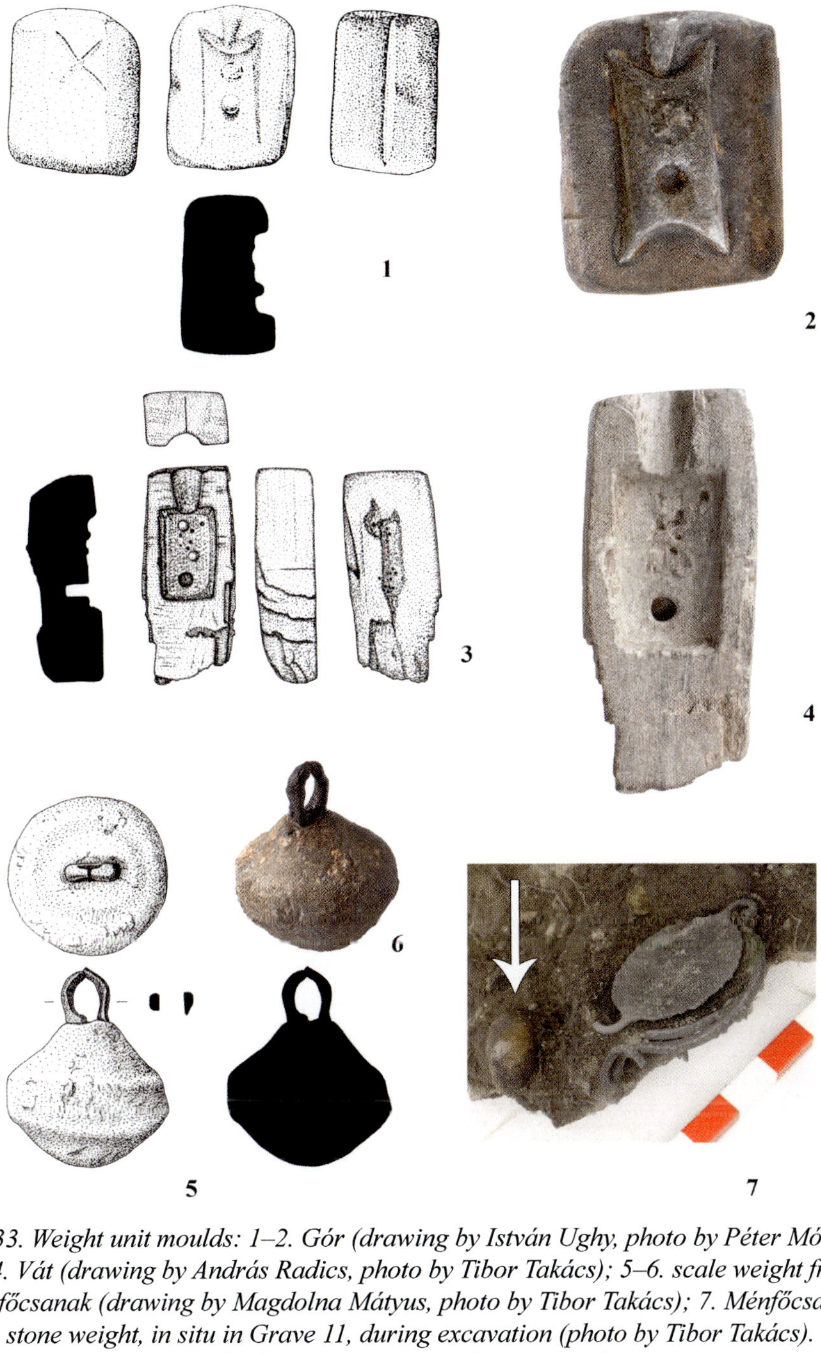

Fig. 33. Weight unit moulds: 1–2. Gór (drawing by István Ughy, photo by Péter Móricz); 3–4. Vát (drawing by András Radics, photo by Tibor Takács); 5–6. scale weight from Ménfőcsanak (drawing by Magdolna Mátyus, photo by Tibor Takács); 7. Ménfőcsanak, stone weight, in situ in Grave 11, during excavation (photo by Tibor Takács). The drawings are not to the same scale

Site	Győr, Ménfőcsanak–Széles-földek			
Inventory number	1.34305.1.163.			
Artefact	Lead weight			
Sampling point				
Measurement number	#2	#3	#4	#6
Setting	Alloy Plus	Alloy Plus	Alloy Plus	Alloy Plus
	%			
Mg	ND	ND	ND	ND
Mg ±				
Al	4.02	2.81	ND	ND
Al ±	0.11	0.11		
Si	7.1081	5.8445	4.93	4.23
Si ±	0.0441	0.0417	0.16	0.11
P	2.8913	2.3991	ND	ND
P ±	0.0181	0.0175		
S	ND	ND	ND	0.2933
S ±				0.0196
Ti	ND	ND	1.66	0.88
Ti ±			0.14	0.08
V	ND	ND	ND	ND
V ±				
Cr	ND	ND	ND	ND
Cr ±				
Mn	ND	ND	ND	ND
Mn ±				
Fe	**1.1188**	**1.0219**	**92.55**	**93.78**
Fe ±	0.0363	0.0355	0.56	0.41

Fig. 34. The results of the XRF analysis of the weight found at Ménfőcsanak

Site	Győr, Ménfőcsanak–Széles-földek			
Inventory number	1.34305.1.163.			
Artefact	Lead weight			
Sampling point				
Measurement number	#2	#3	#4	#6
Setting	Alloy Plus	Alloy Plus	Alloy Plus	Alloy Plus
Co	ND	ND	0.86	0.63
Co ±			0.16	0.12
Ni	ND	ND	ND	ND
Ni ±				
Cu	ND	ND	ND	ND
Cu ±				
Zn	ND	ND	ND	ND
Zn ±				
Zr	ND	ND	ND	ND
Zr ±				
Nb	ND	ND	ND	ND
Nb ±				
Mo	ND	ND	ND	ND
Mo ±				
Ag	ND	ND	ND	ND
Ag ±				
Sn	**2.33**	**3.31**	**ND**	**ND**
Sn ±	0.06	0.07		
Sb	ND	ND	ND	ND
Sb ±				
Hf	ND	ND	ND	ND
Hf ±				

Site	Győr, Ménfőcsanak–Széles-földek			
Inventory number	1.34305.1.163.			
Artefact	Lead weight			
Sampling point				
Measurement number	#2	#3	#4	#6
Setting	Alloy Plus	Alloy Plus	Alloy Plus	Alloy Plus
Ta	ND	ND	ND	ND
Ta ±				
W	ND	ND	ND	ND
W ±				
Re	ND	ND	ND	ND
Re ±				
Pb	**79.37**	**79.63**	**ND**	**0.1912**
Pb ±	0.22	0.22		0.0299
Bi	0.3222	0.4054	ND	ND
Bi ±	0.0455	0.0473		
Au	ND	ND	ND	ND
Au ±				
Pt	ND	ND	ND	ND
Pt ±				
Ir	2.85	4.58	ND	ND
Ir ±	0.21	0.22		
Pd	ND	ND	ND	ND
Pd ±				
Rh	ND	ND	ND	ND
Rh ±				

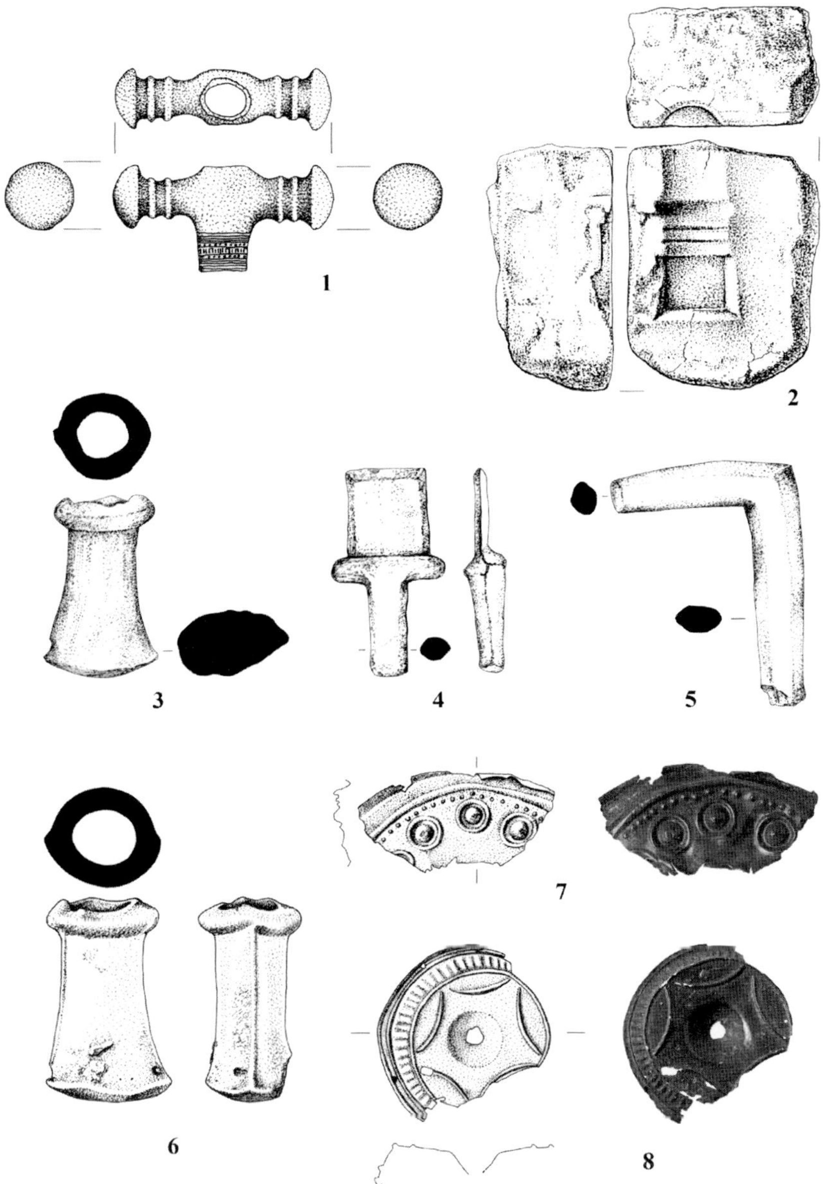

Fig. 35. Metal tools and products from Vas County: 1. the "Szombathely" hammer (drawing by Ágnes Nagy); 2. hammer mould from Gór–Kápolnadomb (drawing by István Ughy); 3–6. hammers found on St. Vid Hill, anvils for cutting and embossing (drawing by Ferenc Gelencsér); 7–10. bronze sheet artefacts (drawing by Magdolna Mátyus, photo by Tibor Takács). The drawings are not to the same scale

Fig. 36. Goldsmith's pitch from an Early Iron Age bronze hoard found at Ikervár (photo by Gábor Papp)

1

2

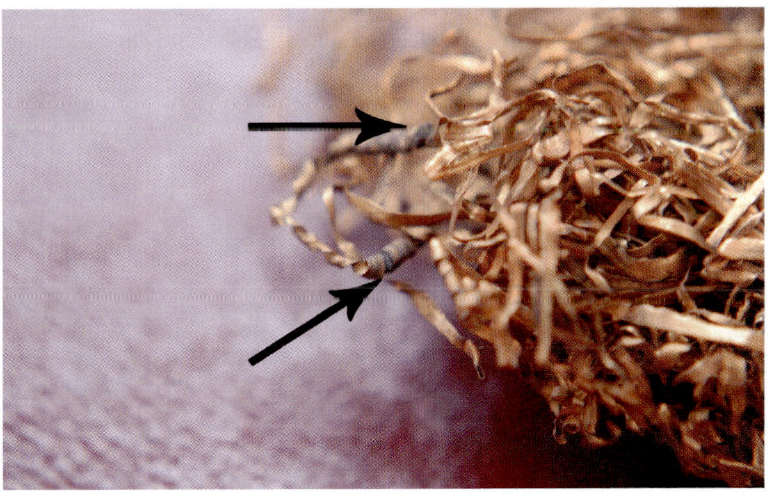

3

Fig. 37. The wires of Gold Hoard 2 at Várvölgy, in situ *and after lifting (photos by Róbert Müller, 2005, 2012)*

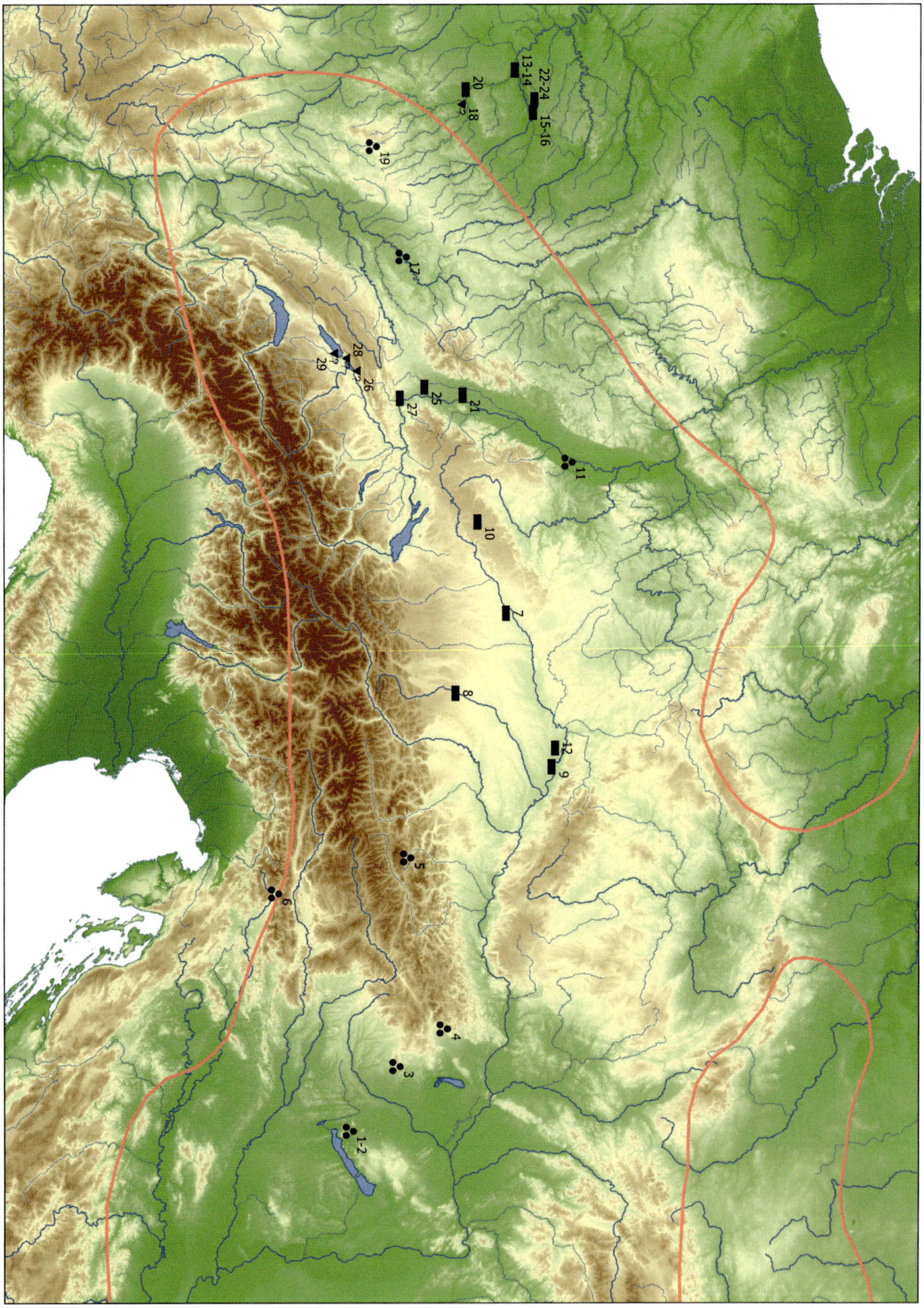
1-2
3
4
5
6
7
8
9
10
11
12
13-14
15-16
17
18
19
20
21
22-24
25
26
27
28
29

Fig. 38. Pectorals of the Late Bronze Age in Central Europe (after KOSSACK *1995, Abb. 1;* LEHRBERGER *1995, Fig. 1, made by Tibor Takács based on the author's data collection)*

Legend: ■ *grave/burial;* ♣ *hoard, treasure;* ▼? *unknwn context*

1–2. Várvölgy–Felsőzsid, treasure; 3. Velem, St. Vid Hill, treasure; 4. Rothengrub (Lower Austria), treasure; 5. Koppental (Styria), treasure; 6. Bled (Slovenia), treasure; 7. Aislingen (Bavaria), burial; 8. Grünwald (Bavaria), Grave 1; 9. Straubing (Bavaria); Grave 31; 10. Gammertingen (Baden-Württemberg), double grave; 11. Karlsruhe–Neureut (Baden-Württemberg), hoard (Einzelfunde), Rhine; 12. Taumering (Oberpfalz), Grave 51; 13–14. Barbey, Cent Arpents (France), Graves 4, 26; 15–16. Barbuise-Courtavant (France), two pieces from burials; 17. Beaujeu (France), hoard; 18. Beaumont, Crot aux Moines (France), context unknown to the author; 19. Blanot (France), hoard; 20. Champlay-la-Columbine (France), Grave 101; 21. Durrenentzen–Haut-Rhin (France), burial; 22–24. La Saulsotte (France), Graves 38, 43, 52; 25. Rixheim (France), Grave 2; 26. Bienne (Switzerland), context unknown to the author; 27. Binningen (Switzerland), burial; 28. Twann–Petersinsel (Switzerland), context unknown to the author; 29. Vallamand–Les Ferrages (Switzerland), context unknown to the author

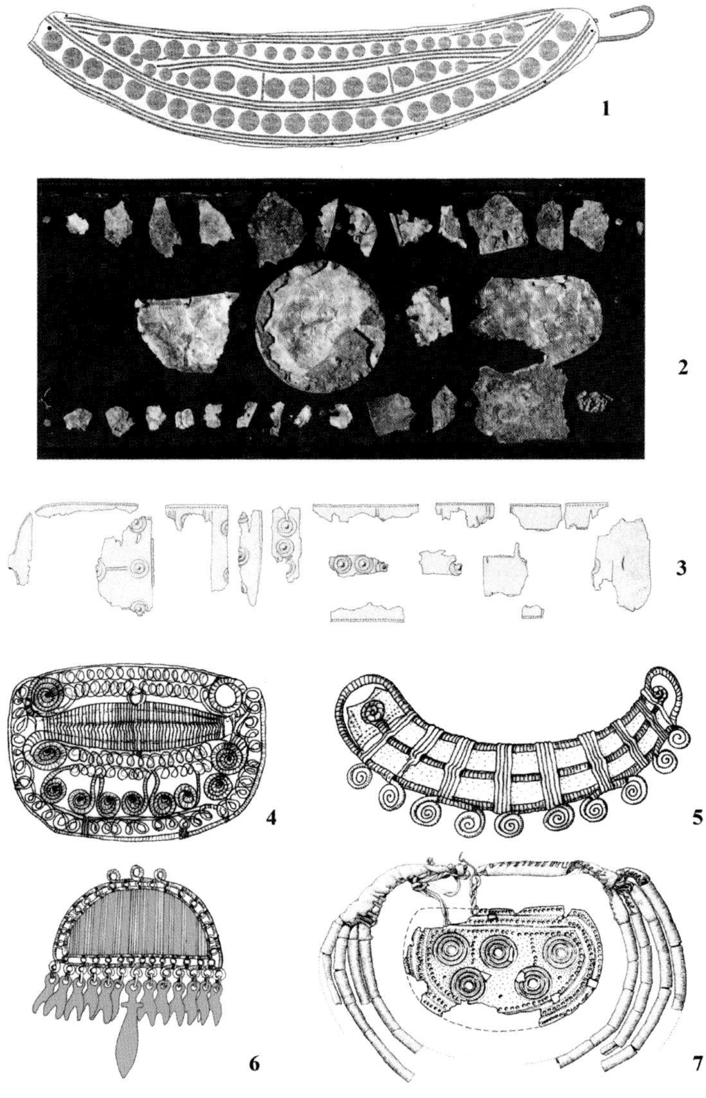

Fig. 39. Plate jewellery: 1. Diadem: Museum of Berlin (after HÄNSEL 2003, Abb. 2); 2. Gold plates and bronze backplates of Hoard II from Ság.hegy, pre-restoration condition documented in Lázár's album (SM Archaeological Archives inv. no. 2378-08); 3. Belt plaque: Budinščina (after KILIAN-DIRLMEIER 1975, Taf. 46-47. 460). Pectorals: 4. Rothengrub (after PITTIONI 1952, Taf. 1); 5. Champlay-la-Columbine, Grave 101 (after PIETTE 1998, Fig.1.1); 6. Aislingen (after WELSWEYRAUCHT 1995,. Abb. 1. 2–4.); 7. Blanot (after THEVENOT 1991, Figs 54 and 63). The drawings are not to the same scale (drawing by Magdolna Mátyus)

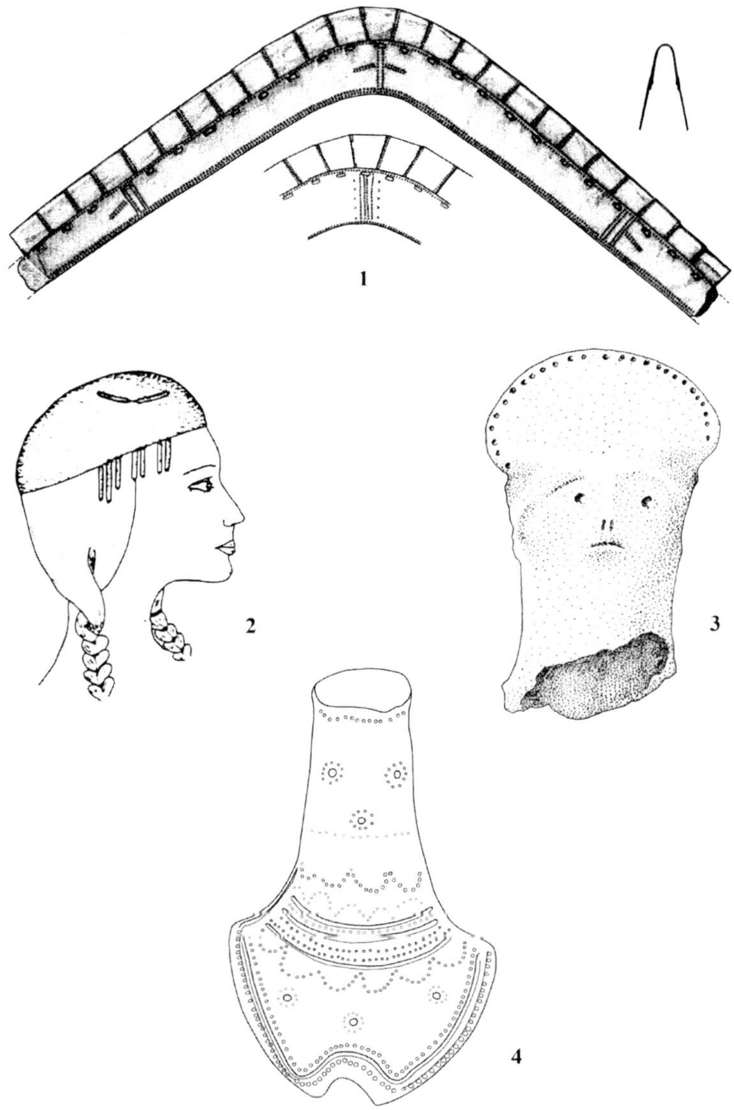

Fig. 40. Female headbands and breast ornaments of the Bronze Age: 1. Unterwölbling culture, Franzhausen I, Grave 110 (after NEUGEBAUER *1994, Abb. 40. 4, Abb. 41. 1–2); 2. Ordacsehi, Grave 400, Kisapostag culture (after* SOMOGYI *2004, Abb. 16. A–C); 3. Budapest–Kőérberek, Early Bronze Age figurine fragment (after* ZSIDI *2005, 84); 4. Ludas–Varjú-dűlő, Late Bronze Age figurine with roundels on the chest (after* DOMBORÓCZKI *2012, Fig. 196). The drawings are not to the same scale (drawn by Magdolna Mátyus)*

Fig. 41. 1–6: Reconstructions of how the gold sheet jewellery from Velem was worn (drawing by Magdolna Mátyus)

Fig. 42. 1–6: Reconstructions of how the gold sheet jewellery from Velem was worn (drawing by Magdolna Mátyus)

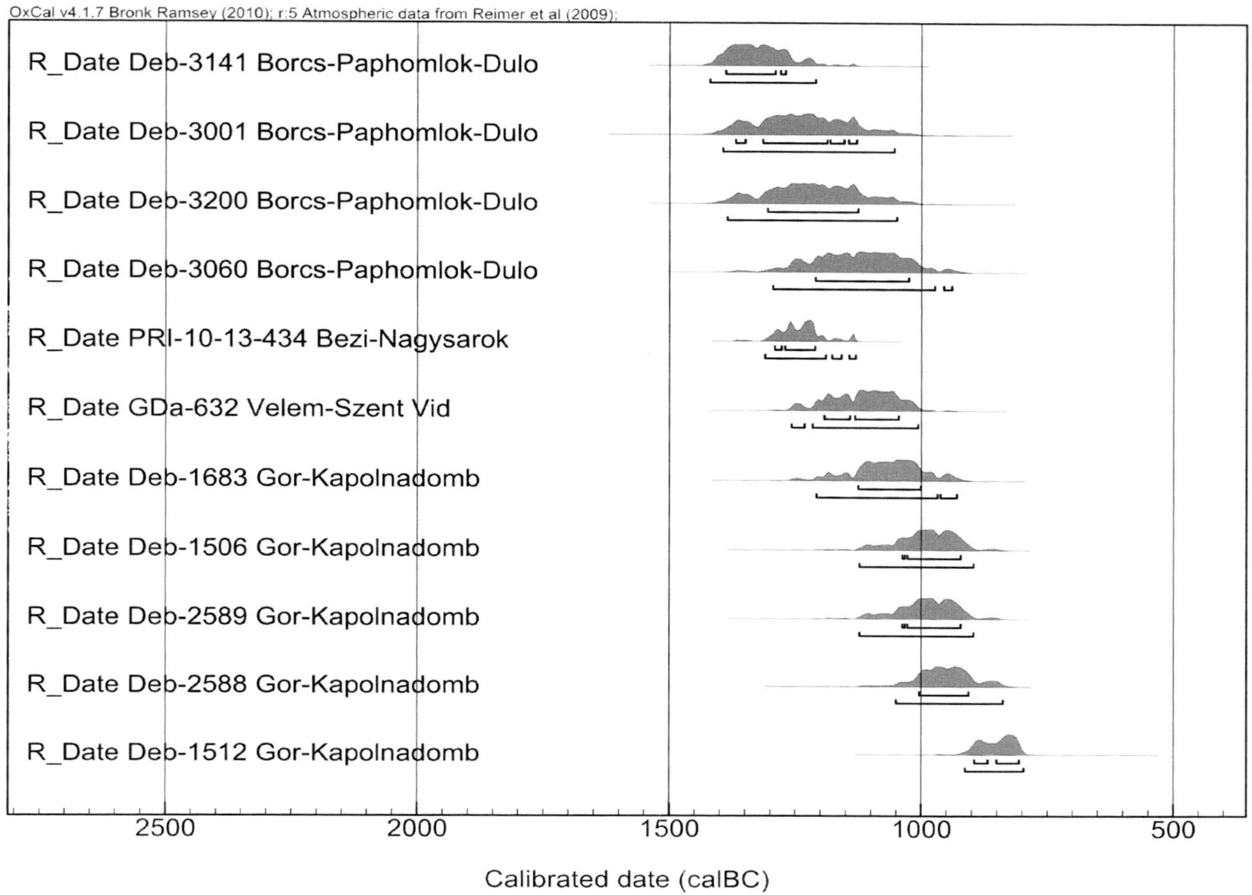

Fig. 43. Radiocarbon dates from Western Hungary for the Urnfield period (with the exception of the Németbánya data)

ARCHAEOLINGUA

Edited by
ERZSÉBET JEREM and WOLFGANG MEID

Main Series

27. **The Medieval Royal Palace at Visegrád.** Edited by Gergely Buzás and József Laszlovszky. 2013. 398 pp. € 66.-. ISBN 978-963-9911-39-0.
28. **Explorations in Salt Archaeology in the Carpathian Zone.** Edited by Anthony Harding and Valerii Kavruk. 2013. 332. pp. € 60.-. ISBN 978-963-9911-44-4.
29. **Textiles from Hallstatt / Textilien aus Hallstatt. Weaving Culture in Bronze Age and Iron Age Salt Mines / Gewebte Kultur aus dem bronze- und eisenzeitlichen Salzbergwerk (bilingual).** Edited by Karina Grömer, Anton Kern, Hans Reschreiter and Helga Rösel-Mautendorfer. 2013. 572 pp. € 65.-. ISBN 978-963-9911-46-8.
30. **Transitions to the Bronze Age. Interregional Interaction and Socio-Cultural Change in the Third Millennium BC Carpathian Basin and Neighbouring Regions.** Edited by Volker Heyd, Gabriella Kulcsár and Vajk Szeverényi. 2013. 358 pp. € 60.-. ISBN 978-963-9911-48-2.
31. Paul R. Duffy: **Complexity and Autonomy in Bronze Age Europe. Assessing Cultural Developments in Eastern Hungary.** 2014. 402 pp. € 60.-. ISBN 978-963-9911-52-9
32. **The Medieval Royal Town at Visegrád. Royal Centre, Urban Settlement, Churches.** Edited by Buzás Gergely, Laszlovszky József and Mészáros Orsolya. 2014. 272 pp. € 40.-. ISBN 978-963-9911-58-1.
33. **Aspects of the Design, Production and Use of Textiles and Clothing from the Bronze Age to the Early Modern Era. NESAT XII. The North European Symposium of Archaeological Textiles 21st – 24th May 2014 in Hallstatt, Austria.** Edited by Karina Grömer and Frances Pritchard. 2015. 374 pp. € 64.-. ISBN 978-963-9911-67-3.
34. Attila Gyucha: **Prehistoric Village Social Dynamics. The Early Copper Age in the Körös Region.** 2015. 352 pp. € 54.-. ISBN 978-963-9911-68-0.
35. **Persistent Economic Ways of Living. Production, Distribution, and Consumption in Late Prehistory and Early History.** Edited by Alžběta

Danielisová and Manuel Fernández-Götz. 2015. 243 pp. € 50.-. ISBN 978-963-9911-70-3.

Series Minor

1. Wolfgang Meid: **Gaulish Inscriptions. Their interpretation in the light of archaeological evidence and their value as a source of linguistic and sociological information.** 2014. (Third edition, revised and enlarged) 74 pp. € 20.-. ISBN 978-963-9911-61-1.
28. Sofia Pescarin: **Reconstructing Ancient Landscape.** 2009. 264 pp. € 36.-. ISBN 978-963-9911-09-3
30. **A History of Central European Archaeology.** Edited by Alexander Gramsch and Ulrike Sommer. 2011. 219 pp. € 24.-. ISBN 978-963-9911-23-9.
31. **Archaeological Imaginations of Religion.** Edited by Thomas Meier and Petra Tillessen. 2014. 404 pp. € 38.-. ISBN 978-963-9911-24- 6.
32. Mária Bondár: **Prehistoric Wagon Models in the Carpathian Basin.** 2012. 142 pp. € 20.-. ISBN 978-963-9911-34-5.
33. **Appropriate narratives. Archaeologists, publics and stories.** Edited by Elisabeth Niklasson and Thomas Meier. 2013. 298 pp. € 34.-. ISBN 978-963 9911-47-5.
34. Alexander Falileyev: **In Search of the Eastern Celts. Studies in Geographical Names, their Distribution and Morphology.** 2014. 173 pp. € 28.-. ISBN 978-963-9911-56-7.
35. Magdolna Szilágyi: **On the Road: The History and Archaeology of Medieval Communication Networks in East-Central Europe.** 2014. 250 pp. € 36.-. ISBN 978-963-9911-57-4.
37. András Patay-Horváth: **The Origins of the Olympic Games.** 2015. 156 pp. € 24.-. ISBN 978-963-9911-72-7.

Please address orders to:

ARCHAEOLINGUA

H-1250 Budapest, Pf. 41.
Fax: (+361) 3758939
e-mail: kovacsr@archaeolingua.hu
http://www.archaeolingua.hu www.hungarianarchaeology.hu